David Der-wei Wang

Why Fiction Matters in Contemporary China

Brandeis University Press
Waltham, Massachusetts

Brandeis University Press

Manufactured in the United States of America
Designed by Eric M. Brooks
Typeset in Quadraat by Passumpsic Publishing

Library of Congress Cataloging-in-Publication Data
appears at the end of the book

5 4 3 2 1

Why Fiction Matters in Contemporary China

The Mandel Lectures in the Humanities at Brandeis University

Sponsored by the Jack, Joseph and Morton Mandel Foundation

Faculty Steering Committee for the Mandel Center for the Humanities

Ramie Targoff, chair; Brian M. Donahue, Talinn Grigor, Fernando Rosenberg, David Sherman, Harleen Singh, Marion Smiley

Former Members
Joyce Antler, Steven Dowden, Sarah Lamb, Ann Olga Koloski-Ostrow, Eugene Sheppard, Jonathan Unglaub, Michael Willrich, Bernard Yack

The Mandel Lectures in the Humanities were launched in the fall of 2011 to promote the study of the humanities at Brandeis University, following the 2010 opening of the new Mandel Center for the Humanities. The lectures bring to the Mandel Center each year a prominent scholar who gives a series of three lectures and conducts an informal seminar during his or her stay on campus. The Mandel Lectures are unique in their rotation of disciplines or fields within the humanities and humanistic social sciences: the speakers have ranged from historians to literary critics. From classicists to anthropologists. The published series of books therefore reflects the interdisciplinary mission of the center and the wide range of extraordinary work being done in the humanities today.

For a complete list of books that are available in the series, visit www.brandeis.edu/press/

David Der-wei Wang, *Why Fiction Matters in Contemporary China*
Wendy Doniger, *The Donigers of Great Neck: A Mythologized Memoir*
Ingrid D. Rowland, *The Divine Spark of Syracuse*
James Wood, *The Nearest Thing to Life*
David Nirenberg, *Aesthetic Theology and Its Enemies: Judaism in Christian Painting, Poetry, and Politics*

Contents

Preface

This book is derived from the Mandel Lectures in the Humanities that I presented at Brandeis University in the spring of 2018. I am grateful to the Mandel Center for the Humanities at Brandeis, and in particular Ramie Targoff, its director, for inviting me to join the lecture series. I also wish to express my deep appreciation for everyone who attended my lectures and shared their thoughts and questions, which informed and improved this book.

As the first of its kind, the book represents an effort to address the power of fiction in relation to China and the rest of the Sinophone world from the millennial turn to the present. I have defined "fiction" not only as a narrative genre in print or other media but also as an amorphous process of fabulation at every layer of our society, something that energizes our capacity to imagine and act, for good and for ill. In China, fiction has been invoked as a key factor of nation building at the beginning of the twentieth century and an apparatus of postsocialist governance in the new millennium. Fiction provides one of the most polemical ways to engage with Chinese realities.

Accordingly, the book takes as its point of departure the call of President Xi Jinping of the People's Republic of China (PRC) in 2013 to "tell the good China story" and not only explicates the fictional turn of contemporary Chinese cultural politics but also traces its genealogy from early modern times. By using the phrase "fictional turn," I do not mean to observe Chinese reality as a mere simulacrum. Rather, I am more concerned with the tangled relationships between ideological imperatives and emancipatory yearnings, and between empirical contingencies and narrative interventions, in contemporary China.

In five chapters, the book highlights the variety and vitality of fictional works from both China and the rest of the Sinophone world—in genres ranging from science fiction to political allegory, from erotic escapade to utopias and dystopias, and from social exposés to psychological thrillers—and examines the way they have intrigued, fascinated, puzzled, and scandalized readers. The book also introduces a series of discourses by critics within China (such as Liang Qichao, Lu Xun, and Shen Congwen) and from the West (such as Hannah Arendt, Walter Benjamin, and Gilles Deleuze). These critics have tried to explain modern narrativity from ethical, political, and affective perspectives and have offered their observations of its agency, or lack thereof, and consequences.

The book follows three thematic threads. Transgression identifies the deviant subjects and soundings that contest the legal, ethical, and cognitive terms in reading and writing fiction. Transmigration calls attention to the necrological and natal cycles beneath and beyond the anthropomorphic horizons, questioning the feasibility of humanism when encountered by multiple forms of being in time and space. Transillumination takes issue with the extant paradigm of realism in relation to luminosity and enlightenment, eliciting instead the typology of "the beam of darkness" that sheds light on the invisible and unthinkable. The three thematic threads are each represented by the emblematic figures of aliens, the phantasm, and posthuman beings.

To conclude, the book offers its own theoretical take on fiction in terms of modernity and monstrosity. And it argues for a literary ecology in which ideological doctrines and individual eccentricities, as well as conventional forces and speculative impulses, interact in such a way as to constitute a kaleidoscopic structure of feeling in contemporary China. It contends that where history fails to address the consequences of atrocities, fiction arises to bear witness to the immemorial and unforeseeable.

Selected passages are drawn from my previous work: *Fictional Realism of 20th-Century China: Mao Dun, Lao She, Shen Congwen* (Columbia University Press, 1992), *Fin-de-Siècle Splendor: Repressed Modernities of Late Qing Fiction, 1849–1911* (Stanford University Press, 1997), and *The Monster That Is History: History, Violence, and Fictional Writing in 20th-Century China* (University of California Press, 2004). All referenced passages have been adapted in the context of the new arguments in this book.

As this book went to press, the coronavirus outbreak was dominating the headlines. At the peak of the health crisis, the Chinese people were asked to stand in solidarity against the virus and to "tell the good China story of fighting the pandemic." Meanwhile, numerous good and not-so-good stories were flooding the virtual and actual media and were quickly hailed or censored. This book inadvertently bears witness to how fiction is invoked to narrate a state of emergency in China today as it was at the beginning of the modern era.

Acknowledgments

I would like to thank my colleagues at Brandeis University and other institutions—Ramie Targoff, Pu Wang, Ralph Thaxton, Mingwei Song, Yuyang Li, Jing Li, Jingling Chen, and Hsiu-mei Liu, among others—for their valuable thoughts and comments at different stages of this project. I would also like to thank my current crop of students at Harvard University, particularly Dylan Suher, Fangdai Chen, Jannis Jizhou Chen, and Tu Hang, for their critical feedback and editorial assistance. Special thanks are due to Sue Ramin, director of Brandeis University Press, as well as the production team: Ann Brash, Mary Garrett, and Jeanne Ferris. Last but not least, I thank Vivian and Jonathan Wang for their inspiration and continued encouragement. This book is dedicated to my mother, Yun-chung Chiang (1916–2020).

I

"Tell the Good China Story"

On August 19, 2013, Xi Jinping 習近平, president of the People's Republic of China (PRC), gave an important talk at the National Conference on Thought and Propaganda. In it, Xi declared that in response to "global changes and developments, new material and circumstances worldwide, and new thoughts, viewpoints, and knowledge of each country, we need to . . . create our best propaganda forms, striving to mold new concepts and new expressions." Above all, Xi stated, the Chinese people were encouraged to "tell the good story of China, disseminate the good voice of China."[1]

At Xi's decree, a campaign to "tell the good China story"[2] was quickly launched at every level of Chinese society. Topics such as "What makes the good China story?" and "How can we tell the story well?" have been addressed in a wide array of fields, from international politics to bureaucratic ethics, and from the entertainment industry to everyday life practices. Xi has continued to pursue this idea with rigor, reiterating his mandate dozens of times. On February 3, 2020, at the height of the coronavirus outbreak in Wuhan, Xi gave a talk to the Standing Committee of the Political Bureau. He called the outbreak "a major test of China's system and capacity for governance," urging the Chinese people "to relate the touching cases of those who fight on the anti-virus frontline; to tell the good China story of fighting the pandemic."[3] Amid international concerns about China's possible missteps in preventing the pandemic, calls for "expediting the core narrative of combating the coronavirus" abound: China has made a major sacrifice for all mankind; China is comparable to the "plague village" Eyam rather than Chernobyl; China must convey the sense of "graininess of truth" to the world.[4] Above all, China's success in combating the pandemic is said to contribute to the "myth" of revolutionary leadership.[5]

Xi has even made his own contribution to the good China story campaign by publishing *Xi Jinping jiang gushi* 習近平講故事 (Stories told by Xi

Jinping) in 2017. The book features 109 tales, anecdotes, and allegories either related directly by Xi or extracted from his talks and writings. Some references take the reader as far back as to the incorruptible official Yang Zhen 楊震 (?–124) of the Eastern Han Dynasty (25–220), but others are as contemporary as the American television drama *House of Cards*. All of the stories in the book are said to address the "way" (*dao* 道; the same word used to name the philosophy of Daoism) of national reform and development, foreign diplomacy, self-cultivation, and interpersonal engagement. A national bestseller, Xi's book won a special book prize that year for reconstructing Chinese spiritual civilization.

It is indeed a rare occurrence in recent decades to witness a Chinese national leader place such an emphasis on storytelling. We could dismiss "tell the good China story" as just another mass media campaign concocted by the party or state: after all, Xi introduced the slogan at an internal conference on thought and propaganda. Nevertheless, judging by the spread, variety, and vitality of the campaign to date, we need to think more seriously about the messages embedded therein. By "story," Xi obviously means more than a fictional account for entertainment. Rather, the "story" that Xi wishes to tell points to a narrative sequence informed by moral dogma and political mandate, narrated (or performed) in such a way as to be intelligible and accepted as legitimate in both public and personal spheres. Xi's "story" aspires to a symbiosis of nation and narration.

The Story and the Nation

The Chinese term for story, *gushi* 故事, has multiple definitions. It can refer to bygone events and accomplishments in lived memory, literary, and historical allusions, or it can refer to something novel, with a strong connotation of inventiveness and surprise—an imagined narrative, a fictional account. The last definition (*gushi* as a fictional narrative related or enacted by storytellers and the media) is the definition most commonly used in modern colloquial Chinese. If we reverse the order of the two characters *gu* and *shi*, we have another word entirely: *shigu* 事故, which connotes an accident or something anomalous. *Gushi* is the inverse of this word in multiple senses. Where *shigu* is accidental, an event or story that exists outside of plot, *gushi* is narrated and always informed by historical specificities.

Insofar as story and storytelling constitute the fundamental elements of narrativity, what concerns me here is how they can be brought to bear on the dialogue between fictionality and historicity in China as the nation re-emerges as a world power in the new millennium. More specifically, I ask why fictional narrative—from storytelling in the conventional oral context to its latest variations in the digital world—matters so much that China's national leader is compelled to assert its power in relation to nation building.

To begin with, Xi's call to "tell the good China story" took place amid a series of events aimed at revalidating the literary tradition of the PRC. In May 2012, a hundred leading literati, including the Nobel Prize winner Mo Yan 莫言 (b. 1955), wrote out by hand Mao Zedong's 1942 "Talks at the Yan'an Conference on Literature and Art" in commemoration of the talks' seventieth anniversary—an undertaking reminiscent of the transcription of religious texts in medieval China. Between May 2 and May 23, 1942, Mao delivered three talks to the cadres and cultural workers in Yan'an. In the talks, Mao proclaimed that literature and the arts should serve revolution, and he urged cultural workers to find media most accessible to the people so as to facilitate mass communication. Popular narratives and performing arts in the folkloric tradition were seen as particularly viable methods to nurture a new national form. Mao's Yan'an talks have since served as the foundation and standard for the Chinese Communist Party's cultural policy. In the wake of the Yan'an anniversary event, more literary sounding campaigns were launched. In November 29, 2012, during a visit to the "Road to National Rejuvenation" exhibition at the National History Museum, Xi introduced the vision of the *Zhongguomeng* 中國夢 or "Chinese Dream." The term has since been widely disseminated across the globe.

On October 15, 2014, one year after his appeal to "tell the good China story," Xi called a national meeting of cultural, artistic, and literary leaders and demanded that Chinese literature be once again undertaken in the spirit of Yan'an. Echoing Mao, Xi asked the newest generation of cultural workers to intertwine discipline and blessing, asceticism and aestheticism, self-denunciation and self-fulfillment, and this-worldly travail and the coming of utopia so as to describe and realize the Chinese dream.

Xi's call to tell the good China story came as part of a well-planned move to assert the legacy of Mao's Yan'an talks. As the editor of *Stories Told by Xi Jinping* notes, "a talent for storytelling is a characteristic shared by famous politicians and thinkers of the past and the present, in China and in the world. In particular, it is the supreme talent of Chinese communist party leaders."[6] It is undeniable that Mao Zedong pioneered the communist tradition of storytelling in China. One of the stories he told during the Yan'an era is "Yugong yishan" 愚公移山 (The foolish old man moves the mountain), about a ninety-year-old man who strives against all odds to remove the two mountains that are "seven hundred miles square and seven hundred thousand feet high" that block access to his house. His determination finally touches God, who has the two mountains moved away. Mao borrowed the story from the fifth century BCE Daoist text *Liezi* 列子 and used it to allegorize the Chinese communists' determination to overcome all impossibilities during the revolutionary crusade:

> Today, two big mountains lie like a dead weight on the Chinese people. One is imperialism, the other is feudalism. The Chinese Communist Party has long made up its mind to dig them up. We must persevere and work unceasingly, and we, too, will touch God's heart. Our God is none other than the masses of the Chinese people. If they stand up and dig together with us, why can't these two mountains be cleared away?[7]

Even more famous is Mao's retelling of the story of the farmer and the viper from *Aesop's Fables*. On December 30, 1948, when the communists were nearing the point of victory, Mao delivered the speech "Jiang geming jinxing daodi" 將革命進行到底 (Carry on the revolution to the end).[8] He asserted his resolution to accept no compromise with the opposition, because kindness to evil nourishes only betrayal. He reminded his audience of the Greek fable in which a farmer rescues a viper freezing in the snow by placing it in his coat. The viper, revived by the warmth, bites his rescuer, who dies realizing that his merciful deed has caused his own destruction.[9] Mao's story is said to have hit home in the final thrust of the revolution.

Involved in the Maoist tradition of storytelling is what Michel Foucault would call the making of the "truth regime,"[10] a discursive form designed in such a way as to embody a specific system of knowledge and truth claims.

Echoing Mao's approach, Xi and his followers intend to revive storytelling as a quintessential tool for communicating with the people, laying bare the "truth" hidden underneath reality. Telling (and learning) "the" good China story is expected to be both an act of interpellation (a calling of sorts, through which national subjectivity is consolidated and the global community inculcated with the soft power of the socialist regime) and an act of self-assertion (through which political sovereignty is authenticated and the personal integrity of the leaders is reinforced).

The issue of truth claims leads to the ambiguous connotation of the Chinese character *hao* 好 (good, correct, positive, or well) used to qualify Xi's storytelling. "Tell the good China story" can also be translated into either "tell the correct or right China story" or "tell the China story well." Therefore, depending on how *hao* is interpreted, Xi's slogan takes on a different charge: descriptive, interlocutory, imposing, or even imperative. The questions boil down to one: who gets the final say about the "goodness" of a story?

Nevertheless, at a time when "all that is solid melts into air," in the words of Karl Marx and Friedrich Engels in *The Communist Manifesto*, in both rightist and leftist camps, Xi's storytelling campaign is bound to face challenges. For one thing, to a generation of Chinese oversaturated with the "phantasmagorias"[11] of both postcapitalism and postsocialism, Xi's campaign risks belying the fanciful nature of the good China story at the outset. Or, more intriguingly, one might suggest that the campaign has proven successful so far because it positions the national leader as "the greatest storyteller of China," setting the political stakes so high that no one can afford to question its credibility. Here the fable of the emperor's new clothes may come to mind. In other words, Xi's campaign functions in two ways. As a simple call for storytelling, it aims to rekindle the yearning for a genuine socialist truth. But at the same time, the campaign hints at the performative nature of truth making, something that hinges on the willing and willful suspension of disbelief on all sides of society. Slavoj Žižek, who is known for his observation of the menacingly playful nature of ideology, would welcome such vertiginous flip-flops of the China story wherein truth and its disavowal become interchangeable to facilitate the ideological underpinning of the master narrative.[12] It recalls the double meaning of the

Chinese term *gushi* as both a truthful testimony and a wishful and willful fabulation; both communication as authentication and a fantastic flight from that which is intelligible and representable.[13]

Nevertheless, just as "tell the good China story" has become a national craze, the Chinese people have been welcoming a plethora of not-so-good stories, "told" in print culture, the performing arts, visual media, computer games, intellectual property industry, and online gadgets—to say nothing of the rumor mill and voices of dissent online. These are not the kind of stories Xi and his cohort want to see told. Whereas science fiction has suddenly become the most popular genre in China since the turn of the millennium, fantasies, utopias and dystopias, queer erotica, and exotic escapades are flooding the internet, drawing audiences of millions. Even in the more traditional domains of literature, young writers have been churning out works that test ideological borders. Meanwhile, Sinophone communities outside the PRC are contesting "the good China story," telling stories that bring into question what makes China "China."

In this book, I posit that although the government is tightening its control on informational and conceptual freedom and mandating the telling of the monolithic "good" story, stories of all sorts are proliferating often where least expected and are registering other realities. My goal, nevertheless, is not to debunk Xi's storytelling campaign in favor of heterogeneous voices. To do so would simply replicate the tired scheme of hegemony versus spontaneity or fabrication versus truth. Rather, I am more concerned with a literary ecology in which ideological doctrines and individual eccentricities, as well as suppressive forces and avant-garde impulses, interact in such a way as to constitute a kaleidoscopic structure of feeling in contemporary China. This ecology generates both productive and counterproductive outcomes that inform the extant horizon of knowledge and its containment versus dissemination. More importantly, I take "tell the good China story" as a prompt for pondering the unlikely literary turn of political discourse in China and its implications.

To better circumscribe the phenomenon, I focus my study on recent developments in narrative fiction (*xiaoshuo* 小說) in both China and other Sinophone communities. I focus on narrative fiction because it is not only the most popular genre of modern Chinese literature but also the venue in which "tell the good China story" takes on historical and theoretical dimensions. The Chinese fictional tradition originates, after all, in storytelling. *Xiaoshuo* literally means "small talk," a clear reference to a culture of orality. It manifests itself first and foremost in various forms of storytelling such as hearsay and street talk.

Three Stories

To explain how narrative fiction became modern in China by means of "telling the good China story," I will now introduce three stories, all written in an early stage of modern Chinese literature. They are by Liang Qichao 梁啟超 (1873–1927), Lu Xun 魯迅 (1881–1936), and Shen Congwen 沈從文 (1902–88). Each offers a distinctive direction for telling a good story through the medium of vernacular fiction.

Xi's decree uncannily brings to mind Liang's ambitions over a century earlier. Exiled in Yokohama in 1902 after his role in the aborted 1898 political reform of the Qing dynasty, Liang set out to promote "new fiction" as the key to Chinese reform. In the inaugural issue of *Xinxiaoshuo* 新小說 (New fiction), Liang published "Lun xiaoshuo yuqunzhi zhiguanxi" 論小說與群治之關係 (On the relationship between fiction and ruling the people), which begins:

> To renovate the people of a nation, the traditional literature of that nation must first be renovated. Thus to renovate morality, we must first renovate fiction; to renovate religion, we must first renovate fiction; to renovate manners, we must first renovate fiction; to renovate learning and the arts, we must first renovate fiction; and even to renew people's hearts and remold their character, we must first renovate fiction. Why? It is because fiction exercises a power of incalculable magnitude over mankind.[14]

As a harbinger of the modern Chinese politics of fiction, Liang Qichao's campaign for new fiction was premised on his commitment to revolution. Since fiction had been regarded as a base genre in the traditional Chinese literary hierarchy, Liang's elevating it to a position of principal importance was itself a revolutionary engagement. He believed that to "tell the good

China story" of his time or any time was the key to reforming the Chinese nation and the Chinese mind. At some mysterious point of time, as Liang would have it, fiction and nation—or, for our purposes, utopia and history—become exchangeable notions.

Such a statement highlights one of the unique features of literary practice and the political imaginary in modern China. The literary practice described by Liang reflects the time-honored conceptual chain of being from *wen* 文 (literary manifestation) to *dao* 道 (the way),[15] but at the same time, it points to the inextricable tension between the imaginable and the realizable in realistic terms. This tension became all the more poignant during the subsequent decades when Western discourses of fiction, narrativity, and polity were introduced to China.

To promote the new fiction, Liang set out to compose new fiction of his own, such as *Xinzhongguo weilaiji* 新中國未來記 (The future of new China, 1902). The novel opens with an overview of a prosperous China in 2062, sixty years after the novel's fictional publication date of 2002. As citizens of the Republic of Great China (*Da Zhonghua minzhuguo* 大中華民主國) celebrate the fiftieth anniversary of the country's founding, a revered scholar, Kong Hongdao 孔宏道, a seventy-second-generation descendant of Confucius, is invited to give a lecture at the Shanghai World Exposition on the way Chinese democracy has been implemented. His lecture draws a huge enthusiastic audience, including thousands of people from overseas.

The extant narrative of *The Future of New China* relates, via flashback, the interaction between Huang Keqiang 黃克強 and Li Qubing 李去病, the two protagonists of the novel. Incited by the humiliation of the Qing dynasty by the Empire of Japan in the First Sino-Japanese War in 1895, both Huang and Li decide to go to England in pursuit of new thought, and they end up studying at Oxford University. When news about the aborted Hundred Day Reform of 1898 (the failure of which was the cause of Liang's exile) reaches them, the two friends are faced with another crucial decision. When Li considers the immediate and radical action of revolution, Huang cautions his friend against the consequences of futile violence and sacrifice. The two then part ways: Huang travels to Berlin to learn the latest theories of political science and statecraft, and Li heads to Paris to witness the effect of the French Revolution on French society. The two are reunited on their way back to China, yet they still cannot solve their disagreement regarding how to renew China. The novel ends there.

Many late Qing novels came to a similar abrupt stop, a fact that attests to the volatile circumstances of reading and writing fiction at the time.[16] What makes *The Future of New China* special is that its unfinished form complicates its utopian scheme. Insofar as it promises to tell how the bright future will have been reached over a span of fifty years, the unfinished project of *The Future of New China* exposes a short circuit in its narrative and historiographical mechanism. If the future serves as the goal of Liang's fiction or revolution, its realization presupposes that a passage of time, along with the plot, will unfold so as to lead to the fulfillment of the goal. As the novel stands now, China in the future has been reached in advance (through a flashback), and the history and narrative that would have filled the gap between now and then is nowhere to be found.

If the grand opening of *The Future of New China* feels uncanny, perhaps it is because that future seems to have become reality in the new millennium. At a time when China is a leading political and economic power worldwide, having hosted not only a World Exposition but also the Olympic Games; having launched an ambitious "One Belt, One Road" project, a trade network that will bring the world to China; and, most impressively, founded hundreds of Confucius Institutes in places as far from China as Pakistan and Liberia, Liang Qichao's futuristic utopia may prove to have already been realized by socialist China. Indeed, as if taking up where Liang left off more than a century earlier, Xi's speech on the "Chinese Dream" in 2012 projects the future of new China as one thriving on "the way of socialism," "the spirit of nationalism," and "the force of ethnic solidarity."[17] To be sure, there are important differences between Xi's injunction to "tell the good China story" and Liang's campaign for new fiction. Whereas Liang was taking refuge in Japan as a political dissident, Xi is the supreme ruler of contemporary China; and whereas Liang was projecting his wish to reform China from a prerevolutionary age, Xi tries to "harmonize" (*hexie* 和諧) the Chinese society in a postsocialist era in which any revolutionary attempt to shake up the status quo has become taboo. What is nevertheless similar is their attention to the politics of literature—or, for our purposes, the relationship between narrativity and governance. If Liang's statement is imbued with a sense of moral persuasion and historical urgency, Xi's decree smacks of a Foucauldian brand of discipline: to tell the good China story is to tell the correct China story.

I have elsewhere described the narrative short circuit of Liang's novel in terms of the future perfect tense—a projection of an episode expected to happen before a certain time of reference in the future. In other words, the novel deals not with what may happen but what will or should have happened in the years to come.[18] Xi's campaign has the same agenda. Whereas Liang's visit to the future follows a secret itinerary through the fantasies of the past, Xi's proposed "good story" indicates not so much a discovery of a new temporal horizon as the fulfillment of the Chinese dream. When the remote future turns out to be uncannily familiar, or when the mystical apocalypse proves to be preconceived news, both Liang and Xi risk turning their visions of the future into paradoxically nostalgic anticipation.

Between Liang's and Xi's provocations, we witness the twists and turns of the "China story" as related by Chinese writers over the past hundred years. Lu Xun and Shen Congwen present a useful contrast. In 1918, Lu Xun wrote "Kuangren riji" 狂人日記 (The diary of a madman), arguably the first Chinese story in the modern, vernacular form. Inspired by Nikolai Gogol's story with the same title as well as premodern Chinese accounts of wayward figures, Lu Xun's Madman has a clinical case of schizophrenia and happens to discover the secret that the society in which he lives thrives on cannibalism. The Madman is eventually cured so he can rejoin normal societal functions—and become a cannibal.

What is significant to us is the story's framed narrative structure. Its short introduction is provided by an anonymous narrator in classical Chinese, while its central text—the diary of the Madman—is rendered in vernacular Chinese. The linguistic contrast between the classical frame and the vernacular center symbolizes the conceptual confrontation between the traditional and modern *epistemes*. It gives rise to the most ambiguous moment of the story: when the Madman engages in reading Confucian classics at night, all he sees popping up "between the lines" of the sages' teaching is the Chinese phrase *chiren* 吃人, "eat people." Hence he discovers that the four-thousand-year-old civilization has taught us only one lesson: how to consume each other's flesh in the name of virtue and propriety.

Through the metaphor of cannibalism, Lu Xun casts a pessimistic look at the intertwined relationships between civilization and savagery as well as textuality and orality. Nevertheless, if Lu Xun sees cannibalism figuratively as the repressed real demanding to be emancipated, he has to deal with a result not unlike an opened Pandora's box. The Madman's radical discovery cannot be conveyed simply through a straight narrative but must be contained within the frame; it has to be continually subjected to an allegorized, socially acceptable reading and rereading. In other words, the Madman can discern the cannibalistic nature of Chinese history because he himself is nourished by that ghoulish tradition.

As the story's frame indicates, the nomination and exclusion of the mad and the irrational is necessary for a society to differentiate the conscious from the unconscious, and the real from the unreal. By contrast, the story at the center of the frame triggers a vertiginous interplay between madness and rationality, illusion and reality. The story ends with the Madman's cry, "Save the Children!" It is followed by ellipsis points, as if the diary itself is cannibalized by the narrative frame in the end.

The tenor of Lu Xun's story is thus very different from Liang's tone just a few years earlier. Liang recognizes the crisis of China and chooses to cling to a new narrative paradigm as a remedy. But Lu Xun turns the paradigm inside out so as to flaunt his radical iconoclasm. While inviting us to allegorize the Madman as a psychopath, a social outcast, or even a prisoner of political conscience, Lu Xun simultaneously questions the validity of any of these labels. Indeed, it is his deep-seated skepticism about narrative fiction or *xiaoshuo* as a viable form of communication that makes his story a sharp critique of modern Chinese fictional discourse even at its inception.

This critique is even more significant when contextualized within the incident that apparently prompted Lu Xun to become a writer, a story he told in 1922. In 1906, as a medical student studying in Japan, Lu Xun saw a slide show in which a Chinese crowd idly watched as one of their compatriots was beheaded for spying on the Japanese army during the Russo-Japanese war (1904–5), which was fought largely on territory technically under the rule of the Qing dynasty. What ensued has become a well-known story. Dumbfounded by the scene of decapitation, Lu Xun realized that before saving Chinese people's bodies, he had first to save their souls. Hence, before practicing ordinary medicine, he had to tend to the broken spirit of China with the medicine of literature:

> The people of a weak, backward country, even though they may enjoy sturdy health, can only serve as the senseless material of an audience for public executions. . . . Our first task was surely to transform their spirits, and I thought at that time that literature could best meet the task of spiritual transformation. I then began to think about promoting literary activities.[19]

This moment thus triggered the most crucial turn in Lu Xun's life, changing him from a modern student of medicine into a traditional member of the literati. He did not adopt a clinical anatomical perspective on the beheading of this Chinese person but instead treated it as an allegorical scene that illuminated China's fate.

I have pointed out in my earlier study of modern Chinese realism that Lu Xun's decapitation complex may have created an ontological vacuum, creating a desire to write and reinstate reality.[20] Here, I want to call attention to a narratological crack in the way in which Lu Xun writes about the decapitation event. This recollection of watching the decapitation slide show appears only in the 1922 foreword to his collection *Nahan* 呐喊 (A call to arms). The belated reminiscence has already been given a figurative meaning, dramatizing an anxiety about a primordial loss of origin—meaning and life symbolized by the head, and loss symbolized by the mutilated body. Lu Xun's effort to retrospectively add an origin story for his literary career suggests such an anxiety. Critics such as Leo Lee have pointed out that the traumatic slide has never been found and suggested that Lu Xun may have fabricated the whole incident,[21] giving an allegorical form to his abstract conception. The case of the decapitation slide suggests that fiction and (private and public) history might have become inextricably confused at the (textual) beginning of modern Chinese (literary) history.

Lu Xun's storytelling thus introduces a set of entry points for narrating Chinese modernity and reveals a modern writer who was also a frustrated intellectual revolutionary, a radical historian, an ideologue, and perhaps something of a Madman. Lu Xun's success should be found not in his versatility but rather in his inability to play all these roles. The Madman's story becomes his own story—that of a self-cannibalistic storyteller.

Yet at the same time Lu Xun's story tells us something else. It tells us that, despite—or because of—the vicious impediments of history, the story must be told. In the wake of the elliptic ending of "The Diary of a Madman," in which the Madman's cry seems to vanish, the silence was quickly filled with a tremendous volume of narrative fiction in China that, at its most provocative, formed an alternative discourse to official accounts. Even during the most coercive years of the Maoist era, forbidden stories circulated underground or surfaced in the least expected ways, testifying to the power of narrating how things could be otherwise.

The third case I wish to present is that of Shen Congwen, a born storyteller of the manners and morals of his native region, western Hunan. A rebellious son from a military family with some ethnic minority ancestry, Shen had an early life that was full of rough-and-tumble adventures in the Chinese hinterlands, and he became a teenage soldier in a warlord's army. This young rural solider was nevertheless inspired by the May Fourth movement and made his way to Beijing to pursue a literary career. His writing captures some of the most volatile moments of modern China in crisis, yet he is able to render them lyrically.

Shen's lyricism is far more than an expression of romantic whims and pastoral yearnings. His lyrical sensibilities lead him to ponder the historical contingencies and human imperfections underlying the experience of modernity. For him, literature's most productive relationship with the world is not mimetic realism but evocative configuration, an aesthetic and ethical capacity to abstract values from human experience and give a form to that which otherwise is obscure and mercurial. He is keenly aware of the menacing threats of reality and hopes to redeem that reality through lyricality, rather than eschew it.

In the 1930 story "Sange nanzi he yige nüren" 三個男子和一個女人 (Three men and one woman), purportedly based on Shen's personal experience, three young men—two soldiers and the owner of a tofu store—compete for a young woman's love in a border town where a warlord's troops are stationed. While the two soldiers' fight draws more of the reader's attention, the tofu store owner turns out to be the unexpected winner of the woman's love. Just as everything seems to be working out fine for the young couple, the woman mysteriously commits suicide. Soon after her funeral, the woman's body is found missing from its tomb. The thief is caught—and it turns out to be the tofu store owner, who dug out the body, took it to a nearby cave, and slept with it for three nights.

With its necrophiliac subject, the story might easily have been made into an erotic thriller. But Shen turns it into a story about passion at its most mysterious (framed by a rustic, brutal background) as well as an inquiry into the art of storytelling that transcends human foibles. The first-person narrator, who is one of the two soldier suitors, offers to tell us a story at the outset and then ushers his audience step by step into a world enshrouded by Eros and Thanatos. It starts with a military incursion into a mountain town and ends with gothic horror and insanity. Yet Shen's narrator relates the woman's story in such a way that when her dead body is found, it is "completely naked on a stone ledge, with blue chrysanthemums scattered all over her body and on the ground." The power of storytelling, we are told, "turns the obscene into the divine."[22]

As I have discussed elsewhere, Shen actually wrote three versions of this story: one in the context of his biography, one in a travelogue about his hometown region, and then this explicitly fictional version. What drove Shen to retell the story? At the end of "Three Men and One Woman," Shen writes,

> I am forever restless because the past returns to haunt me often. To each his own destiny: this I know. Some things of the past perpetually gnaw the inside of me. When I talk about them you would only say they are stories. Nobody can understand how a person feels who lives day after day under the weight of hundreds of stories like this one.[23]

Shen has noted that his writing is motivated by a profound emotional and cognitive impediment, which he sees as a result of the poetic subject's frustrating encounter with the world. He associates this impediment with *yuan* 怨, a classical poetic concept denoting the discontent induced by the loss of origin and plenitude.[24] This emotional lacuna nevertheless serves as the (traumatic) cause of creativity. *Yuan* can be politically motivated, but it intimates a more profound ontological ressentiment. It drives the writer either to the abyss or to fantastic escapades, without ever promising a resolution. At its most intense, it brings forth a preemptive mourning for what is yet to be lost or what has never existed. The result is a state of "restlessness" that is vividly expressed in the quote above.

"Three Men and One Woman" lays bare Shen's philosophy of storytelling. His desire to emplot realistic events becomes more than just an entertainment, and repetition represents a continued attempt to articulate an obscured master plot. Just like Samuel Taylor Coleridge's Ancient Mariner (in *The Rime of the Ancient Mariner*), Herman Melville's Ishmael (in *Moby-Dick*), and Joseph Conrad's Marlow (in *The Heart of Darkness*), Shen's first-person narrators have to tell the same story over and over again to ease their mental burdens. To tell a story is to translate memory into art. Storytelling is not only a ritual of exorcism, an attempt to expel demons, but also a form of incantation, taking the storyteller again and again into the cavern of memory and throwing different lights on its sunken passages. Storytelling, above all, may bring not only catharsis but also new pains and pleasures.

Thus, by the early 1930s, one can already discern three intertwined approaches to narrating China. Liang Qichao concerns himself with the politics of storytelling, which structures his engagement with the Chinese people. Lu Xun is equally committed to the cause of reforming China by retooling the China story, but he appears more concerned about the ethics of storytelling. His stories instantiate the irreconcilable tensions between civilization and savagery; the human and the inhuman; and, most poignantly, the efficacy and futility of storytelling. Finally, writing from the margins of Chinese culture and ethnicity, Shen Congwen dedicates himself to the poetics of storytelling by exploring the heart of darkness and employing lyricism as a form of catharsis. All three stories discussed above betray the untenability of narrating modern China: Liang's *The Future of New China* remains unfinished; Lu Xun's "Diary of a Madman" ends with an elliptic cry for an impossible hope; and Shen's "Three Men and One Woman" unveils the traumatic core of storytelling.

It has never been easy to tell a "good" story of China, even from the beginning of modern Chinese literature. Both Liang and Lu Xun passed away in the midst of the chaos of the Republican era. Shen survived a suicide attempt on the eve of the 1949 revolution and lived long enough to witness the ups and downs of the new China in its first four decades, but he abandoned literature in the 1950s because he understood that what the authorities might authenticate as a "good story" at one time could turn out to be a bad story at another. Meanwhile, censorship, confiscation, persecution, incarceration, exile, and execution constitute the leitmotifs of storytelling and literary writing throughout twentieth-century China.

Still, stories about China have to be told. Liang Qichao, Lu Xun, and Shen Congwen not only told stories in their own time and on their own terms, but their stories live on to be retold and emulated by storytellers in the following generations. *One Thousand and One Nights* comes to mind: Princess Scheherazade has to relate one story after another to survive, given the impending threat of execution that "a Sasanian King ruling in India and China" imposes on her.[25] To tell stories is to sustain the narrative as life. Through narrating the unthinkable and unforeseeable, storytelling calls forth the creative power of "becoming other" in such a way as to sustain or anticipate hope.

Storytelling and Sociality

In this book, I argue that a more productive way to engage with the call to "tell the good China story" is not to stigmatize it but to understand it in the broader historical context of Chinese narratology. More significantly, I intend to bring this campaign to bear on modern theories of storytelling and social bonding, thereby opening up a new horizon for the dialogue between China and the West.

I contend that "telling the good China story" is not a completely new project but a reinstatement of the narratological legacy of the Chinese communist revolution in the early days. In their research about the rise of Maoist discourse during the Yan'an era, David Apter and Tony Saich describe how storytelling was employed in such a way as to facilitate what they call "exegetical bonding." For Apter and Saich, "storytelling" refers not only to a variety of narrative genres (from folk tales to anecdotal accounts, and from personal confessions to public manifestos) but also to the shared sentiment of connectivity forged through narrative and performance. Whatever the format, "storytelling in this sense requires an agent with a special ability to lift the burden of storytelling from the shoulders of the individual by enabling that person to share it with others—an act of *communitas* as an act of cognition; an 'imagined community,' as [Benedict] Anderson puts it."[26]

Apter and Saich noticed that this form of storytelling became institutionalized around 1942–44, a time that coincided with Mao's talks followed by the rectification campaign—a thought reform ending with massive purges. Mao's delivery in his talks was as pragmatic as it was spellbinding, and in practice it led to some of the harshest moments in the history of the literature of socialist China in subsequent decades. As Apter and Saich note, in this process of storytelling, "the agent must assume a role vis-à-vis the collectivity somewhere between the theocrat, who is realizing the divine will, and the psychoanalyst, who represents the agency for the individual."[27] Through sharing with each other stories about bygone misdeeds or looming misgivings, or repentant feelings or epiphanic discoveries, members of the interlocutory community come to the moment of mutual understanding: "In this sense storytelling is a catharsis touched with mystery. It is a cathartic narrative that reduces the need for, and the urgency of, the individual story as a driver. By such acts of cognition, the property of the story becomes the property of the discourse community."[28]

This process—which, as noted above, Apter and Saich call "exegetical bonding"—gives rise to an apocalyptic sentiment suggestive of a religious calling, but its binding principle is none other than a this-worldly commitment: it is meant to "convert the revolutionary simulacrum from a community of lost souls into a chosen people and, if necessary, consign the rest to the historical scrap heap."[29] More importantly, it operates through information control and the modulation of emotional affect, serving the goal of ideological solidarity.

Apter and Saich also call attention to the mirage-like, insubstantial quality of the communist imaginary such as the "myth" of Yan'an, describing it in terms of Jean Baudrillard's notion of "simulacrum,"[30] a hypnotic projection of collective desire. Their inspiring analysis notwithstanding, the two scholars may have too readily couched their argument in postmodern discourse. Above all, they cannot exempt themselves from the tautological circle by calling something a simulacrum while granting themselves a vision of the real by default.

I would suggest an alternative approach. Instead of using the term "simulacrum," one should take the ambitions of revolutionary enlightenment seriously and understand them as a different kind of truth claim. To that end, the old Weberian model of enchantment versus disenchantment may prove more viable than the Baudrillardian model of simulacrum.[31] As I note in chapter 2, for Max Weber, modernity emerges through the disenchantment of the premodern episteme.[32] If this is the case for modernity, the Maoist brand of modernity takes on an additional dimension. It enacts enlightenment not merely through disenchanting Chinese people from traditional values but also by simultaneously reenchanting them by calling on the divine power of the real.[33] Involved here is the "fusion of horizons" between iconoclasm and idolatry, modernist mythologies and "primitive passions,"[34] rationality and volition. When enlightenment engenders enchantment, and enchantment substantiates enlightenment, a Maoist solidarity—rather than a simulacrum—comes into being, exuding a defiant power beyond the modernity we might imagine.

The Maoist use of storytelling brings to mind Walter Benjamin's famous discussion of the storyteller in 1936, at roughly the same time the Chinese Communist Party was establishing its utopia at Yan'an. In view of the malaise resulting from the advancement of modernity—such as alienation, efficacy at the cost of intimacy, and not just the saturation but the oversaturation of information—Benjamin invokes the tradition of storytelling, which he believes is not only a narrative skill but also a symbolic form of social communication and inquiry into the surrounding world. Benjamin describes how in ancient times, an itinerant raconteur would be summoned to relate bygone events to a community, heroic tales that would allow the community to reckon with the passage of time and the cycle of life and death, as well as the "moral occult" embedded therein.[35] The storyteller is not a creator of fantasies but a transmitter of universal wisdom: allowing "the wick of his life [to] be consumed completely by the gentle flame of his story," he is "the figure in which the righteous man encounters himself."[36] By way of contrast with the modern media of the novel and the news, which are paradoxically ephemeral and reproducible, the storyteller sheds light not on information but on the meaning of life and death, whose fecundity remains inexhaustible.

One can draw a few parallels between Benjamin's version of storytelling and its Chinese socialist counterpart. Both stress storytelling as a way to resist the modernist symptoms of social fragmentation, and both solicit "openly or covertly, something useful" so as to realize the hidden lessons of the human condition and sustain the sensuous vibration of life. But one can quickly point out that the exegetical bonding created by Maoist storytelling is a world away from the Benjaminian ideal type of sociality. If the former seeks to assert authority on behalf of the party line, the latter is concerned about the authenticity of life as a holistic experience. Numerous records indicate that during the rectification movement, stories were told in such a way as to create both intimacy and hierarchy, both individual awakening and collective unison, both discipline and punishment. Above all, the size and scale of the Maoist interlocutory community are far greater than those of Benjamin's folk gathering.

On the one hand, the contemporary "tell the good China story" campaign evokes a nostalgia for the (Benjaminian) storyteller who spontaneously utters the truth of life. On the other hand, it relies on post-Mao and -Deng Xiaoping, as well as postmodern, technologies—from cultural industry to media control—to facilitate storytelling. As "the good China story" is disseminated into every layer of the society, the wisdom it aims to convey smacks of dogma.

Our assessment of the "storytelling turn" of contemporary China may also benefit from Hannah Arendt's theory about natality and narrativity. To be sure, Arendt has been known for her harsh criticism of totalitarianism, leftist and rightist alike, and her firm stance in favor of liberal universalism. Arendt focused mainly on Europe, but John Treat has nevertheless ventured to ask about "Arendt in Asia," applying her theory of storytelling to "responsibility and judgment in Nanjing and Hiroshima."[37] Similarly, we can imagine how Arendt might have commented on Xi's campaign.

Arendt strives to develop "a conception of political theory as 'storytelling.'"[38] For her, one way to define the "human condition" is to highlight the symbiosis of action and narrativity, a symbiosis that she identifies as the incipient sign of "natality." In other words, to be born is to become part the continuum of time, which is underpinned by the creative power of narrativity as action. With the city-states of ancient Greece as her ideal,

Arendt contends that utterance in the form of storytelling in a public space engenders communication and sociality. Storytelling is a political action, as it creates an open space in which the public and the personal, as well as the past and the future of a community, are brought into view, allowing the passions and shared historical vision of a community to be contested and interwoven. A vibrant society thrives on its narrative power, since to tell stories is to act out new beginnings for the human condition.[39]

In the broader philosophical context, Arendt's understanding of storytelling is connected to the Kantian engagement with imagination. Storytelling suggests that "private conditions condition us; imagination and reflection enable us to liberate ourselves from them and to attain that relative impartiality that is the specific virtue of judgement."[40] Through storytelling, one realizes the human ability to begin, since "a being whose essence is beginning may have enough of origin within himself to understand without preconceived categories and to judge without the set of customary rules which is morality."[41] In other words, storytelling, like action, is beginning. It brings out the new and is distinguished by its plurality and unpredictability, hence the promise of freedom: "Every action occurs in a plural context and in a web of already-existing relationships and references; it always goes further and puts in relation and motion more than the agent can predict."[42]

Arendt's emphasis on narrative plurality leads us to Mikhail Bakhtin's concept of heteroglossia, though the latter addresses his concern in a different theoretical context. Bakhtin pits narrative fiction (in his case, the novel) against poetry, attributing to the former the power of heteroglossia. For the Russian critic living through the Stalinist age, the novel is capable of generating the polyphonic energy of a society, culminating in a carnivalesque outburst of linguistic forces. In his 1934 "Discourse in the Novel," Bakhtin develops the concept of heteroglossia, which highlights the coexistence and conflation of distinct voices within a single language. He considers the novel to be the site in which multiple types of utterances made by the characters and narrators are brought into play to capture social interaction at its most dynamic. Bakhtin calls attention to heteroglossia not only in the dialogue between characters but also within the direct and singular articulation of the author. He thus opens up the monolithic authorial identity to the possibility of intersubjectivity.

Bakhtin finds an exemplary case of heteroglossia in the medieval carnival, in which authorities are turned upside down, grotesquery triumphs over decorum, and collective laughter renews social communion. This festive impulse is full of revolutionary momentum as it threatens to overturn the status quo. One notes the ambivalent undercurrent of Bakhtin's carnival: it is framed by a preordained calendar and spatial terrain and is therefore susceptible to authoritarian containment, but it always includes an impulse toward excess that may lead to a violent denial of any kind of order.[43]

We may also take into consideration Gilles Deleuze's concept of "fabulation." Deleuze derives this concept from Henri Bergson, who considers "to fabulate" to be a social propensity to shape the meaning of life —mythmaking—vis-à-vis the flux of time. Whereas Bergson is critical of the term's projection of an overtly anthropocentric, closed, and traditional society, Deleuze emphasizes its potential to break open imaginative horizons. Originally translated as "storytelling,"[44] fabulation as Deleuze defines it refers to the aesthetic capacity to invoke the power of becoming as opposed to the stasis of utopia. In Ronald Bogue's words, "when novelists engage in fabulation, when they diagnose the impasses of the present and their historical causes, and then instigate disruptive becomings-other and lines of flight toward a people to come, they are experimenting on the real."[45] Hence, fabulation underscores creation by initiating its transformative powers.

More provocatively, in his discussion of cinematic images, Deleuze relates fabulation to "storytelling" that endorses the "powers of the false."[46] Instead of associating the notion of "false" with fakery or counterfeiting, Deleuze identifies it with "virtual" forms and forces that have to be actualized within the "real." Storytelling for Deleuze is the conduit through which a certain disruptive becoming manifests itself in the real world.

I have traced the discourse of "tell the good China story" to the Yan'an era in light of Apter and Saich's study. While welcoming the two scholars' observations, I have taken issue with their theoretical model of Baudrillardian simulacrum. Instead, I have offered four critical perspectives of storytelling—by Benjamin, Arendt, Bakhtin, and Deleuze—from which to engage this "China story" campaign. If the campaign is more than a propaganda stunt, I argue, it deserves a serious inquiry into its cultural logic and political potential. From the perspective of world literary culture, the campaign may well add a new dimension to the time-honored studies of storytelling and narratology.

Lastly, insofar as the following survey examines the "China story" campaign in terms of the genre of narrative fiction (*xiaoshuo* 小說), we need to situate the campaign in the Chinese tradition of *xiaoshuo* to better gauge its genealogical trajectory. *Xiaoshuo* can be traced back as far as to *Zhuangzi* 莊子, a text from the Warring States period (476–221 BCE). In ancient China, the genre was associated with rootless gossip and street talk as well as inauthentic accounts and unofficial histories. These possible origins point to three distinctive features of traditional *xiaoshuo*: it is allegorical and entertaining, thrives in public and plebian spaces, and serves as an anomalous form of historiography. Narrative fiction was traditionally looked down upon despite its popularity in both textual and oral forms. The fact that *xiaoshuo* literally refers to "small talk"—fantasy, hearsay, and, unofficial history—bespeaks its "minor," unstable position vis-à-vis the elite culture.[47]

Narrative fiction in the popular vein—transmitted in the vernacular, with a wide range of subjects from the chivalric to the perilous and the gothic—became mature during the sixteenth and seventeenth centuries. That period saw a huge advancement of fiction in terms of elite participation, narratorial craftsmanship, and circulation, as evinced by the compilation of "imitation storytelling" tales such as *Sanyan* 三言 and *Erpai* 二拍,[48] the Four Great Classical Novels[49] and numerous other original works of fiction. Even then, fiction was treated as something vulgar and contrasted to refined genres such as poetry. Fiction was, after all, regarded as the incubator for decadent thoughts and forbidden desires, anathema to the Confucian didacticism underlying the official literary paradigm.

Perhaps for this reason, when elite writers engaged in fiction writing, they felt compelled to offer apologia. Most pertinent to our concerns is Feng Menglong's 馮夢龍 (1574–1646) preface to *Illustrious Tales to Instruct the World* (also titled *Gujin xiaoshuo* 古今小說 [Stories old and new]), one volume of the magisterial *Sanyan* collection of storytelling-imitation short stories that made Feng's name almost synonymous with late imperial vernacular short fiction. In the preface he wrote:

> Fiction began to rise when the tradition of historiography showed signs of decline. With Han Fei [circa 280–233 BCE] and Lie Yukou [circa 450–375 BCE] as its progenitors, it started to take shape toward the end of the Zhou dynasty [circa 1027–256 BCE], flourished in the Tang dynasty [618–907], and became widespread in the Song dynasty [960–1279]. . . . Song writers used the colloquial attuned to the common ear. Now common ears outnumber literary minds in our world, and fiction draws less from the elegant than from the colloquial style. Just ask the storytellers to demonstrate in public their art of description: they will gladden you, astonish you, move you to sad tears, rouse you to song and dance; they will prompt you to draw a sword, bow in reverence, cut off a head, or donate money. The faint-hearted will be made brave, the debauched chaste, the unkind compassionate, the obtuse ashamed. One may well intone the *Classic of Filial Piety* [Xiaojing] and the *Analects* of Confucius every day.[50]

In the preface, Feng starts by observing that the genesis of fiction coincided with the decline of history, and he ends by celebrating the affective power of fiction over Confucian classics. By juxtaposing fiction with historiography and the Confucian canon, Feng must have meant to vindicate the debased position of fiction with regard to the orthodoxy of history (史統 *shitong*). But insofar as he traces the beginning of the decline of history to ancient times, he seems to insinuate something more subversive—that is, that history was incomplete and imperfect from its very genesis, and fiction was already created to be its supplement, if not its replacement. Thus, history and fiction have always already been implicated in each other's existence.

Accordingly, the title of one of Feng's *Sanyan* volumes (*Stories Old and New*) may serve as a sign of a budding modern consciousness in late imperial China. Feng finds in fiction a momentum that can transcend history, propelling humanity in a way that even Confucian learning cannot emulate. Feng lived at the end of the Ming dynasty, a time that saw a drastic shake-up in cultural and social values. His declared aim was to collect stories from various sources and times, revising them in such a way as to construct a fictional order that could emulate the orthodoxy of history—hence his comparison of fiction with Confucian classics.

Nevertheless, by traversing historical limitations in search of a lasting moral schema articulated through fiction, Feng may at the same time have called forth the opposite outcome: an existential sensation that everything —history and fiction, the real and the false—has a fleeting coexistence with everything else. By associating fiction with history, Feng introduces a paradox, achieving not only his stated agenda but also its disavowal: fiction can be as much a close derivation of history as it is a deviation from history. *Stories Old and New* has always been praised as an exemplar of late Ming mimetic realism. But I contend that Feng achieves the realistic effect of his fiction elsewhere, by spelling out a deep-seated sense of crisis about the capriciousness of time and the untenability of history.

Feng's provocative statement that "fiction began to rise when the tradition of historiography showed signs of decline" can invite a more radical interpretation in the modern era. In 1902, when Liang Qichao asserted that vernacular fiction was the most powerful remedy for a China in decline, he was referring to its power to tell a new story about China. Replacing Confucian orthodoxy, this new story is supposed to incite action, in the name of revolution, to topple all establishments. In Bakhtin's terms, this was a carnivalesque enterprise. But we are unfortunately all too aware of the consequences of the tangled relations that Liang establishes between history and fiction. Ironically, Liang's desire to "fabulate" history was taken up by Mao's communist hegemony, while Liang's effort to safeguard history against the excess of fiction remains a challenge to the Chinese authorities to date.

Why Does Fiction Matter in Contemporary China?

For all their distinct motivations to tell the good China story, Liang Qichao, Mao Zedong, and Xi Jinping among others would have been amazed at the fictional extravaganza that alternately shocks, repels, enchants, and disenchants the Chinese people of the new era. Extraterrestrial creatures from another galaxy are seen invading the earth, and fairies, ghosts, and humans travel through the tunnel of time to live out alternative histories. Grotesque exposés of social vice win as much popularity as decadent romances. While realism is still the privileged form of fictional discourse, the reality in writers' treatment has become more equivocal than ever. The internet has fostered enormous contact zones outside of conventional publication venues where multiple narrative experiments—from serialized cycles to fiction turned into games—are made possible. Meanwhile, television and cinema adaptations of popular works have given rise to intellectual property fever.

This book will focus on the China stories told in the form of narrative fiction through the medium of print. To be sure, narrative fiction may no longer enjoy the kind of popularity and prestige that it did in the twentieth century, but this loss of importance has granted it some leeway, enabling it to regain freedom and energy as when Liang conceived of new fiction at the beginning of the twentieth century. Above all, as discussed above, fiction manifests its essence by continuously upsetting its own foundation as a genre. In the following chapters, even with a limited number of cases drawn from narrative fiction both in China and in other Sinophone regions, one can already tell this has been an eye-opening era in which multiple story lines and experimentations have prevailed.

Before moving forward, I need to qualify the three keywords of this book: "contemporary," "China" (or "Chinese"), and "fiction." First, "contemporary" is often taken to mean temporal occurrence at its most instantaneous and acute, but it may also suggest the crystalized moment of time and its eternal return. Since the founding of the PRC in 1949, "contemporary" has been adopted as the sacrosanct moment of a post-1949 "now"—a moment that, according to the ideology of the regime, represents China's final stage of historical development and should last forever. "Contemporary literature" (*dangdai wenxue* 當代文學), therefore, is used to describe literature produced since 1949. This is contrasted with ideas of "early modern literature" (*jindai wenxue* 近代文學) and "modern literature" (*xiandai wenxue* 現代文學), which are used to refer to literature of the late Qing (1840s–1910s) and the May Fourth (1919–49) periods, respectively. This periodization, with each era representing a supposedly more advanced stage in the development of literature, has been used to embed a progressive, revolutionary agenda in the historiography of modern Chinese literature.

However, such a definition of "contemporary" tends to freeze the flux of time, eternalizing that which is supposed to be fleeting and changeable. "What is contemporary?" the Italian thinker Giorgio Agamben asked in an essay by that title at the end of the twentieth century. Citing Roland Barthes and Friedrich Nietzsche, Agamben contends that the contemporary is the "the untimely."[51] In other words, the contemporary is someone who refuses to conform to social norms, straddling multiple temporalities—either "too soon" or "too late," either "already" or "not yet"—in such a way as to see "the obscurity" arising from the folds of time. In light of Agamben's and other critics' insights into time and temporality, I attribute the status of "contemporary" to those writers who hold their gaze on their own time to "perceive not its light, but rather its darkness," all the while searching for some unlikely "beam of darkness" that projects into the time yet to come.

Second, "China" in my treatment signifies at least four phenomena: China as a political entity, as a historical process of continuities and breakups, as a cultural and intellectual topography, and as an "imagined community" to be desired or feared. Since Liang's *The Future of New China*, how to represent and re-present China has been the primary concern of Chinese writers. In 1971, C. T. Hsia (1921–2013) coined the term "obsession with China" to describe the ambivalent attitude of modern Chinese literati toward Chinese modernity. Hsia holds that modern Chinese literati are so obsessed by national crises as to turn their repugnance for the status quo into a masochistic mentality. These literati see any given social or political malaise as a sickness unique to China, and thus grapple with Chinese modernity only negatively, by denouncing it.[52] To remedy this syndrome, Hsia calls for a cosmopolitan engagement with Western literature.[53]

Now, almost five decades after Hsia's critique, "obsession with China" still casts a shadow over Chinese discourse, but the phenomenon has developed in unexpected ways. Whereas writers and readers on the mainland have turned their "obsession" into something more complex—from fanaticism to cynicism, and from passion to nonchalance—in the wake of "China is peacefully rising," as the popular propaganda goes, their radical counterparts in Taiwan (or what is increasingly rarely referred to as the Republic of China) have come to love hating everything about China, so that in an ironic way, they demonstrate the classic symptoms of "obsession" with China. Even more polemical is to think critically about what has been described as "Sinophone literature" in recent years: Chinese-language literature produced in the regions of "greater China" that include Taiwan, Hong

Kong, and the Chinese communities in countries such as Malaysia and Singapore, as well as by Chinese-speaking subjects in the diaspora. In contrast to the term "overseas Chinese literature," which connotes a geopolitically peripheral position with regard to literature centered on the Chinese mainland, Sinophone literature refers to a heterogeneous body of texts related, but not necessarily subjected, to the dominant discourse of China in the name of nation, territory, and ethnicity.

Third, as discussed above, I see "fiction" as a narrative form based not only on fabrication but also on fabulation. I argue that fiction takes on a different dimension in the Chinese context, as both a continuation of and an intervention in history. The intertwined relationships between Chinese history and fiction cannot be reduced to the antithesis between authenticity and its disavowal. I argue that the tension between history and fiction brings to the fore the most engaging and most disturbing aspects of modern Chinese literature. As will be discussed in the following chapters, we must ask how fiction, as a form purportedly catering to the low end of human desires, can miraculously transform itself into the remedy for the malaise of history. Do contemporary Chinese intellectuals' and political leaders' continued efforts to narrate the nation demonstrate the complicitous power of fiction, or its treacherous nature?

In what follows, I introduce three of the most exciting aspects of contemporary fiction in the Chinese and Sinophone world in three related terms—transgression, transmigration, and transillumination. To begin with fiction as transgression, I argue that contemporary Chinse fiction became modern first and foremost because of its transgressive capacity, in a generic, affective, and conceptual sense. Through the prism of transgression, writers and readers launch their call to arms, conjure up utopian and dystopian dreams, and gauge the parameters of subjectivity versus alterity. I focus on the way contemporary writers describe the intrusion of the alien —be it a foreigner, a social outcast, an ethnic minority, a people's enemy, or an extraterrestrial creature—into a harmonious society and the way they use these encounters to test the boundaries of moral decency and political rectitude.

If fiction as transgression touches on the polemics of narrativity and governance, fiction as transmigration engages with narrativity, chronology, and bio- and eco-ethics. Through a series of cases on haunting, spectrality, reincarnation, and metamorphosis, I look into the way in which writers and readers turn the chronological line of a life or story into cyclic tales of transformation, unchronological fantasy, or anachronistic carnival. When ghosts come and go in everyday life, or when animals and humans become exchangeable creatures, the chain of being is disturbed, and a shake-up of human values is called for. I argue that today, more than at any moment in the twentieth century, Chinese fiction writers are willing to venture beyond the sanctioned domain of the real in search of the virtual. Although "obsession with China" still reigns in mainstream discourse, it is a new vision of China, ingrained in a reflection on anthropocene at large that distinguishes avant-garde writers' intervention with the status quo.

Finally, I argue that the most contested area of Chinese fictional writing is represented by fiction as transillumination. "Transillumination" is originally a medical term, referring to the passing of a strong beam of light through tissues or a body cavity for medical inspection. However, I am using this term to evoke something more poetic. I suggest that at its most provocative, contemporary Chinese fiction drives us to contemplate the optic of invisibility as well as the power of immanence.[54] I call attention to works that rethink the "moral occult" of narrative fiction by questioning the tenet of enlightenment and exploring the magic power of mythology and "divine thought." In Lu Xun's words, the writer's capacity to illuminate lies nowhere else but in "inhabiting the dark so as to see the darkness of the dark."[55]

To conclude this chapter, let us return to the "tell the good China story" campaign. One wonders if Xi's repertoire of storytelling would include Liang Qichao's or Lu Xun's inaugural attempts at telling the good China story more than a century ago. I am not simply critiquing the propagandist intent of Xi's campaign, but rather suggesting that the campaign induces the same aporia as Feng Menglong's campaign in the late Ming and Liang Qichao's in the late Qing. The "tell the good China story" compels us to reckon anew with the power of narrative in public life.

I am therefore reminded of another president's musing on the meaning of storytelling. Václav Havel (1936–2011) was a playwright before he participated in the democratic moment of Czechoslovakia. In the late 1980s, he published "Stories and Totalitarianism" to explain the seemingly harmonious society of his country, one in which no "stories" take place:

> What bothers me is something else: the fact that this remarkable absence of newsworthy stories is not an expression of social harmony, but merely the outward consequence of a dangerous and profound process: the destruction of "the story" altogether. Almost every day I am struck by the ambiguity of this social quiescence, which is essentially only the visible expression of an invisible war between the totalitarian system and life itself.[56]

Havel's observation of the last days of socialist Czechoslovakia offers an intriguing perspective from which to view contemporary China. I want to believe that China is not a totalitarian nation, and that as much as it is a harmonious society, there are many stories, good ones and not so good ones, to be told. In what follows I try to introduce my own list of "good" stories that have been told by contemporary fiction writers in China and other Sinophone societies.

2

The Aliens Are Coming

Fiction as Transgression

In 1899, a young Italian priest of the Franciscan order named Giovanni Martino was killed in a skirmish between local Catholics and rioters in a town in Shanxi, in northwest China. In response, Bishop Vescovo Licovino, the local representative of the Roman Catholic Church, demanded that the riot leader be arrested and quickly put to death. What the Chinese did not know, however, was that Martino did not die but regained consciousness after three days. Appalled by Bishop Licovino's decision to continue to conceal the fact of his "resurrection," Martino challenged the Church and ended up being excommunicated. Later that winter, when Martino had been reduced to begging, he encountered an insane woman who, it turned out, was none other than the widow of the riot leader.

In 2066, a Chinese chess prodigy named Tang Long first sets foot on American soil. By then the United States has suffered a series of economic and political disasters, while China has become the world superpower. Tang has been sent to America to participate in a chess championship, but he becomes caught up in the country's Second Civil War. Tang has a series of adventures in the following months, including encountering transgenic humans and surviving a deluge on a ship named *Noah*, before finally returning to China. But the crisis looms ever larger. China is already controlled by the artificial intelligence called Amanduo (阿曼多), which is in turn succumbing to an invasion by Martians.

The stories of Martino and Tang—one from Li Rui's 李銳 (b. 1952) *Zhang Mading de dibatian* 張馬丁的第八天 (The eighth day of Zhang Mading, 2012) and the other from Han Song's 韓松 (b. 1962) *2066: Huoxing zhaoyao meiguo* 2066: 火星照耀美國 (2066: Mars over America)—are two stories that illustrate the scope and provocative nature of Chinese fiction since the beginning of the new millennium. Despite pervasive censorship, a digital media boom, and decreased readership, contemporary Chinese writers have been seeking to inscribe the unspeakable and the improbable in a way that often outshines the writing of their predecessors. They construct in their works utopias and uchronias, and they ponder historical trauma and posthuman apocalypse.

As the dominant genre of modern and contemporary Chinese literature, narrative fiction has exerted enormous influence at various moments of China's search for modernity. For instance, it projected the Chinese dream of utopia in the 1900s, lashed out at institutional cannibalism in the 1920s, indicted social injustice and imperial invasion in the 1930s and 1940s, launched revanchist and socialist campaigns from the 1950s to the 1970s, and evoked the cultural fever (*wenhuare* 文化熱) in the aftermath of the Cultural Revolution (1966–76). Above all, it dramatizes what C. T. Hsia calls the "obsession with China," a sentiment mixing both unconditional nationalism and extreme self-depreciation with regard to historical crises.[1] While narrative fiction since the millennial turn may still perform some of these functions, it no longer enjoys the same momentum or even raison d'être that was ascribed to the genre in the last century. Many literary scholars even suspect the age of fiction has come to an end.

Contrary to such common wisdom, however, I argue that narrative fiction has gained rather than lost its energy in contemporary China, if only for paradoxical reasons. On the one hand, internet literature has engaged millions of writers, readers, bloggers, and fans in a cybernetic revelry hitherto unseen in any other culture: China boasts the largest volume of online literature worldwide.[2] On the other hand, the governmental apparatus of propaganda and censorship is more pervasive and technologically sophisticated than ever. Both the internet and propaganda challenge how we read and write fiction in the conventional format. Nevertheless, both appear to be deriving their rhetorical skills, tropes, and plots from the extant repository of narrative fiction.

As suggested in chapter 1, at a time when even China's national leader is calling for proficient storytelling, one witnesses fiction infiltrating the texture of everyday life and political provocation betraying its own brand of what Gilles Deleuze calls the "power of the false." Meanwhile, fiction proves unruly. Just as President Xi Jinping is fashioning himself as the greatest storyteller of the party or state, a plethora of conventional and new-wave forms of fiction—including online literature, games, and social media—has introduced a carnival that sidetracks, mocks, and defies the narrative of monoletheism.

In this chapter, I propose to look at contemporary Chinese fiction as a form of transgression. By transgression, I refer not only to the violation of the legal, moral, or cognitive paradigm of a community, but also to the politics of boundary crossing—or, in the terminology of Gilles Deleuze and Félix Guattari, the tactics of "deterritorialization" and "reterritorialization."[3] The two novels introduced above serve as good cases in point. Where Martino's untimely "resurrection" touches off a conflict related to religious salvation, colonial hegemony, and extraterritorial manipulation at the beginning of modern China, the Martians' attack in the twenty-first century realizes a premonition of extraterrestrial holocaust. Indeed, contemporary Chinese writers are more inclined than their predecessors to traverse the horizons of China. If traces of "obsession with China" are still discernible, this obsession is made to reckon with much broader concerns, from the possibilities of communicating with aliens to planetary apocalypse.

I contend that the global circulation of bodily, technological, and epistemological forces has called forth a new spatial apparatus, one that activates the phenomena of assimilation, dissemination, situatedness, and transgression in a format far more complex than ever before. It has given rise to a unique *nomos*—a normative universe in which right and wrong, lawful and unlawful, and valid and invalid are deliberated in a narrative form.[4] In some ways, modern Chinese fiction's engagement with nomos is nothing new, as the genre has been associated with the agency of transgression since the beginning of the twentieth century. It has harnessed the power of iconoclasm to debate the recognized and recognizable codes of the body, law, and knowledge. Once unleashed from the shackles of convention, however, fiction reveals its monstrous potential.

Transgression is linked to the dialogue between justice and violence. Here, justice refers to a social institution that is implemented in many ways—from legal codes to administrative norms, from consensual conventions to mythical taboos, and from disciplinary measures to revolutionary action

—to define and curb natural and human forms of violence.[5] Violence is understood as a demonstration of natural, social, or individual power that crosses the consensual boundary of the rational and results in physical or psychological damage to the victim.[6] Nevertheless, justice is contingent on the "state of exception," and violence can be justified as "divine violence."[7]

In what follows, I examine novels drawn from both Chinese and other Sinophone contexts to demonstrate how fiction as transgression can alternately offend, scandalize, enchant, and titillate the reader in such a way as to shed new light on the politics of justice and violence in contemporary China. To that end, I focus on the trope of alien—the foreigner, the enemy within, or the outlandish being—whose (accidental) intrusion from outside Chinese horizons brings about a crisis of territoriality. Let us begin, however, with a genealogical review of the fictional discourse of modern China, against which the contemporary cases can be gauged.

Four Paradoxes

Modern Chinese fiction evolved alongside an incessant debate about the relationship between nation and narration. Realism—as an effort at mimetic representation through language, a cognitive and ideological construct of reality, and a truth claim—was the focus of contestation. There are at least four moments when the debate over the "order of mimesis"[8] became highly contentious: the beginning of the twentieth century, the post–May Fourth era (1930s), the founding years of the People's Republic of China (PRC; 1950s), and the decade after the Cultural Revolution (1980s). Both writers and readers in these eras engaged in the polemics of reality and its fictional representation, often risking both their artistic and political integrity. Indeed, the history of twentieth-century Chinese fiction is punctuated by numerous negotiations of the boundary lines between the real and the unreal, and truth claims and their violation.

When Liang Qichao called for a fiction revolution in 1902, he inaugurated the discourse of new fiction. Liang argued that fiction, however contemptible in the eyes of conservative intellectuals, was capable of renovating China because the genre has an incalculable power to affect the Chinese mind. Liang's advocacy of a fiction revolution was preceded by similar calls from reform-minded intellectuals such as Yan Fu 嚴復 (1854–1921) and Xia Zengyou 夏曾佑 (1863–1924). For them, fiction was the genre that most emphatically dealt with heroism (*yingxiong* 英雄) and romance (*ernü* 兒女), the common denominators of a universal humanity (*gong xingqing* 公性情). Accordingly, whereas history may fall short in showing what life should be, fiction can rectify history to ensure the perpetual commemoration of the heroic and romantic ideals of humanity.[9]

Liang's campaign for a fiction revolution culminated in his 1902 manifesto on the relationship between fiction and ruling the people.[10] In a hyperbolic tone, he suggested that the future of new China hinged on the reform of fiction, and he preempted any skeptical response by arguing that "fiction is endowed with an incalculable magnitude of power to transform the mentality and morale of the Chinese people."[11] Moreover, Liang argued that fiction exerts its influence on people in four ways: by diffusing (*xun* 熏), permeating (*jin* 浸), piercing (ci 刺), and lifting (*ti* 提) the reader. Although he derived these concepts from Buddhist thought, his emphasis on the affective—even contagious—power of fiction is anything but transcendental: fiction is meant to disturb the equilibrium of human feeling.

Critics have noticed a strong didactic and utilitarian logic in late Qing fiction discourse, one reminiscent of the orthodox Confucian principle that "*wen* 文 [literature and culture in the broad sense] . . . carries the Way."[12] But this didacticism was in fact a hybrid discourse. Yan and Xia drew inspiration from social Darwinism, and Liang was indebted to the Japanese and European traditions of the political novel.[13] Despite their shared dedication to using fiction for moral inculcation, each gave the discourse an additional twist by pondering its ethical bearings: all three authors uttered harsh words about the decadent potential of fiction generally before setting out to promote new fiction. Yan and Xia believed that fiction incites thoughts of cupidity and lust.[14] Liang blamed fiction for spreading all the corrupt ideals and superstitions of traditional Chinese society: "Whence comes the Chinese habit of overprizing the successful scholar and prime minister? It comes from fiction. Whence the Chinese vice of fancying oneself as a talented beauty or gifted young scholar? It comes from fiction. Whence the Chinese admiration for brigands and thieves of the rivers and lakes? It comes from fiction. Whence the Chinese fascination with demons, shamans, fox spirits, and ghosts? It again comes from fiction."[15]

If fiction is a genre that has poisoned Chinese society for hundreds of years, why would someone like Liang want to embrace it? Why would he believe that this poisonous genre would transform itself into a miraculous potion capable of curing Chinese society? While Plato drove poets out of his republic for fear that their works would weaken the morale of its citizens, late Qing critics followed a similar argument to a rather different conclusion. Liang and his like-minded peers welcomed fiction, asserting that its incredible power allowed it to be cleansed of its own poisonous nature and then administered to revive the audience it had earlier poisoned—a seemingly homeopathic therapy reminiscent of the Derridean case of *pharmakon*.[16] Or, to stick closer to China, it is a literary immunology based on the old Chinese medical concept of *yidu gongdu* 以毒攻毒, to fight poison with poison.

Juxtaposing fiction's incalculable power to corrupt and its incredible power to rehabilitate, Liang and his contemporaries pushed traditional critics' fear of and fascination with fiction to the extreme. If practitioners of traditional fiction defended its moral value in a tongue-in-cheek manner, their modern counterparts did so seriously. In their willing suspension of disbelief about the future of literature, they are the pious advocates of the literary values they should have been skeptical about.

However, a quick glance at the oeuvre of late Qing fiction shows that for every item of new fiction, there appear many counterexamples, works later to be called novels of depravity, black screen novels, chivalric romance, fantasy, and so forth. Although the target audience of new fiction was the general public, Xu Nianci 徐念慈 (1875–1908), Liang's contemporary, estimated that the common people constituted no more than 10 percent of its total readership.[17] This was not only a problem of literacy and affordability but also popular taste. In the essay "Gao xiaoshuojia" 告小說家 (To fiction writers), Liang admits that "the past ten years saw the tremendous degeneration of social morals and manners, and what aspect of that degeneration has not been traceable to an influence of the so-called new fiction?"[18] Since that statement was made in 1915, the alleged decline of new fiction could be traced back to 1905, the year Liang's magazine, *New Fiction*, folded.[19]

This vicious cycle of the immunization and contagion of fiction continued into the 1920s and 1930s, giving rise to what I call the second paradox of modern Chinese fictional development. In the wake of the May Fourth movement, engaged writers pursued a fictional discourse that could both reflect social malaise and point to the hope of salvation, thus both issuing a call to arms and cultivating a space for individual sensibilities. Fictional realism—be it labeled critical, revolutionary, or socialist—became the privileged form of this discourse, not merely because of its efforts at mimesis but also because of its adherence to a rationalist agenda and its claim of total truth: the order of mimesis was implicated in such a way as to become an ideology.

Nevertheless, close analysis reveals that the end and the means of this fictional poetics did not coalesce: its inherently rationalist agenda called for justice and humanity, but in practice it was subject to spells of fanaticism and mannerism. Thus, in picturing the development of modern Chinese fiction, one should be always alert to the gaps between what the writers and critics thought they achieved and what they really did achieve and between what the elite expected their readers to like and what their readers actually liked.

In particular, since the ultimate goal of a fiction revolution is to prepare for the arrival of reform or revolution, writing is expected to evoke a yearning for that imminent revelatory moment. Fictional realism becomes an act of anticipation, but it can also be an act of procrastination. If realism is first and foremost an effort to depict the status quo in its immediacy, post–May Fourth writers quickly found themselves in a dilemma: the more accurately and poignantly they depicted sociopolitical vices, the more they projected —wittingly or unwittingly—the evil, stagnant nature of humanity and the hopelessness of any change. The bitterest question of Lu Xun in "The Diary of a Madman" comes to mind: "Perhaps there are still children who have not eaten men? Save the children . . ."[20] Can children really be saved if they are nourished by their cannibalistic parents?

Marston Anderson has identified this dilemma as a problem of "the morality of form." Using works by Lu Xun, Mao Dun, and Ye Shaojun as evidence, he suggests that the success of critical realism brings about only a negative dialectic. That is, fiction writing can best be defined as an act of self-denial, if not self-cannibalization: a desperate naming of what reality cannot become.[21]

Mao Zedong's 1942 Yan'an talks were intended to be a cure for this dilemma. The talks derived their power from a utopian agenda for a revolutionary literature. As if echoing Liang, Mao asserts the "power of an incalculable magnitude" of literature, but he believes that this power cannot be fully employed unless the literature in question has been programmed —or disciplined—by the party.[22] At its most provocative, Maoist literature is said to be able to bridge the gap between the elite writers and the illiterate audience, the literary subject and the everyday event, individual talents and dogmatic tradition, and deplorable past and irresistible future. Liang's fiction dream came true, in a most unlikely way.

How to compose fiction the right way in relation to revolutionary history was already a contentious issue by the Yan'an period. Fiction was expected not only to reflect but also to rectify reality. Moreover, it was expected to project reality—the socialist state of plenitude, as promised by the success of the revolution. A new narratology was developed, and new politics and ethics of writing were made institutional. Zhao Shuli 趙樹理 (1906–70) was hailed as a model writer of the era for his ingenious welding of progressive ideology and the party line with grassroots performing arts traditions. At the same time, established writers were undergoing an enormous metamorphosis. One prominent case is Ding Ling 丁玲 (1904–86), who before her conversion first became popular for her portraits of the decadent lives of urban women. In 1941, Ding wrote "Wozai xiacun de shihou" 我在霞村的時候 (When I was in Xia village), describing a female communist's painful negotiation between gender and revolution. In the story, a village girl, a victim of rape by Japanese soldiers, volunteers to serve as a comfort woman for the Japanese troops to collect information for the revolutionary forces. She contracts syphilis and returns to her village, only to be ostracized by the villagers, and her cure remains uncertain. For this and several other writings, Ding was rectified on the ground that she spread decadent thought and sentimentalism. When she reemerged in 1948, with *Taiyang zhaozai sanggan heshang* 太陽照在桑乾河上 (The sunshine over the Sanggan river), Ding had become a cadre writer in submission to Mao's formula. Even her new style—impassioned yet restrained—reflected the shake-up of her political bearings.

By the end of the Yan'an era, one can already discern at least three themes arising from revolutionary literature: the dialectic of revolution and history, the fashioning of an enlightened and progressive subjectivity, and the projection of a utopian vision. The first theme has to do with authenticating nationhood and enforcing the party line, the second highlights the epistemological and affective transformation of individuals as well as communities, and the third helps realize the imaginary as promised by the ideology.

When the PRC was founded in 1949, it created a new image for writers. A new ethics of writing also emerged, which demanded that writers descend to the proletarian world and mingle with the people they were delegated to portray, so as to tell the people's stories firsthand—a most literal practice of realism. One discerns a new narrative typology of realism that merges fiction with politics and pedagogy with entertainment. But what has been downplayed is the fact that to implement socialist realism, ink and blood were often mixed to produce a most brutal ecology of writing and reading.

This fact brought about the third paradox of modern Chinese fiction. On the one hand, it informed the writers that the revolution had succeeded, and thus the conditions for the existence of prerevolutionary literature had disappeared. If modern fiction was first occasioned by social and political injustice before 1949, it had become a redundant undertaking in the new society, except for its role in recalling the bad old days and reaffirming the happy new days. On the other hand, writers were told that the revolution was still going on: there were more class enemies that needed to be eliminated and more anticapitalist wars that needed to be fought. However, if writers resumed the critical positions of their prerevolutionary days, they would have only recapitulated the second aspect of the paradox of realism—postponing rather than hastening the completion of the revolution. Either way writers were forced into a corner, where they had to submit to the role prepared for them by the party. The result is a hollowing out of the rationale behind the moral courage and theoretical rigor of the fiction for revolution before 1949.

The dialectic of revolution and history resulted in two trends in fictional writing from the 1950s to the 1970s: the revolutionary historical romance, or *geming lishi xiaoshuo* 革命歷史小説, which chronicles the prehistory of the founding of the PRC; and the peasant novel, which narrates the radical changes in Chinese rural communities resulting from land reform and other agricultural policies.[23] Neither trend should be taken merely at face value. Both point to a well-orchestrated temporal scheme that advocates the inevitable triumph of the future over the past; the eternal return of lost justice; and an intricate spatial symbolism representing the loss, recovery, and redistribution of the homeland at both national and personal levels.[24]

Yet the transgressive potential of fiction continuously surfaced in the new China, sometimes in a most unlikely manner. By the mid-1950s, a literature that presumably had sublated all previous revolutionary writings was well on its way to becoming a grand praxis. When writers competed in filling their works with propagandistic plots and exemplary figures, they adhered to a socialist narratology of excess. Formally, that sanctions rather than avoids hyperbole and redundancy; conceptually, it is devoted to ideological dogma to the point of conjuring up a new mythology of socialist virtues.

Thus, one finds works such as Du Pengcheng's 杜鵬程 (1922–91) *Baowei Yan'an* 保衛延安 (Guarding Yan'an, 1954), crowded with heroes ready to die for the nation, and works such as Zhao Shuli's 趙樹理 *Sanliwan* 三里灣 (Three mile bay, 1955) that feature model peasants fighting tirelessly against class enemies in an almost Sisyphean manner. Socialist realism induces socialist melodrama, flooded with the Manichean scheme of characters, episodes, and values, as well as the deus ex machina of the Communist Party. When transgression takes an inward turn, the revolution described by realist fiction seems instead to be an uncanny involution.

However, one must learn to appreciate the ideological and rhetorical acrobatics in fiction writing at this time, as any misstep could lead to fatal consequences.[25] Thus, as censorship and the demand for bowdlerization escalated, so did the enthusiasm for imagining and inscribing the Maoist sublime. The fervor gives rise to a unique aesthetic. Those who discerned the irrational quality of this new literature either willingly suspended disbelief, hoping that things would take a turn for the better, or mutely protested, engaging in a form of internal exile by ceasing to write. However, there were writers who engaged in quixotic combat, at the expense of their careers and lives.

Take a look at Wang Meng's 王蒙 (b. 1934) *Qingchun wansui* 青春萬歲 (Long live youth, 1979). This novel describes the life of a group of high school girls and their dreams, misgivings, visions, and hesitations on the eve of graduation. Their education culminates in a nocturnal visit to Tian'anmen Square, where they run into a giant figure who turns out to be none other than Chairman Mao. A chance encounter becomes a miraculous moment of encountering the messiah of socialist China, without which the girls' initiation into communism would be incomplete.[26]

Wang was fifteen when he joined the Communist Party in 1948 and twenty-three when he finished *Long Live Youth*. In a way the novel is something he wrote for and about himself—his own ideal bildungsroman. However, the novel was censored, and Wang Meng was exiled to Xinjiang for sixteen years. When *Long Live Youth* was finally published after the Cultural Revolution, it was already inscribed with a subtext about enlightenment turned into forbidden knowledge and enchantment transformed into precarious enthrallment.

In the aftermath of the Cultural Revolution, as Chinese society tried to come to terms with the causes and consequences of the so-called ten-year holocaust, fiction again became an arena for debate and experimentation. The new era began with a genre called scar literature (*shanghen wenxue* 傷痕文學), which treated the scar of the Cultural Revolution as a contested sign of both injury and healing, both a reminder and a remainder of violence. However, to many people realism became the impediment to probing the true cause of the scar.[27] Writing at a time when revolution had lost its mandate and reality had become a pretext for bad faith, writers could not take up the two subjects without pondering their obscurity. Thus, whereas the root-seeking (*xungen* 尋根) movement called for excavating the repressed and oppressed roots of the socialist paradise, the avant-garde (*xianfeng* 先鋒) movement paraded radical forms and concepts from modernism to postmodernism to represent the unrepresentable.

Above all, this is an era of posthistory, in which history—be it as an ideology, episteme, institution, or narrative form—is thrown into question. Ge Fei's格非 (b. 1964) "Mizhou" 迷舟 (Misty boat, 1987) envisions revolution as a labyrinthine game of desires, whims, and mishaps that ends up nowhere; Mo Yan's *Honggaoliang jiazu* 红高粱家族 (Red sorghum family, 1986) depicts revolutionary history as a regressive rather than progressive sequence of national and family memory; and Yu Hua's 余華 (b. 1960)

"1986" of the same year simply likens revolution to a gory theater of corporeal mutilation and insanity. Thus, the works seek to dissolve the spell of "Maoist discourse"[28] that has dominated the conception, production, and consumption of literature in China since the 1940s.

However, this leads to the fourth paradoxical moment of twentieth-century Chinese fiction. As much as the writers of new era manage to disrupt the paradigm of socialist realism, the way in which they engage with Maoist discourse only reinstates the familiar swing of fictional politics. In other words, in their attempt to exorcise the Maoist ghost, the writers only prove the extent to which they are haunted by it. In a case like Yu Hua's fiction, hysteria, insanity, and violence are depicted in such an uninhibited manner that one wonders whether the author is not indicting Maoist discourse by cynically giving in to all its cannibalistic impulses.

In a previous work, I have pointed out three directions in which Chinese fiction traveled at the end of the twentieth century. First, in opposition to Western formalist theory, which values "defamiliarization" as key to the "literariness" of literature, contemporary Chinese fiction distinguishes itself ironically by means of "re-familiarization of the uncanny."[29] If defamiliarization refers to adopting a critical approach to the banal, repetitious continuum of life, making use of the techniques of disruption or even parody, refamiliarization turns such a strategy upside down. It recognizes the facts that Maoist reality is already full of absurdities and abnormalities and that literature can intervene by making reality more intelligible rather than more strange.

When the horrors and grotesqueries of everyday experience are not repressed but legitimated and even promoted, the result is a condition that Sigmund Freud has labeled the uncanny: "something familiar and old-established in the mind that has been estranged only by the process of repression."[30] Chinese writers of the post-Mao era have given the Freudian concept a twist. They are compelled to explore the paradoxical question of why things that would be seen as dreary and repressed in a Western and Freudian context have been presented as natural in China. If their works can be called uncanny, they are uncanny in the sense that they represent the cognitive flip-flop necessary to make comprehensible the banality of quotidian horror.

Second, as described above, contemporary Chinese writers have adopted a highly subjective, even idiosyncratic, approach to history as a master narrative. Facing the gap between what has happened and what should have happened, the writers try to make sense of the past by retooling the memory machine, using *poesis* (the art of imaginary evocation) as a way to critique the grand historical narrative.

I call this intervention the "lyricization of the epic," in light of the Czech Sinologist Jaroslav Průšek's view of Chinese modernity as constituted by the two poles of the lyrical and the epic.[31] For Průšek, a lyrical sensibility enables modern Chinese writers and intellectuals to articulate their feelings of nonconformity with respect to any establishment, but this individual attempt cannot prevail until it is substantiated by the communal momentum of the people—the epic sensibility. Chinese revolution can succeed only through the fusion of the lyrical and the epic. However, history seems to have proven that such a synthesis is difficult if not impossible to achieve, and Průšek himself became a victim of the "epic" power of the Prague Spring in 1968. He was put under house arrest and deprived of all privileges, and he led an isolated life until his passing in 1980.

If Průšek's view makes sense to contemporary writers, it is not because the lyrical and the epic form the totality of the literary approaches to the nation but because, through their continued conflict, they have illuminated each other's aesthetic and political assumptions. History may still be the primary concern of the Chinese nation-state, but epic discourse has often been appropriated by its lyrical other, resulting in a history that is either fragmented or anachronized. While this lyrical tendency may point either to the neoliberal desire to make personal what used to be communal or to the schizophrenia of broken historical subjectivity, there is an even stronger force behind it. With its emphasis on the figurative power of language, the new lyrical mode affirms a critical position that refuses to be confined by the referential, deterministic imperatives of epic (or historical) discourse. This emphasis on language and literary expression is a confirmation of the human ability to independently figure, and figure out, the world. If one looks at Yu Hua's exposé of the socialist absurd or Can Xue's 殘雪 (b. 1953) celebration of the macabre and ghastly in everyday life, one is intrigued by the total—if not totalitarian—manner in which they deconstruct the past.

Third, late twentieth-century Chinese fiction is characterized by a state of unbearable lightness. C. T. Hsia has famously criticized modern Chinese literature for its "obsession with China," a mentality that drives writers to focus on China at the expense of the world, obsessing about Chinese malaise nearly to the point self-flagellation. However, contemporary writers have tried to break away from such an obsession by heading in the opposite direction and ending up with what we could label a "flirtation with China." These writers adopt an attitude of frivolous yet harmless eroticism to any serious subject—above all, to the most serious of all subjects, China. Writing becomes a facetious gesture or playful action that titillates rather than teaches and flirts rather than indicts. Laughter is the dominant, but ambiguous, emotional register.

"Flirtation with China," however, must be treated with no less caution than the deadly gravity of earlier generations. For one thing, it reflects writers' ambivalent contemplation of literature's status in a postmodern world where simulacra deconstruct realities and morals boil down to mere manners. From another angle, the flirtation with China reveals the strategic political repositioning of the writers. Through their light writing, they either tease the apparent solemnity of the state and censorship or bid farewell to such forerunners of modern Chinese literature as Liang Qichao and Lu Xun. In this vein, Zhang Dachun 張大春 (b. 1957), a leading novelist in Taiwan, calls the fiction writer nothing but a master liar (大說謊家 *dashuohuangjia*), and Wang Shuo王朔 (b. 1958) creates hooligan literature (*pizi wenxue* 痞子文學) that subverts the canon of socialist literature in toto. More noticeable is the case of *Huangjin shidai* 黃金時代 (The golden time, 1992) by Wang Xiaobo 王小波 (1952–97), a novel about a "sent-down" youth's initiation on a farm during the Cultural Revolution, in which political fanaticism amounts to mass hysteria about sexual perversion. Meanwhile, it reveals the melancholia underneath sexual escapades and the sound and fury resulting from the three-ring circuses of political scandals.

Since its inception, modern Chinese fiction has been closely bound to the cultural politics of reforming and re-forming China. It is defined by a mimesis-oriented canon of realism, an affective equation between ink and blood, a censorious impulse to direct libido into ideology, the combination of writing and revolution, and its instrumental use to reinforce the orthodox implication of history and truth. But in facing the four paradoxes I have described above, writers of different generations have aimed at upsetting these discourses in such a way as to question their tenability, if not legitimacy.

This is where fiction demonstrates its power as an imaginative exercise that always escapes the prescribed boundaries of writing and thought. Such fictional power has never disappeared, not even at the most precarious moments, and it has manifested itself once again in the new millennium, bringing to the fore its inherent transgressive potential. Where the state power nurtures a haunting eternal return of ideological bondage, fiction begets hopes of transgression and creation.

The Adventures of Padre Giovanni Martino and Inspector Morris Davison

How does narrative fiction regenerate its transgressive power in China at the turn of the millennium? Did the paradoxes of modern Chinese fiction described above resolve themselves by the end of the twentieth century, or did they emerge ever more invigorated? In the rest of this chapter, I describe the changing configuration of the alien—the actor of alterity who crosses the racial, ethical, religious, political, and even anthropocentric boundary lines of a community—and gauge the gamut of transgressions in the act of imagining China in the new millennium. I begin in this section with the intrusion of two foreigners (a missionary and a colonial officer) into China. Their incursion demonstrates how xenophilia and xenophobia help define modern territoriality in spatial, institutional, and bodily senses. In the following section, I discuss two Chinese intellectuals in exile, one in an exile imposed by the government and the other self-exiled, and ponder how the alien was created within China as the result of political and ideological mutations. In the section after that, I turn to science fiction, the most popular genre of the new century, and examine how the advent of extraterrestrial beings has enabled Chinese fiction to venture into the zones of the unknown and unknowable. By traversing racial, legal, gender, national, and even cognitive boundaries, contemporary Chinese fiction showcases the turbulent streams of political consciousness flowing beneath a regime otherwise labeled as unified and harmonious.

We begin with Li Rui's *The Eighth Day of Zhang Mading*, which takes us back to the beginning of the twentieth century. As noted above, in 1899, a young Italian priest, Padre Giovanni Martino, was accidentally beaten to death in a skirmish between local natives and churchgoers in a small town in Shanxi. This was a clash between two belief systems: the centuries-old cult of the goddess Nüwa, the archdeity of creation and birth, and the monotheism demanded by the Catholic Church. The bishop in charge of local missionary affairs, Vescovo Licovino, loves China and has vowed to die for the salvation of the old Orient; he tolerates no indigenous heresy. Meanwhile, the local administration has been so intimidated by foreign powers that it agrees to Licovino's demands whenever possible.

The Western missionary movement played an extremely complex role in the making of modern China. It brought about the profound shake-up not only of Chinese spiritual life but also of China's sociopolitical infrastructure. In late Qing China, Shanxi Province was a site where foreign and domestic belief systems frequently met in drastic confrontations. Li Rui starts *The Eighth Day of Zhang Mading* in late 1899, when local conflicts were already escalating at the instigation of the Boxers, insurgents purportedly endowed with a mysterious power and supported by the Chinese court in their resistance to foreign powers. The situation was intensified in March 1900, as Yuxian 毓賢 (1842–1901), a conservative, was appointed governor of Shanxi. On July 9, a massacre of missionaries and their family members occurred in Taiyuan, igniting a massive antiforeign fervor. By the end of the summer, hundreds of foreigners and thousands of Chinese had been killed in the province—so many that their deaths were described as "the greatest single tragedy in the history of Christian evangelicalism."[32] As a leading instigator of the Boxer Rebellion, Yuxian was executed in early 1901 to pacify the foreign invaders.

With this background, Li Rui could have made his novel yet another chronicle of the Boxer Rebellion, an incident that hurled China into the modern world in a traumatic way. But he chooses to direct our attention instead to an accidental murder case. At the center of his narrative are Padre Giovanni Martino; the riot's leader, Zhang Tianci; and his wife, Woman Zhang Wang. Born in Varallo in northern Italy, Martino decided to serve God for good in his teenage years, and he was barely twenty when Bishop

Licovino brought him to China. He has adopted a Chinese name, Zhang Mading (張馬丁), and a Chinese lifestyle. By contrast, Zhang Tianci is a peasant who, together with his fellow townspeople, has long been agitated by missionary activities and the county magistrate's favoritism. As the novel begins, he is awaiting execution for leading the riot and killing Martino when Woman Zhang Wang sneaks into the jail. She hopes to have sex with her husband before his death so she can continue the family line.

Meanwhile, Bishop Licovino has demanded immediate revenge for Martino's purported death because he sees the young priest as his successor and surrogate son. But Martino's untimely "resurrection" disturbs Licovino's plan. Instead of stopping Zhang's impending execution, the bishop decides to take advantage of Martino's "martyrdom" to consolidate the Church's power. "Zhang Mading" must die for the church, and Martino is asked to grow beard and assume a new identity. What ensues is a roller coaster of a plot. Martino resists Licovino's scheme and is eventually excommunicated, "deprived of everything. . . . In this foreign and remote country, among the heretics who don't believe in God, he has no way out but begging."[33] On a snowy night that winter, Martino is found collapsed at the entrance of the temple of the goddess Nüwa by a woman, Zhang Tianci's widow.

A veteran writer known for his austere, realistic portraits of the historical turmoil of modern China, particularly the Cultural Revolution, Li Rui startles his reader with a new kind of novel charged with melodramatic tension and sensuous details. He contends that to trace the origin of China's modern experience, one must narrate against its grain and engage its primal scenes at their most intricate and painful. The realism sanctioned by the authorities cannot serve this purpose. He instead must yoke the mimetic to the fantastic to depict the violence and irrationality of the Shanxi incident.

The theme of contagion and hybridity haunts *The Eighth Day of Zhang Mading*. This is a novel that presents the mutual penetration of superstition and belief; legal justice and divine justice; fanaticism and Machiavellianism; and above all, China and the West. In describing Martino's coming back to life, Li Rui hints at the blurry line between mythical reincarnation and Christian resurrection. But even more perplexing is the climax of Martino's suffering. In a state of frenzy, Woman Zhang Wang rescues the dying Martino as if he had been sent by heaven, which she believes he was. She believes the young priest to be the incarnation of her husband, arranged by the goddess Nüwa to alleviate her suffering and complete her wish to carry on the family line.

The two characters never find out each other's identity. At her most delirious, Woman Zhang Wang forces Martino to have sexual intercourse with her in such a way as to completely demoralize the young priest. Imbued with abject eroticism and gothic revelry, the scene is easily one of the most disturbing moments in contemporary Chinese fiction. It challenges the limitations of narrating China: are we expected to learn from it the lesson of radical mercy, coming at the cost of the complete downfall of both characters, or that of historical monstrosity, which defies any attempt at salvation?

Martino dies a pathetic death a few days later, after being forced to have sex not only with Woman Zhang Wang but also a few other widows yearning for offspring. They all believe that Nüwa has answered their wishes by sending them a foreign man. Before his death, Martino jots down a few words as his own epitaph:

> Your world settles on the Seventh Day,
> My world starts on the Eighth Day.

The novel ends on a chilling note. In the aftermath of the Boxer Rebellion, five babies appear in this provincial town, all with blond hair and Eurasian looks. They are the creations of Martino on the "eighth day," a dubious allegory for the arrival of the Chinese modern age.

We now turn to a different case. On December 25, 1941, Sir Mark Aitchison Young (1886–1974), governor of Hong Kong, surrendered the British crown colony to Japan, eighteen days after the beginning of the Japanese attack. During the following three years and eight months, Hong Kong was subject to the brutal rule of Japanese imperial forces. It was a dark time for both the British colonizers and the Chinese people in the colony. Among those stranded on the island are Morris Davison and Lu Nancai. Davison is a Scot working for the colonial government as a police inspector, while Lu is the head of the local triad gang and Davison's informant. The two carry on a clandestine love affair. The fall of Hong Kong not only throws them out of the set trajectories of their lives, but it also sends their political and romantic relationships into crisis.

Davison and Lu are characters in *Longtou Fengwei* 龍頭鳳尾 (Dragon head, phoenix tail, 2016) by the Hong Kong writer Ma Ka-fai 馬家輝 (b. 1962). Ma considers the Japanese occupation period (1941–45) the turning point in Hong Kong's colonial history. However, to describe the time at its most capricious, he gives up the traditional form of historical saga and focuses instead on a slice of the life of an unlikely couple, Davison and Lu. Both had been brought to Hong Kong by chance. Whereas Davison leaves his wife and children in Scotland to make a career in the Far East, Lu, a native of Guangdong, starts out as a rickshaw boy and eventually becomes the most powerful man in the underworld. For both, Hong Kong turns out to be a place that liberates their forbidden desires.

By situating the fall of Hong Kong in the context of a homoerotic romance between a Chinese godfather and a British colonial officer, Ma casts a harsh light on the volatile and skewed nature of the colony's society. Lu and Davison are drawn to each other's exotic and erotic appeal, and their affair becomes possible only in the extraterritorial domain of Hong Kong. One can of course draw a parallel between the two men's affair and the heterosexual formula of colonial Orientalism: stories about the likes of Suzie Wong come to mind. But Ma means to do more. He probes how the island can generate a vortex of unpredictable confrontations across gender, racial, class, legal, and political boundaries. After all, Lu is not a stereotypical Oriental effete out of *M Butterfly* but a robust and reckless gangster. In a colony where sodomy laws are enforced, Davison and Lu keep alternating roles, reveling in the intertwining of lust, ambition, sadomasochism, and romantic yearning and cheating.

As the crisis in East Asia escalated in the late 1930s, Hong Kong became a shelter for people from all factions, trades, professions, and classes—including such prominent figures as Wang Jingwei 汪精衛 (1883–1944), the most infamous traitor of the Second Sino-Japanese War; Song Qingling 宋慶齡 (1893–1981), the widow of Sun Yat-sen and a communist sympathizer; and Du Yuesheng 杜月笙 (1888–1951), the godfather of the Shanghai underworld. Davison and Lu find themselves mingling with people from all walks of life, and taking high-stakes risks. Gambling and sex spread metaphorically across both the text and the Hong Kong society it depicts. The novel's title (*Dragon Head, Phoenix Tail*) refers to a Chinese gambling game, but it also takes on an erotic connotation. Indeed, promiscuity provides the thematic matrix for the interlinking of the worlds of commerce, politics, warfare, and romance.

After the fall of Hong Kong, thousands of British soldiers and colonial officers are sent to a concentration camp, while Lu survives by serving both the Japanese and the underground Chinese resistance forces. It is at this point that Ma adds another layer of moral and romantic ambiguity. Moving among the warlord forces, the nationalists, the communists, and the colonial authorities, Lu has never harbored any qualms about not having a political allegiance. As he claims, in the fallen Hong Kong, "all residents are traitors": "whatever happens, we are ruling the underworld."[34] Yet Lu is devastated to learn that Davison is having a new affair while trading classified information with the Japanese for money. This turns out to be the last straw. Lu permanently falls out of his (unrequited) love for the Scottish officer and launches a lethal scheme for revenge.

For Ma, the challenge lies in how he can bring a forbidden romance to bear on the epic moment of Hong Kong history. Compare Ma's scenario, for example, with Eileen Chang's 張愛玲 (1920–95) famous novella *Qingcheng zhilian* 傾城之戀 (Love in a fallen city, 1943). In that novella, an average but unusually calculating couple consummates their love affair amid the bombing of Hong Kong, a romance that otherwise would have already reached a dead end. The outbreak of war in Hong Kong serves as the unexpected deus ex machina that rescues a romantic shipwreck. Chang casts an eschatological look at the fate of Hong Kong with both irony and compassion: "millions of lives perished as if only for the happy ending of the couple."[35] More than sixty years after Chang's Hong Kong fable about the unbearable lightness of being, Ma gives the plot another twist, rendering a queer version of history and a "love in a fallen city." There is an eye for an eye, and a betrayal for a betrayal. Something harrowing looms ever larger, as the novel closes on a dark note. But the questions can be asked: Written in the postcolonial time when Hong Kong has been under the control of China, does Ma's novel present a different political innuendo from Chang's? If so, what is it?

By juxtaposing two foreigner characters, Giovanni Martino in 1899 and Morris Davison in 1942, against the historical foils of the Boxer Rebellion and the Japanese occupation, respectively, I call attention to two factors that profoundly affected the making of modern China, Christian missionary culture, and colonialism. These two characters are both described as arriving in mainland China or Hong Kong at a critical moment, and they inadvertently ignite the inherent xenophobic or xenophilic tension between China and the West on all fronts. Their adventures are so spectacular as to overturn conventional Chinese imaginaries of the foreigner. Whereas Martino embodies the missionary enterprise at its most precarious and perverse, Davison is the personification of the colonial hegemony turning against itself.

More significantly, both characters are seen as the agents and victims of (religious and political) extraterritoriality that is closely related to colonial government. Extraterritoriality justifies the application of a colonial sovereign's law outside of its territory; it creates an enclave that legitimates a certain value system otherwise deemed unacceptable by the locals. Thus, in the *Eighth Day of Zhang Mading*, Bishop Licovino can demand the instant execution of the Chinese riot leader so as to assert the law of his God on Chinese soil; and in *Dragon Head, Phoenix Tail*, Inspector Davison can use his immunity from judgment to better control the Chinese residents in Hong Kong. Nevertheless, in breaching the "state of exception,"[36] both Li Rui and Ma Ka-fai aim to unveil the encounters that subvert the enclosed extraterritorial autonomy of either the church in Shanxi or the colonial government in Hong Kong. In other words, they try to find the exceptions to the state of exception. They discern in tabooed eroticism something that erodes the establishment of either religion or sovereignty. The result is a very ambiguous presentation of the two foreigners' fates in China. One can no longer be sure if Martino dies as an unconditional sacrifice to God or an unsolicited degeneration into depravity or if Davison meets his downfall because of his colonial overreaching or his wayward romance.

The way Li and Ma describe the two foreigners also leads us to speculate on the connections of their works to contemporary China. In the epilogue to his novel, Li states in a tongue-in-cheek manner that he has no intention of writing a national allegory: instead, he intends to create an allegory that subverts any prescribed formula of allegory. Indeed, by revisiting the site of the Boxer Rebellion or by retelling the fall of Hong Kong into Japanese hands, the writers refer the reader to the nationalist narrative of recent years, according to which China's trauma during the past century has transformed into China's triumph in this one. But Li and Ma have something different to tell us. Whereas *The Eighth Day of Zhang Mading* prods one to ponder the terms of belief systems that have less to do with religion than with political theology, *Dragon Head, Phoenix Tail*, written twenty years after the handover of Hong Kong to the PRC, understands Hong Kong's fate as the aleatory consequence of mutual betrayal in the past and the present. Thus, through the fictional adventures of two foreign figures, one comes to unlearn the lesson of history by recognizing in it the treacherous exercise of heresy and betrayal.

Transgression and Freedom

In contemporary Chinese literature, the alien is not necessarily someone who comes from outside of China. Over the past decades China has created numerous strangers out of its own people. Whether they are called class enemies, black elements, dissidents, counterrevolutionaries, or simply traitors, they are deprived of their citizenship for alleged political and intellectual deviations from the correct course of nation building. Out of fear of their pernicious influence on society, the party has terminated their existence either literally or figuratively, by segregating these people by means of incarceration, exile, and re-education through labor. Insofar as they are excluded in such a way as to affirm the party's absolute power, they are perfect Chinese examples of "bare life," or *homo sacer*—a social scapegoat deprived of all rights in Giorgio Agamben's terminology.[37] From Zhang Dongsun 張東蓀 (1886–1973), purportedly the first intellectual charged with the crime of treason in the PRC, to Liu Xiaobo 劉曉波 (1956–2017), the Nobel Peace Prize recipient who died in custody in 2017, numerous cases testify to the PRC's will and ability to turn a citizen into an enemy of the people.

Chinese fiction since the late 1970s has not been short of examples that expose the punishments imposed on intellectuals who venture to think and write beyond the "truth regime."[38] The new era's literature of reflection (*fansi wenxue*, 反思文學) began with Dai Houying's 戴厚英 (1938–96) *Ren ah, ren* 人啊, 人 (Man, ah, man, 1981), a biographical novel based on the persecution of the poet Wen Jie 聞捷 (1923–71) during the Cultural Revolution and Dai's romance with Wen, which ended with Wen's suicide. Once hailed as a model Red poet, Wen was found guilty of being a counterrevolutionary in the heyday of the Cultural Revolution. His interrogator was none other than Dai Houying, then a young radical activist. Dai lost her status and power in the next round of the power struggle and was sent down to a cadre school where, against all odds, she found a kindred spirit in Wen. The two planned to marry but were refused permission by the party. Worse, after Wen killed himself in despair, he was posthumously accused of doubly betraying his nation. Maoist biopolitics denies "bare life" any rights, including the right to self-annihilation, and suicide was considered a crime against the revolution.[39]

Most works about prisoners of conscience move us because they are exposés. They tend to be either a recollection of personal suffering or an indictment of the state's brutality. A recent case in point is Fang Fang's 方方 (b. 1955) *Ruanmai* 軟埋 (Soft burial, 2016), a novel describing the massive killing of so-called class enemies in the land reform campaign during the 1950s. The novel ignited a heated debate over its political motivation, even though as a former president of the Writers' Association of her home province of Hubei, her political credentials should have been beyond reproach.[40] The novel was banned in 2017. Fang Fang's online diary about the outbreak of coronavirus in Wuhan and bureaucratic missteps in the spring of 2020 came under severe attack and censorship for violating the national interest.

It is in this context that two recent novels merit our attention: Yan Geling's 嚴歌苓 (b. 1958) *Lufan Yanshi* 陸犯焉識 (Convict Lu Yanshi, 2011) and Gao Xingjian's 高行健 (b. 1940) *Yigeren de shengjing* 一個人的聖經 (One man's bible, 1999).[41] Both are based on the authors' personal stories: *Convict Lu Yanshi* is said to be inspired by the labor education experience of Yan's grandfather, Yan Chunen 嚴春恩; and *One Man's Bible* refers to Gao's expatriate pilgrimage to self-discovery. To that effect, both writers relate a good deal of firsthand knowledge about intellectual life during the decades of Mao's republic. But the reader will quickly discover that the two writers are not content only to report this raw material, however (melo)dramatic, to general readers. Instead, they seek to reckon with the metaphysics of storytelling by deliberating the raison d'être of fiction. In different ways they come to the conclusion that fiction is nothing if not the articulation of freedom.

In Yan Geling's novel, Lu Yanshi is an intellectual condemned to a life sentence in a labor camp in Qinghai Province during the late 1950s. Before 1949, Lu had been a flamboyant liberal Shanghai intellectual known for his witticisms and outspokenness. After the founding of the PRC, he finds himself trapped in a Kafkaesque circle of strictures and is arrested during the antirightist movement of 1957. Lu has never enjoyed his marriage to his wife, Wan yu, which had been imposed on him as a result of a family intrigue. It is not until after he has been jailed and exiled, followed by an extremely harsh experience in the labor camp, that he comes to realize his wife's virtues. He falls belatedly in love with her, so much so that he risks his life escaping from Qinghai to Shanghai just for the sake of seeing her and their family one more time.

There is a long tradition of making class enemies in the Communist Party. In her study, Haiyan Lee has called attention to the "obsession with purity" that creates "class enemies," an obsession produced through moral imperatives and ideological strictures.[42] One also is reminded of Giorgio Agamben's investigation of the "bare life"—in which human lives are reduced to the status of less than human—as a prerequisite for authoritarianism of any kind. In his study of the class system in socialist China, Michael Dutton presents a diagram of stratification, from party officials and members to the advanced masses, ordinary masses, and class enemies.[43] To be labeled a class enemy is to become an "alien 'race,' immutable and expendable—in Agamben's words, entering 'the zone of indistinction.'"[44] Numerous accounts have described the purgatorial experience that the so-called malignant elements have experienced, from the rectification campaign of the Yan'an era to the antirightist movement of 1957, to say nothing of persecutions throughout the Cultural Revolution. These experiences follow a standard pattern that includes interrogation, confession, a public trial, incarceration, reeducation, exile, and execution. Concentration camps—and their euphemistic counterparts such as the labor education farm, the reform camp, and the cadre school—constitute the facilities that detain and reform the "bare lives" rejected by the socialist sovereignty.[45]

In contrast to the typical dark and dreary narrative about the concentration camp, Yan's novel is full of sensuous, sentimental details and verges on the melodramatic. By interweaving various moments of Lu's past and present, Yan manages to produce a full portrait of a modern Chinese intellectual: his complacency and vanity, his romantic dreams and realistic setbacks, and his courage in facing disgrace and suffering. Yan holds nothing back in describing the ghastly circumstances of the labor camp, from chronic constipation to the fatal threat of the Great Famine of 1959–61, and she relates it in such an exuberant style that it seems almost a spectacle in the theater of cruelty. In doing so, Yan challenges the formula of stark realism that often characterizes such descriptions of victimhood and endurance. She seems determined to use her rhetorical power lavishly, adding unexpected color to the harrowing reality of her descriptions.

For all his foibles, Lu is a resourceful and imaginative man. The novel reaches its first climax at the moment when he sneaks back into Shanghai at great risk, only to decide at the last minute not to reunite with his family for fear of causing them trouble. His escape and consequent arrest bring him a life sentence. However, an unlikely hope is born out of despair. All along Lu has been known for his good memory. Now, thrown into a situation without an exit, he starts to exercise his mnemonic power and literary imagination. He reviews in the dark the correspondence he had had with his wife, which he used to think nothing of, and composes imaginary responses to her. He lets thousands of words proliferate in his mind day and night, building an enormous memory palace of his own. In a section that is easily the most touching part of the novel, he processes and classifies the words into countless mental files that refer to one another in a most spectacular network—both bleak and blissful, both hopeful and desperate. As Lu develops a fantastic epistolary escape from the labor camp through remembrances of things past, he falls deeply in love for the first time with Wanyu—or rather with the Wanyu he creates through his words.

By turning the letters from the prison into a lover's discourse, Yan tells a most compelling tale of narrative as freedom—freedom from the panopticon of socialist control. One of the charges against Lu is that he is a liberal, despite the fact that he used to care little about liberalism. However, Yan seems to suggest that Lu may be a liberal after all, inasmuch as he believes in the individual's right to a life free of any bondage. Hannah Arendt has discussed the necessity of narrative as "the form of life," something that creates one's contact with the world by giving it a new beginning and thereby creating new possibilities of life.[46] Where the totalitarian regime deprives Lu of his rights to citizenship and reduces him to the state of "bare life," Yan stresses his capacity to remember and fabulate—at least in his mind—to resist the propagandist noise on the one hand and the shroud of censorship and silence on the other hand.

Lu's story takes another twist in the last part of the novel. In the wake of Mao's death in 1976, Lu and thousands of other camp laborers are declared to be rehabilitated and set free. After years of separation, nevertheless, Lu is returning home a stranger. Not only does he feel alienated from the society and family he has yearned to rejoin, but he is also thrown by the fact that Wanyu has developed serious dementia and can no longer recognize him. Thus, the romance he has tried to remember—or conjure up—in prison for so many years has ultimately been futile. Or has it? As Yan would have it, this turns out to be the moment for Lu to truly prove his capacity to love. At the end of the novel Lu discovers a family secret: years before, Wanyu had willingly offered herself to an official in exchange for the commutation of her husband's sentence. Released from prison, it is now his turn to guard his wife, who behaves like a stranger at home until the end of her days.

If fiction about concentration camps and persecution is often marked by motifs of destitution, Yan has overturned convention by favoring its opposite: her story of Lu is couched in the narrative mode of excess. Not only does Yan enrich her style with meticulous detail, but her plotline tends to melodramatize moments to the point of distortion. Like her character Lu, she seems determined to remind us that language is not necessarily confined by realist determinism and that the "order of mimesis" can be overwritten by the will to imagine.

At the end of the novel, Lu disappears from Shanghai with the urn containing his wife's ashes. As Lu tells his children in a letter he leaves behind, "they" are returning to Qinghai, a place that Lu had once found unbearable. Compared to the hustle and bustle of Shanghai in the new era, the wasteland of Qinghai surprisingly turns out to be the space that promises freedom—a land free from domestic trifles, political interference, and the recent imposition of capitalist culture. Needless to say, given the circumstances of life in China, this is a liberal dream.

If in *Convict Lu Yanshi* Yan describes the multiple conditions of transgression and incarceration in socialist China, Gao Xingjian goes one step further by pondering the politics of territoriality in global terms. Gao won the Nobel Prize for his novel *Lingshan* 靈山 (Soul mountain, 1990), in which an intellectual writer takes a solo pilgrimage to a legendary Soul Mountain in the Yangtze valley and ends up venturing into the hinterland of southwestern China. Through chance encounters and fragmentary memories, Gao (or his fictional alter ego) tries to reorient himself after recent political and medical crises, construing the meaning of Soul Mountain. The novel is full of Buddhist references, and Gao particularly stresses the Chan Buddhist practice of seeking epiphanic enlightenment amid mundane trivialities.

Gao continues to explore the themes of political diaspora and spiritual wandering in *One Man's Bible*, but there he adopts a more radical strategy. The novel features no distinct settings but instead takes place in a series of transient spaces, mnemonic sites, and imaginary occasions. Like Gao, the protagonist of *One Man's Bible* is an artist trying to negotiate his identity in the realms of the transcendental, political, and domestic. No longer rooted in China and deprived of Chinese nationality, he is always on the road. Invitations to events on the international cultural circuit take him to Hong Kong, Sydney, New York, Perpignan, and elsewhere. None of it seems to mean much to him compared with the traumatizing experiences of his early years, and he is haunted by memories of his mother. Wandering from one place to another, the narrator strives to understand his relations with his nation, his family, and above all himself—only to realize that he cannot do so even by traversing all defined boundaries. As a result, we have a perplexing narrative tapestry in which bygone memories and existential sensations as well as imagined dialogues and dramatic monologues crisscross to produce a heteroglossia.

One Man's Bible starts with an explicit description of the narrator's rendezvous in Hong Kong with a German Jewish woman with whom he collaborates on an experimental play. What follows is a series of interwoven narratives of the narrator's erotic adventures, philosophical contemplations, and biographical reminiscences. Gao gives a vivid account of growing up during the turbulent years of new China, his literary pursuits in defiance of iron socialist law, and his marital crises during the Cultural Revolution. Contrasting with his mainland experiences are his subsequent romantic escapades in the diaspora, his efforts to become a citizen of the world, and his frustration at the limits of cosmopolitanism. He pulls all of the narrative strings together in a dramatized dialogue among his alter egos, represented by the pronouns he, she, you, and I as if psychological schism can be resolved only through a theatrical reinstatement.

Critics have faulted *One Man's Bible* for its "residual bourgeois sentimentalism and misogyny."[47] In response to criticism, Gao claimed that his philosophy of writing has two tenets: "cold literature" (*lengde wenxue* 冷的文學) and "no-ism" (*meiyou zhuyi* 沒有主義): "Cold literature . . . exists simply because humankind seeks a purely spiritual activity beyond the gratification of material desires. This sort of literature of course did not come into being today. However, whereas in the past it mainly had to fight oppressive political forces and social customs, today it has to do battle with the subversive commercial values of consumerist society. For it to exist depends on a willingness to endure the loneliness."[48]

Whereas cold literature pits itself against the ardent, engaged literature produced under both socialism and capitalism, "no-ism" denounces any ideological or conceptual fixation within literature. One may discern in Gao's philosophy an indebtedness to Western modernism, which has long fascinated him. But one should not overlook his adherence to Chan Buddhist teachings, an adherence to which aligns his novel with a different kind of freedom—one that hinges on free play without any worldly attachment to life or language. Accordingly, by *meiyou* Gao means not only negation but also, in light of Buddhist thought, emptiness (*kong* 空; in Sanskrit, *Śūnyatā*). While negation may suggest either Nietzschean defiance or existential nihilism, emptiness points to the capacity to both contain and erase all, including nothingness—hence, the genesis of freedom: "Instead of saying that Buddha is in the heart it would be better to say that freedom is in the heart and it simply depends on whether one makes use of it. If one exchanges freedom for something else then the bird that is freedom will fly off, for this is the cost of freedom."[49]

This is how Gao realizes his poetics of transgression and freedom. For him literature is nothing if it is unable to offer new horizons, beyond the reach of this-worldy rationality and sensibility. In his Nobel Prize speech, Gao said: "Born at the start of human civilization, like life, language is full of wonders and its expressive capacity is limitless. It is the work of the writer to discover and develop the latent potential inherent in language. The writer is not the Creator and he cannot eradicate the world even if it is too old. He also cannot establish some new ideal world even if the present world is absurd and beyond human comprehension. However, he can certainly make innovative statements either by adding to what earlier people have said or else starting where earlier people stopped."[50]

Instead of merely letting things be, literature addresses freedom by ironically intensifying the "fault lines,"[51] as Paul Ricoeur would have it, in human conditions. As Gao puts it in his Nobel Prize speech, "It is not the writer's duty to preach morality and while striving to portray various people in the world he also unscrupulously exposes his self, even the secrets of his inner mind. For the writer truth in literature approximates ethics, it is the ultimate ethics of literature."[52]

One such case is the protagonist's continued carnal encounters with women both in China and elsewhere. While it may raise feminists' eyebrows, a close reading shows that through the erotics of writing, Gao is pondering the terms of radical mercy in gendered, textual, and political terms. That is, insofar as both male and female characters in *One Man's Bible* are wandering in a world bereft of values, physical intimacy—however painfully transient—becomes one way to assert their relatedness to each other, and hence offers a flickering hope of redemption.

Thus, in his study of the novel, Carlos Rojas calls attention to the symbiotic symbolism of Gao's sexual and textual pursuits, particularly the strong Freudian urge "from the act of writing as a secondary displacement of a prohibited erotic desire for the mother, to fantasizing oneself as being a free-floating spermatozoa within a vast maternal womb."[53] According to Gao:

> You . . . float lightly, having lost all of your weight. You travel between different nations, different cities, and different women, not wanting to find a resting place. Floating along, you merely chew playfully on words, thus leaving behind traces of life just like drops of ejaculated semen.[54]

Gao proposes that, because of its creative potentiality, literature cannot be constrained by social, ethical, or ideological strictures, and thus it always entertains challenging options. As he presents the questions literature raises:

> The true freedom, in the final analysis, boils down to individual choice: should one choose freedom or well-being? And the choice of freedom presupposes one's reflection on the necessity of freedom. Therefore, one's recognition of freedom comes prior to choice, and as such freedom is that which enacts the challenge of human consciousness to existence.[55]

Implied here is Gao's indebtedness to both the Kantian tenets of liberal autonomy and the Chan Buddhist epiphanic awakening to total emptiness. Thus, where *Soul Mountain* ends with the revelation of the *dao* in the momentary blink of a frog, *One Man's Bible* hints that the much searched for sanctuary of selfhood can be found nowhere but in the protagonist's continued departures from familiar surroundings and accidental encounters.

When read side by side, *Convict Lu Yanshi* and *One Man's Bible* form a dialogue on how an intellectual can survive tyranny and censorship through language. However, such a language can be uttered only in the most secretive, ventriloquial manner—a Chinese brand of "esoteric writing."[56] Thus, Lu Yanshi constructs his memory palace in which he indulges his romantic fantasy, and Gao Xingjian's protagonist stages a monological theater that nevertheless stars an endless cast of personas. Yan Geling opts for a melodramatic style to create a spectacle of the most desolate situation of starvation and death, while in contrast, Gao Xingjian adheres to the opposite end of "cold literature" and "no-ism." Nevertheless, the two authors have something in common when they articulate the necessity to think and narrate. According to Gao:

> If the writer sought to win intellectual freedom the choice was either to fall silent or to flee. . . . To maintain one's intellectual autonomy one could only talk to oneself, and it had to be in utmost secrecy. I should mention that it was only in this period when it was utterly impossible for literature that I came to comprehend why it was so essential: literature allows a person to preserve a human consciousness.[57]

The Martians, the Trisolarans, and the Man with the Compound Eyes

The above sections have discussed how fiction provides conditions in which national, legal, ethical, and affective boundary lines are crossed by the intrusion of the alien dissident and the exclusion of the alien foreigner, thus playing out the multiple consequences of violation and containment. But the alien figure in contemporary Chinese fiction is not necessarily confined to the human being: the alien may come from outer space, the cybernetic world, or the phantasmal domain. The frequent appearance of extraterrestrial beings and outlandish creatures in contemporary Chinese and other Sinophone fiction is a peculiar phenomenon in a literary tradition otherwise populated with realistic figures of flesh and blood.

The advent of aliens from the domain beyond the human is a result of the boom in science fiction since the beginning of the twenty-first century. As discussed above in the chapter, Han Song's *2066: Red Star over America* ushers in a series of encounters with aliens of various types as the protagonist Tang Long arrives in America to participate in a chess championship. There, he comes across strangers from not only different countries but also outer space. Moreover, we are told that China is already under the control of artificial intelligence, which in turn succumbs to a Martian attack.

2066: Red Star over America is one of the many stories and novels that depict a posthuman condition in China and the world. The Taiwanese writer Wu Ming-yi 吳明益 (b. 1971) introduces a man with compound eyes lost on an island soon to be devastated by a tsunami of garbage (*Fuyanren* 複眼人 [The man with the compound eyes, 2011]).[58] The mainland Chinese writer Chen Qiufan 陳楸帆 (b. 1981) creates a woman-turned-cyborg who is programmed to confront the digital wasteland of postsocialist China (*Huangchao* 荒潮 [The waste tide, 2013]). But few can emulate the terrifying Trisolarans of Liu Cixin 劉慈欣 (b. 1963), projected to attack earth four hundred years from now in a fatal invasion that will destroy human civilization once and for all.

Insofar as Chinese socialist literature has been dominated by realism —be it called revolutionary, humanist, magic, romantic, or new realism— science fiction was seen as an oddity of little note. Until recently science fiction was classified as children's literature, and it was rarely taken seriously by critics. Thus, the sudden surge of science fiction fever in the 2010s represents a shake-up of the realist canon. Indeed, science fiction writers venture to describe the inadmissible and unthinkable in such a way as to stimulate readers to question the tenability of humanity, rationality, and reality. To an extent, the genre sets the terms of China's entry into the new millennium, establishing both a new political agenda and a new national myth. I am more concerned, however, with how science fiction writers fabulate the dystopian vision of China, thereby countering the optimistic official discourse of China's rise.

In Han Song's *2066: Red Star over America*, 2066 marks a turning point in the Sino-American relationship. By then, the United States has suffered a series of economic and political disasters, while China has become an Edenic superpower. A prodigy at the game of chess, Tang Long is sent to compete in the United States, only to be caught up in that country's Second Civil War. Han seems to relate a revanchist fantasy of the type that has obsessed many writers since the late Qing. But Han has more to tell us. Despite its superficial strength and prosperity, China is controlled by Amanduo, an artificial intelligence that programs Chinese citizens' lives and oversees their happiness in every possible way. And even the formidable Amanduo collapses when mysterious Martians descend on earth, turning China into the promised land (*fudi* 福地). Incidentally, the Chinese expression *fudi* is also a euphemism for cemetery—a land for the dead.

Striking as it is, the fiction of Han and his fellow science fiction writers is an uncanny recapitulation of the science fiction fever at the beginning of the twentieth century.[59] What was then known as *kexue xiaoshuo* 科學小說 (science fiction) was one of the new genres promoted by Liang Qichao when he launched the magazine *New Fiction* in 1902. Through the efforts of Liang and his contemporaries, late Qing science fiction consisted mainly of utopian narratives that projected the political desire for China's reform onto an idealized, technologically advanced world. Liang's *The Future of New China* (1902), described in chapter 1, seeks to project the late Qing reformer's vision of China's rejuvenation and eventual ascendency to world power. Although Liang's novel remained unfinished, its sublime vision of China in 2062 presents an immense vista of the nation's future and gave rise to a wave of utopian adventures.

Liang's depiction of China in 2062 and Han's depiction of 2066 form an intriguing dialogue. As Liang would have it, in 2062, fifty years after the founding of the Great Republic of China, China will have become the leading world power—boasting innovative technology, an advanced political system, and a rich culture. A constitutional monarchy and a Confucian edifice join hands in making China a utopian republic that outshines all other civilizations. As if echoing Liang's fictional prophecy, Han Song makes 2066 a year that witnesses China having insurmountable wealth and power. A closer reading, however, reveals that his novel is anything but a celebration of a rich and powerful China: rather, it is a darker projection of China in demise.

Liang's utopia is the consummation of a single linear (but not necessarily evolutionary or revolutionary) development of time. This linear model, which has been so popular with Confucians and positivist Europeans, deprives a novelist like Liang of the freedom to imagine and justify various futures and revolutions. Although *The Future of New China* assumes the structure of a temporal linear progression, it unfolds in the future perfect tense. Thus, the future in Liang's novel appears as the magical moment that stands at the other end of history, without any progressive momentum that leads toward the happening of the moment. As the completion of the prescribed timetable, the future is not a dynamic process of historical forces clashing and crystallizing into an unprecedented constellation, but a mythical moment that transcends time.

Han's novel presents a much more skewed timetable of China's search for modernization. The irony may appear even stronger when Mao's legacy is taken into consideration. As Mingwei Song observes, 2066 is not a randomly chosen number: that year will mark the hundredth anniversary of the outbreak of the Cultural Revolution, the extreme climax of Maoist utopianism.[60] Although *2066: Red Star over America* also seems to project a timeline into the future, Han informs us at the beginning of the novel that 2066 is merely one temporal point in China's futuristic history, after which many other incidents will occur. It turns out that the protagonist recounts his life story retrospectively in 2126, when he is already seventy-six years old and sixty years after the time he narrates the novel. Thus, the future's future—2126—brings not the next stage of Hegelian sublation but a setback. By then, China and the United States, as well as all other civilizations on earth, will have been wiped out by a superior alien species that landed on earth in 2066. A popular motif of the typology of Western science fiction, the Martian is used by Han to denote the ultimate double bind in one's imagination of the alien: a stranger who is from another planet yet, thanks to the recurrent invocation of the Martian in the public imaginary, comes across as a familiar oddity always already inhabiting one's psyche.

What marks the difference between Liang and Han is their diverging takes on human agency with respect to history. As discussed above, for Liang, dreaming of the future new China at the beginning of the modern time, the future unfolds progressively, culminating in the completion of the historical program. As everything will have taken placed as planned, his narration manifests itself in the future perfect tense. Liang yearns for a human subjectivity, epitomized by enlightened intellectuals and revolutionaries, that can take up the Herculean task of transforming reality into a fantastic utopia. His heroes are two young Chinese men returning from the West in the hope of rejuvenating their nation. They represent two different political agendas, constitutional monarchy and democracy, but they both yearn for one unified China. Writing one century after *The Future of New China*, as a new China seems to be rising, Han nevertheless harbors a vision beyond the nation. He seeks the horizons of a China beyond China by conjuring up the figure of the alien anew, as the foreigner, artificial intelligence, and the Martians from outer space.

It is no coincidence that Han's title echoes *Red Star over China* (1937), a work of narrative nonfiction by Edgar Snow (1905–72) that is arguably the first English-language account of life in Yan'an, the wartime Chinese communist mecca. The Chinese translation of Snow's book was released in 1938 under the title *Hongxing zhaoyao zhongguo* 紅星照耀中國 (Red star over China) but was later retitled *Xixingmanji* 西行漫記 (Random sketches on a journey to the West). Both Chinese titles were borrowed by Han for parts of different editions of the novel. Accordingly, "the journey to the west" in *Red Star over China* refers to Snow's venture into northwestern China, where Mao's revolutionary regime was based. There Snow was purportedly enlightened by the fervor of these Chinese guerrillas and taught the truth of revolution. For anyone familiar with the late imperial Chinese fantastic novel *Xiyouji* 西遊記 (Journey to the West), a saga about Monk Tripitaka's pilgrimage to the lands of the West to acquire Buddhist truth, the implication of Snow's "journey to the West" couldn't be more telling. Similar to the Tang monk in search of religious truth west of China, Snow is seen as a modern pilgrim seeking Marxist or Maoist truth in western China. The ironies are complex. For Chinese aspirers to communist revolution, it takes a foreign reporter from the West to testify to the meaning of the Chinese revolution—which after all is inspired by the ideological truth of Marxism, which originated in the modern West.

Han takes this typology of the alien one step further at the beginning of the twenty-first century. He arranges for his protagonist to travel to America, the ideal "West" of modern capitalism, only to witness the decadent and chaotic sides of the erstwhile superpower. As pointed out above, Han's contemplation of the decline of the West does not lead to complacent revanchism but instead to the ominous revelation that China is fully under the control of Amanduo.

A substantial difference has become clear in the transformation from Liang's Confucian New China to Han's China programmed by an artificial intelligence. The late Qing reformer's ideal of national rejuvenation and self-strengthening is subverted by the depiction of the entire nation's submission to a system that manipulates the consciousness, sensibilities, and sensations of every one of its citizens. Behind the postrevolutionary facade, a posthuman technology is at work. Han's cybernetic nightmare may nevertheless have a humanistic motivation. He seems to be insinuating that artificial intelligence gains its hegemonic power only as a result of the total, if not totalitarian, governmental technology first put in place by human beings. In other words, Amanduo can control China and presumably the world so perfectly because it represents the robotic realization of the biopolitics of both capitalism and socialism. The artificial intelligence is not inhuman but all too human, in that once it is set in motion on its own, it acts out the dark forces of the human utopian dream. Moreover, the Martians are said to come after Amanduo, taking over not only China but the whole world. This brings to mind the subtitle of *2066: Mars over America*. The novel is a flashback set in 2126, when all civilizations on earth, both socialist and capitalist, have been terminated. Over the promised land shines Mars, or the fire star (*huoxing* 火星), in place of the red star.

Whereas Han's novel takes issue with the reemerging revanchism in China by imagining a menacing attack by an artificial intelligence and then by extraterrestrials, Wu Ming-yi's *The Man with the Compound Eyes* depicts a world in which ecology is more important than ideology for the well-being of humankind. Wu is a Taiwanese writer and scholar dedicated to environmentalist activism and literature. Over the past two decades, he has won renown in the Sinophone world and beyond for a series of stories, essays, and reportage that presents the mountains and rivers, as well as the human and nonhuman creatures, in Taiwan, in such a way as to connect indigenous subjects to the fate of the earth. Wu is not just an ordinary nature writer: he is a storyteller who manages to mingle natural and supernatural elements, conveying a worldview that is a far cry from the reality we inhabit.

In his prize-winning novel *The Man with the Compound Eyes*, Atile'i, a fifteen-year-old aboriginal boy of Wayo Wayo Island is sent to sea like every second son of his tribe, expected never to return. But Atile'i is swept up by the currents and caught in a gigantic trash vortex that is about to crash into the eastern coast of Taiwan. The vortex hurls him ashore and brings him into contact with a woman named Alice. Alice is a writer in prolonged bereavement years after the mysterious disappearance and supposed death of her husband, Jackson, and their son on a mountain climbing trip. Thus, the two develop an unlikely friendship while they try to probe each other's world.

If in Han Song's world, the sixteen-year-old Tang Long is sent to the United States to receive his first lesson in treacherous international politics, Wu Ming-yi's *A Man with the Compound Eyes* lets the young protagonist undergo tribal rituals, a trash vortex, and environmental calamities. What concerns Wu is the human condition in relation to the dynamics of a global ecology in which humans are only one of a multitude of species. As Wu's novel develops, more and more stories are told related to the two plotlines of Atile'i and Alice: stories about the aboriginal tribes, the birds and butterflies, the fauna and flora, the impending trash vortex, and above all the man with the compound eyes.

Who, or what, is the man with the compound eyes? In the novel, Wu provides many clues to the mysterious character but refuses to draw a definitive picture. The man with the compound eyes is said to appear in the woods, on the mountain paths, on the banks of rivers, and in many other locations. It might be a shadow or a ghost. As a matter of fact, Wu wrote a short story with the same title as this novel, in which the man in question looks much like a Taiwanese aboriginal, with high cheekbones and dark skin. In the novel, however, Wu makes the man's ethnicity less explicit and instead grants him an amorphous and ubiquitous existence. Wu has spoken in interviews about personally encountering the "man" in the wild: "I always feel something around me, but I cannot figure out exactly what it is. I enjoyed appreciating beautiful butterflies with 'that object.' Moreover, 'that object' is ubiquitous; it seems to look like a human figure, but actually [is] not quite fully [human]."[61] The "man" with the compound eyes is so mysterious that the critic Lee Yu-lin concludes that it functions as more of a trope than an actual character, giving aesthetic and ecological significance to the novel. This is especially the case when the character merges with the natural surroundings.[62]

What Wu aims to describe is an experience of encountering the other that can no longer be interpreted in classic anthropocentric terms. The man with the compound eyes could be nonhuman or posthuman. His appearance can be more sensed than seen by ordinary human beings like you and me. Or more intriguingly, as Wu would have it, the man with the compound eyes may well be a projection of the stranger within us, one who is capable of seeing what we fail to see. In other words, through the image of the compound eyes, Wu is invoking a vision of multiple alterities with respect to the world that we assume we confidently inhabit and control. In that vein, Wu provides a vivid description of a mysterious—or imaginary—encounter between Jackson, Alice's husband, and the man with the compound eyes:

> In despair he looks at the man with the compound eyes . . . but all he sees is the man's compound eyes, which seem to change from moment to moment in hallucinatory permutations and combinations. And the scene in each of the tiny ommatidia that compose every compound eye is completely different with each passing instant. Watching carefully, the man's mind is helplessly mesmerized by the instantaneous images playing in each ommatidium: could be an erupting undersea volcano, might

be a falcon's-eye view of a landscape, perhaps just a leaf about to fall. Each seems to be playing a kind of documentary.[63]

As an environmentalist photographer, Wu has doggedly promoted the idea that a human is nothing more or less than an animal and is therefore subject to the all-inclusive ethic of animate creatures. Wu is particularly influenced by the Russian-American photographer Roman Vishniac's photomicroscopy, which Wu calls a visual exemplar of total realism. Vishniac is known for his talent at capturing the movements of all sorts of specimens, from protozoa to amino acids. One of Vishniac's most famous works of photomicroscopy is a series of photographs from the inside of a firefly's eye, behind 4,600 tiny ommatidia, which are presented complexly and out of proportion. Wu notes that through the magnifying effect of photomicroscopy, we come to see a world at its micro and macro levels at the same time. Photomicroscopy exposes the molecular elements of a tiny insect as an awesome spectacle, which achieves an effect of defamiliarization. Inspired by the aesthetics of photomicroscopy, Wu presents his writing in a similar vein, as bringing to light "the mysterious niches of the brain, calling attention to the 'minute' and the 'gigantic' that have always already existed in these lives, both materialistically and conceptually."[64] By extension, he urges us to think about whether "we can look at the world from the angle of a species as low as the fly. The fact is that such [a fly's] angle is not humble but contains a unique perspective on nature from which to interpret the world."[65]

One can see the subtle linkage between Wu's observations of a fly with compound eyes and the man with the compound eyes. For Wu, all species of animals and plants, and even inorganic objects such as stones and soil, are to be included in a community whose members share each other's sensibilities and memories. These sensibilities and memories are beyond the scope of the human language. The man with the compound eyes, therefore, serves less as a human with flesh and blood than as an imaginary agent of what Deleuze and Guattari call "affect," the sensorial momentum that traverses the boundaries of the human and the inhuman, the dead and the living, and the past and the present in such a way as to project the horizons of "becoming."[66]

We can now better understand the triangulated relationships between Alice, Atile'i, and the man with the compound eyes. Whereas Alice is in agony over the loss of her husband and son, Atile'i finds himself doubly homeless when, already banished from the island on which he grew up, the trash vortex sends him to the eastern shore of Taiwan. But their accidental encounter generates ties between them, and the ties deepen as the novel develops to involve other characters, each with a story of a strange encounter to tell. All the stories take us in one way or another to the elusive man with the compound eyes. No one can be sure who or where he is, and yet everyone feels him looming somewhere. As discussed above, at the character's most intriguing, the man with the compound eyes appears endowed with both a certain supernatural power, overseeing numerous human and nonhuman lives as they appear and disappear, and an all-too-natural power, subjecting all lives to the flux of ecological ups and downs. Given his indigenous gift of storytelling, Atile'i can map out a mythological cartography in which Alice is lost in the contingencies of nature. Under the spell of the man with the compound eyes, they try to figure out a way to make sense of their respective existences. Meanwhile, they and other characters are awaiting the doomsday that will occur when the full trash vortex finally hits the eastern seashore of Taiwan.

Shuttling between the worlds of mythology and ecology, Wu has written a novel about the environmental, ethical, and cognitive precarity that entraps all of us in the new millennium. By invoking the man with the compound eyes, he offers a (re)envisioning of a world dominated by the unknowable and invisible and implies that the mission of the storyteller is not to explain everything by explaining it away but instead by inhabiting the multiple sites and sights in anticipation of the arrival of the next stranger.

In contrast to Han Song's antinational allegory and Wu Ming-yi's multitudinous critique of our ecosystem, Liu Cixin impels his readers to gaze at the immense dark cosmos in which neither nationalism nor ecology appear to be anything but trivial. To the artificial intelligence Amanduo, the Martians, and the man with the compound eyes, we may now add another alien figure that transgresses the limitations of human cognition: the mysterious Trisolarans. Liu's *Santi* 三體 (The Three-body problem, 2007),[67] together with *Heian senlin* 黑暗森林 (Dark forest, 2008) and *Sishen yongsheng* 死神

永生 (Death's end, 2010), constitute his trilogy *Diqiu wangshi* 地球往事 (Remembrance of earth's past). The trilogy has an epic scope that spans thousands of years, and it ought to be regarded as one of the most ambitious works in contemporary Chinese fiction. Mixing the Cultural Revolution and the Star Wars movies, historical pathos and extraterrestrial marvels, Liu has created a space and history that his contemporaries can hardly emulate. Liu's works are not only a fantastic spectacle but also an inquiry into the ethical terms of such a spectacle.

The Three-Body Problem begins with the story of a scientist who seeks vengeance for her father's purge and death in the Cultural Revolution by inviting the extraterrestrial Trisolarans to invade earth. A group of Chinese citizens are drafted to help prevent the impending global holocaust. These heroes travel through the tunnel of time, engaging in ingenious tactics and fighting cosmic battles. Meanwhile, it turns out that Chairman Mao foresaw the war long ago and implemented a preemptive plan.

The "three-body problem" refers to the challenge in physics of predicting the motion of three objects whose orbital trajectories and gravitational fields intersect. In Liu's trilogy, humans are threatened by the alien race of the Trisolarans, who are from a planet that has three suns—which cause unpredictable climate changes and, as a result, threaten the planet's sustainability. For every stable era with regular nights and days, there are numerous chaotic eras during which the days can last years and a sun can be so close to the planet that it desiccates everything beneath it. In search of a more stable life, the Trisolarans plot to take over the earth, which has just one sun and therefore enjoys more predictable weather. The only good news is that the Trisolarans are four light years away and traveling in ships that can go only one hundredth of the speed of light, which gives the humans four hundred years to prepare for their invasion.

Because of its grand and majestic style, critics have called Liu's fiction sublime.[68] Indeed, it is the single Chinese science fiction novel since Liang Qichao's time that engages with the fate of humanity as a whole. Liu's works induce awe by introducing an apocalyptic view of world civilization in crisis. He asks if human rationality can generate a political science that is anything but rational; if history presented in the future perfect tense can redeem bygone or ongoing mishaps; if a filial daughter's vengeful wrath can override her professional commitment to the well-being of society; and if a national leader can be both a savior of humanity and a perpetrator of crimes against humanity. Liu refuses to give easy answers to his questions. Instead, he presents them against a gigantic cosmic backdrop, thereby creating an effect that sustains as much as it subverts the Maoist sublime that launches his fictional vision.

The *Three-Body Problem* compels us to consider three aspects of the narratology of transgression. To begin with, the trilogy tells an epic story that begins with the Cultural Revolution, when a secret mission is launched by Mao to establish contact with a hostile alien civilization. During the Cultural Revolution, the astrophysicist Ye Wenjie witnessed her father being persecuted to death, and she was labeled a traitor and sent to a labor camp. After a series of trials, however, Ye ends up working on a secret team for alien communication thanks to her special skills. It is in that capacity that Ye, to avenge her father's death, manages to send a message to outer space inviting the Trisolarans to invade earth.

Here, Liu touches on the politics of transgression in the classical sense. Ye contacts the Trisolarans to avenge her father's death and her own suffering. In so doing, she betrays her nation and indeed the entire world. Her treason nevertheless reveals the tangled relations between filial piety and patriotism, and between professional integrity and personal commitment. PRC fiction has long included a subtradition in which the narrative moves along thanks to conspiracy, espionage, betrayal, internal subversion, and of course treason. In spite (or because) of the call for party loyalty and national solidarity, conspiracy seems to loom everywhere. The enemy within appears to be proliferating in every place and at every moment and must be continually identified and weeded out to consolidate the nation. Liu takes advantage of this stock plotline but pushes it over the brink. Ye makes secret contact not with Western capitalist forces but with Trisolarans from another planet, irreversibly betraying not only China but the entire human race. Last but not least, despite the valiant efforts launched by the authorities and carried out by selfless male and female volunteers, earth is doomed from the outset: no deus ex machina is available as China moves toward her total destruction. The trilogy is the retrospective account of the very few survivors of the end of the world.

If Liang Qichao wrote his science fiction in 1902 to project the future of new China, Liu's trilogy a century later presents the future of no China. This is a bold move, given the prevailing sentiment of China's rise, let alone the teleology of the Chinese socialist vision. Liu can get away with his transgression primarily because he broadens the scope his narrative. His plot is fairly complex, incorporating an international group of misanthropes, outcasts, and opportunists conspiring to contact Trisolarans for their own personal gain; planetary peacemakers striving to find a way for the Trisolarans and humans to coexist; and the Chinese team fighting the tragic battle against the Trisolaran invasion. The doom of China becomes but one part of a fate shared by all civilizations on earth.

Liu's story takes him beyond the bounds of earth and humanity, while never losing sight of fundamental ethics. One of his heroes, Luo Ji, ushers us into the second dimension of Liu's logic of mutual transgression. In the second volume of the trilogy, *The Dark Forest*, Luo learns about the crisis of the three-body problem from his teacher, Ye Wenjie, and vows to defend his nation and the earth against all odds. He joins an elite squad assembled to combat the Trisolarans, while he comes to understand the menacing logic of "Dark Forest theory": that is, the theory that the universe functions in compliance with the law of the jungle, in which a more fearsome predatory species always awaits. Predators and prey are mutually implicated in the eternal cycle of destruction and survival:

> The universe is a dark forest. Every civilization is an armed hunter stalking through the trees like a ghost. . . . The hunter has to be careful, because everywhere in the forest are stealthy hunters like him. If he finds other life—another hunter, an angel or a demon, a delicate infant or a tottering old man, a fairy or a demigod—there is only one thing he can do: open fire and eliminate them. In this forest, hell is other people. An eternal threat to any life that exposes its own existence will be swiftly wiped out.[69]

Trained as a sociologist, Luo Ji, whose name sounds the same as the Chinese word for logic (*luoji* 邏輯), comes to realize the uselessness of his knowledge as he faces the three-body problem. All human engagements, from revolution to civilization, are trivial in the face of the cosmos. He concludes that the only logic of survival is to follow the law of dark forest—namely, the law of transgression.

Luo realizes that the only way to forestall the alien invasion is to threaten to seek out other more dangerous forces capable of destroying even Trisolarans. It becomes clear in *Death's End* that there are civilizations in other galaxies far more powerful and technologically advanced than the Trisolarans. Just as the Martians in *2066: Mars over America* loomed behind Amanduo's seemingly stable rule over earth, these unnamable extraterrestrial creatures are ever ready to clean out humans and Trisolarans alike. And they are merely proxies of the dark force of the universe, which is a moral black hole to begin with.

However, Luo Ji's discovery brings us to the other side of the law of dark forest. From the human perspective, the Trisolarans appear to be an extremely vicious species, but they turn out to have fought for their own survival in conditions hundreds of times more precarious than the mounting crisis on earth. To take over earth, the Trisolarans alter the dimensions of particle physics on which human existence hinges. Having advanced far beyond human technology, they send to earth "sophons," robotic nanoparticles that can be unfolded in two dimensions, with the goal of disrupting the functioning of particle accelerators in the human world. The sophons can gather information and send it back to the Trisolarans, using quantum entanglement that travels faster than light. The cost of perfecting this technology was immense. In the course of developing it, Trisolarans unfolded the protons of the sophons either too thinly, turning them into an infinite one-dimensional string, or too thickly, creating giant three-dimensional geometric solids—spheres, tetrahedrons, cones, solid crosses, and Möbius strips—that fill the galaxy "as though a giant child had emptied a box of building blocks in the firmament."[70] In the end, the earth is reduced to a two-dimensional belt-like existence, with all histories and civilizations minimized into superfluous comings and goings during a transient moment of the cosmos.

It is at this juncture that we are guided to the third level of transgression by Cheng Xin, a tenderhearted female scientist who succeeds Luo Ji to become the chief defender of earth. As the story proceeds to its climax, when the humans and Trisolarans reach a showdown, all Cheng needs to do is to press a button that will set off the mutual assured destruction of both parties, but her nerve fails her. In face of the Trisolarans' approach to earth, she lets her compassion for all the virtues and vices of the human civilization, as well as the comings and goings of all species on earth, cloud her judgment. With a name that sounds the same as "heart of sincerity" (*chengxin* 誠心), Cheng Xin acts in such a way as to intensify rather than dissolve the moral algebra underlining the trilogy. For as the earth will be ruined one way or another, Cheng's decision to abandon her duty represents the final flash of human complexity: the human is a being capable of contradictory inclinations—both hatred and passion, and both cruelty and compassion. If Ye sets out to communicate with the Trisolarans, thus betraying her moral and intellectual commitment to be a human, Cheng acts in such a way as to betray Ye's betrayal—even if both choices result in total destruction.

Near the end of *The Three-Body Problem*, the survivors of the earth's holocaust have moved to Pluto, where they witness the disappearance of human civilization and build their last monument. All is lost, and the future remains unknown. It is here that Liu Cixin demonstrates his own compassion; he lets Cheng Xin narrate an account of what has happened so as to pass on a piece of information about humankind to the next universe. Hence the name of the trilogy: *Remembrance of Earth's Past*.

Is *The Three-Body Problem* a "good China story" by the standards of President Xi Jinping? While debates over the trilogy's content and message continue to proliferate, we may approach the question from a different angle. In 2015, Xi declared at the seventieth anniversary celebration of the United Nations that China has a responsibility to help build the "community of a shared future of mankind" (*renlei mingyun gongtongti* 人類命運共同體).[71] The concept of "community of a shared future of mankind" has since been mentioned on various other occasions and eventually was written into the preface to the 2018 edition of the PRC's constitution. Xi proposes a new model of international relations—one based on the values of friendship, justice, and shared interests—in the hope of forming a new global governance system. The "one belt, one road" (*yidai yilu* 一帶一路) policy is supposedly the cornerstone of such a system, a new manifesto for international diplomacy. For our purposes, we may treat it as an international version of a "harmonious society," a kind of literature of persuasion along the line of such party slogans as "the great nation is peacefully rising," "the great rejuvenation of the Chinese nation," "the Chinese Dream," and so on. In terms of projecting a vision of China and on China's behalf, all of these slogans are part of the campaign of "tell the good China story."

What intrigues us is the fact that before the "community of a shared future of mankind" surfaced in the early 2010s, a writer such as Liu Cixin had ventured to probe the meaning of China and the world not merely at the global but at the cosmic scale. However, his story is less utopian. Combining astronomical fantasy, eschatological prophecy, political innuendo, and moral deliberation, *The Three-Body Problem* presents a bleak vision of the future of the cosmos—of which China occupies merely a tiny if not an invisible sector—thereby pitting itself against the sublime euphoric writings of contemporary political campaigners and wishful intellectuals. Precisely because of Liu's idiosyncratic way of repositioning human fate vis-à-vis the unknown cosmos, he lays bare unspoken possibilities, however speculative, for "the shared future of mankind." Especially in the aftermath of the coronavirus pandemic that swept the whole world in 2020, Liu's China story reads like an uncanny prophecy. He moves beyond the comfort zone of the anthropocentrism that characterizes both socialism and capitalism and offers a sobering vision that truly answers that of the great leader Xi.

From the vantage point of *The Three-Body Problem*, we revisit the thesis of this chapter that fiction can be a social and symbolic form of transgression. With the trope of the alien as the foreigner, outsider, "bare life," and unknown being from another galaxy, we examined how selected contemporary novels imagine various racial, ethical, ideological, and cognitive boundary lines and their transgression. We discussed xenophilia, xenophobia, and extraterritorial disputes in late Qing China and wartime colonial Hong Kong; exilic escapades inside and outside of China, during which political belief and ideological allegiance become matters of life and death; and extraterrestrial dystopias in which the "shared future of mankind" is nothing but total extinction.

The novelists discussed in this chapter have boldly tackled taboos and undermined totems. They write to demonstrate that the novel is an art of imagining if not implicating transgression. They have thus raised an important question. If a "shared future of mankind" is the goal China is striving for, what task could be more urgent a task than solving the "alien" problem, both without and within the nation?

3

Life and Death Are Wearing Me Out

Fiction as Transmigration

The protagonist of *Shensi pilao* 生死疲勞 (Life and death are wearing me out, 2007), by Mo Yan莫言 (b. 1955), Ximen Nao, is a landlord with a reputation for being generous to his tenants. He is nevertheless labeled an enemy of the people in the land reform campaigns of the Chinese communist revolution; his land and properties are confiscated, and he is put to death by the revolutionaries. Ximen descends into the underworld, where he confronts Lord Yama and demands justice. Yama ends up allowing Ximen to return to the human world, but as a donkey, then an ox, a pig, a dog, and finally a monkey. Through these animalistic lives, Ximen witnesses with trepidation the ups and downs of his beloved wife, concubines, and children, as well as village folks in the decades after the revolution. The novel ends with him reborn as a big-headed baby boy.

Mo Yan won the Nobel Prize for Literature in 2012 for *Life and Death Are Wearing Me Out* and other works that chronicle Chinese peasants' lives against the backdrop of the tumultuous history of the People's Republic of China (PRC). The Nobel Prize committee praised him as a writer who "with hallucinatory realism merges folk tales, history and the contemporary."[1] Such a description is circumspect: in a literary culture that sanctions socialist realism, what Mo has done is nothing less than subvert the canon and question the real. He manages to accomplish this subversion by using a time-honored narratology of transmigration.

Mo Yan sets Ximen Nao's story from the first day of 1950 to the last day of 2000, covering exactly the second half of the twentieth century. Each of Ximen's five cycles of transmigration appears to correspond to a defining historical period in PRC history. However, the theme of metempsychosis is not present only at the individual level. Instead, it is brought to bear on the path of national history and the zeitgeist:

> People in the 1950s were innocent, in the 1960s they were fanatics, in the 1970s they were afraid, in the 1980s they carefully weighed people's words and actions, and in the 1990s they were simply evil.[2]

Mo Yan's title, *Life and Death Are Wearing Me Out*, is a phrase borrowed from Buddhist scriptures. It is meant as a critique of the gratuitous cycle of human insatiability and a call for abstinence in pursuit of freedom of the mind and body.[3] To be sure, such a reference is a far cry from both the socialist agenda of progressive history in general and the Maoist brand of volitionism.

By traversing the domains of the human and the animalistic, the living and the dead, and the past and the present, Mo Yan has made his fiction a site of generic transmigration from socialist peasant novel to family saga, historical allegory, religious fable, and farce of the darkest kind. His narrative blends the tone of traditional storytelling with the postmodernist play that has an unreliable narratorial voice. The name of the main character, Ximen Nao, brings to mind Ximen Qing, the Casanova-like hero of the erotic sixteenth-century realist novel *Jinpingmei* 金瓶梅 (The plum in a golden vase), and Ximen Nao's macabre adventures in various reincarnations are reminiscent of late imperial comic ghost fiction. At the same time, one finds in the novel's plot imprints of leftist peasant fiction that can be traced back to works such as Liu Qing's 柳青 (1916–78) *Chuangyeshi* 創業史 (A history of creation, 1960)—only now the Red classic is turned into an animal fable. At his most whimsical, Mo Yan creates a character whose name is also pronounced "Mo Yan" and who joins the novel's parade of reincarnations.

If socialist realism stresses the "order of mimesis,"[4] one that employs the representational power of narrative on behalf of an ideology or a truth claim, Mo Yan's fiction sets in motion the order of metamorphosis. In his world, things are changing in such a way as to project a paradoxical configuration: they either morph and proliferate beyond all control, or else they enact the unlikely rhythm of eternal return. However, Mo Yan's approach is not sui generis. The 1980s saw the first wave of works that subverted socialist subjectivity by introducing then-taboo themes such as haunting and spectrality. In the new millennium, one comes across in both literary and virtual texts a plethora of stories about time travel, transfiguration, and reincarnation. In these works, ghosts, spirits, animals, and animated creatures mingle with humans to generate one unlikely scene after another, but the central theme is always the altered state of reality as a socialist society undergoes the surreal transition to postsocialism, and "all that is solid melts into air," in the words of Karl Marx and Friedrich Engels in *The Communist Manifesto*.

Michel Foucault has contended that bodies represent what we are perpetually imprisoned in: "in the end, all of those utopias only begin to form through a process of opposing and eliminating the body."[5] Foucault explains that within the utopian space that is most deeply rooted in people's hearts, we inevitably find "a fantasy of an incorporeal body"—which is to say that "all non-native spaces" have a "beautiful, clear, transparent, flashing, agile, incomparably strong, endlessly enduring, unrestrained yet invisible body."[6] Different forms and paths are used to "de-realize and transfigure the new world, thereby creating a new relationship with the world." Foucault calls these utopian expressions emerging from the body "heterotopian bodies" and argues that, in contrast to bodies located in "ordinary social space," they "are always located elsewhere, meaning that they are another space within the world."[7] These heterotopian bodies satisfy, stimulate, and complete a utopian imaginary, permitting bodies to escape all sorts of essentializing definitions and realize an alternative ideal in the present moment.

Inspired by, but not limited to, this Foucauldian thesis of the heterotopian body versus reality, this chapter examines the way in which contemporary Chinese and other Sinophone fiction writers "de-realize and transfigure the new world, thereby creating a new relationship with the world." My keyword for this chapter is "transmigration," and I am interested not only in the word's mildly religious undertone in relation to the cyclical movement of a soul after death but also in its bifurcated connotation of both transformation and circulation, both implosion and repetition, as illustrated by Mo Yan's novel.

This chapter is divided into four parts. First, I describe "phantasm"—in terms of the illusory being, apparition, avatar, and karmic carnation—as a postsocialist figure articulated in opposition to the fashioning of modern corporality in Chinese fictional history. Second, in response to Mo Yan's animal allegory, I call attention to the recent fictional engagements with the animal or animus and their biopolitical implications. Third, I discuss the ghostly agency in works that present erratic timelines and aberrant chronologies in such a way as to overturn the conventional discourse of historiography. Lastly, I engage with phantasmal representation in utopias, dystopias, and heterotopias and focus on its necro-political implication.

The Return of Phantasms

There is no shortage of fantastic elements in traditional Chinese literature. Crossing corporeal, temporal, and spatial barriers, ghosts, animate and inanimate spirits, and supernatural beings appear to (dis)embody the spaces between the dead and the living, the unreal and the real, and the unthinkable and the admissible. Instead of serving merely as a reference to ancient superstition, fantastic beings reveal the contested relationship between the modes of verisimilitude and conceptions of historicity.

This fantastic discourse reached its first peak as early as the Six Dynasties period (222–589 CE),[8] and it underwent several major transformations in the following centuries.[9] The conflation of the nonhuman and all-too-human qualities in Ming and Qing narrative accounts about ghosts furnished the necessary repertoire even for writers' configurations of this-worldly affairs. As Lu Xun noted, Ming fiction about gods and demons (*shenmo xiaoshuo* 神魔小說) thrived alongside fiction about social manners (*shiqing xiaoshuo* 世情小說), and in late Ming and early Qing ghost novellas, there arose a remarkable confluence of ghostly and human motifs.[10] Ghost fiction, in Lu Xun's opinion, was one of the progenitors of Qing social satire.[11]

Nevertheless, this tradition came to a halt in the modern era. In the wake of the May Fourth movement, modern literature was expected to highlight themes such as enlightenment and revolution, and art for the sake of life became the goal of progressive writers. In a discourse largely modeled after the nineteenth-century European canon of realism, ghosts—together with other supernatural beings—found no place to dwell.[12] These spectral beings were associated with obsolete superstition, feudal practice, or merely decadent imagination and thus became impediments to modern epistemological and ideological advancement. Zhou Zuoren 周作人 (1885–1967), arguably the most prolific among the May Fourth writers on the subject of the ghostly, summarized the intellectual ethos of the time when he declared himself for "Ren de wenxue" 人的文學 (Literature of the human) in 1921.[13] In the following years Zhou doggedly launched attacks on anything related to the ghostly. "Who are our enemies," he asked in 1924, "but the beasts and ghosts—the beasts and ghosts that have lived off us human creatures?"[14] And speaking of the life-and-death war against the spectral world, one can find no more dramatic a statement than this one made in 1921 by Hu Shi 胡適 (1891–1962):

> Let me rip open my heart and explain to the world: it is only because I believed perfectly well that in the "pile of rotten paper" are numberless old ghosts who can eat people and cast a spell over people. For the harm they can do, they are much more deadly than the germs discovered by Pasteur. But it is also because I believe that though I am powerless against the germs, I take pride in my ability to "chain the demons and subdue the ghosts."[15]

Along with such a realist agenda arose an aesthetics of corporeality that exerted its power over the forming of the national community. The formation of a new Chinese body was a shared cause among late Qing and early Republican enlightened literati and revolutionaries, as evinced by the strong physical imagery of campaigns for military Chinese (*jun guomin* 軍國民) and new people (*xinmin* 新民).[16] Particularly in the tradition of revolutionary literature, from Mao Zedong's first publication "Tiyu zhi yanjiu" 體育之研究 (A study of physical culture, 1917) to the massive campaigns for rehabilitation through labor in the Cultural Revolution, one finds a recurrent logic that links ideological correctness with physical fitness.[17] Yet this call for a massive reform of the Chinese body was shared by the right wing. Chiang Kai-shek and his followers launched the New Life movement in 1934—a campaign that emphasized physical fitness, public and private hygiene, and social discipline—as a way to rescue China from what they called a "ghostly life" (*gui shenghuo* 鬼生活). As Chiang proclaimed, "Modern Chinese life is one full of filth, decadence, laziness and despondency; this is not a life of humanity and it can only be called a 'ghostly life.'"[18] For Chiang as for his followers, the New Life movement was aimed at "fashioning a Chinese body oriented toward militancy, productivity, and aestheticization."[19]

Although ghosts and demons appear to have been kept at bay by enlightened literati, they still lurked not far behind the facade of new literature. Modern Chinese writers and intellectuals cannot carry on their enlightened discourse without invoking, or even inventing, new ghosts. The most prominent case in point is Lu Xun, the pioneer of Chinese literary modernity. For all his efforts to redraw the boundary of the rational world, Lu Xun was fascinated with the dark domain he ruled out, a domain haunted by funeral rites, graves, executions, ghosts, demons, and death wishes.[20] As he once wrote, "I feel very unhappy about the ancient ghosts that I carry on my back. I cannot shake them off. So often do I feel a heavy weight that depresses me."[21]

Lu Xun's fascination with the macabre and the deadly can be discerned at many points in his stories, ranging from the cannibalistic banquet that the Madman hallucinates in "The Diary of a Mad Man" to the illusory light that lures an old scholar to drown himself in "Baiguang" 白光 (White light); the corpse with a grim smile in "Guduzhe" 孤獨者 (The misanthrope); and Xianglin's wife's dubious question, "Is there life after death?" in "Zhufu" (New year's sacrifice).[22] Lu Xun's obsession with ghosts reaches an apex in *Yecao* (Wild grass, 1927)[23] and in *Zhaohua xishi* 朝花夕拾 (Morning flowers plucked at sunset, 1927), an essay collection permeated with his memories of the ghostly ambience—including, for example, family deaths, haunted gardens, exorcism rituals, and gothic theaters—in which he grew up.

The modern campaign to exorcise the ghosts haunting Chinese humanity was charged with even more power in the period of revolutionary literature. The play *Bai Maonü* 白毛女 (White-haired girl, 1946) ends with the maxim, "The old society turned human beings into ghosts; the new society turns ghosts into human beings."[24] But despite communist crackdowns, ghosts kept creeping back into China, and they even seem to have multiplied in number after the founding of the PRC. The collection *Bupagui de gushi* 不怕鬼的故事 (Stories defying the superstition of ghosts), edited by He Qifang 何其芳 (1912–77), was popular in the 1950s. In 1963, Mao's wife, Jiang Qing 江青 (1914–91), banned Meng Chao's 孟超 (1902–76) Beijing opera *Li Huiniang* 李慧娘 (1961) because it promoted the dangerous principle that "ghosts do humanity no harm" (*yougui wuhai* 有鬼無害).[25] The banning of *Li Huiniang* was part of the prelude to the Cultural Revolution, and during the revolution, one of the most most frequently used slogans was "down with ox ghosts and snake spirits."

Exorcism underlies the communist imaginary of the sublime, which is described by Ban Wang as "a discursive dynamic, a psychic mechanism, a stunning figure, a grand image of the body, or a crushing or uplifting experience from the lowest depression to the highest picture."[26] Given the existence of a nationalist discourse that has nervously celebrated the motif of virile corporeality, it is ironic to witness how the banished haunting constitutes that motif's unlikely other. One cannot help asking what the ghosts and ghost-like beings are doing in a socialist society that has reportedly been cleansed of all nonhuman and inhuman creatures. Are they superstitions and heresies to be cleansed in the land of atheism? Are they memories and desires quelled by hegemonic power? Are they the dark forces, madness, and taboos perpetually rejected by ideological hygiene? Are they the ironic self-projections of those oppressed for reasons of class, ethnicity, or gender? Are they the unnamable evil—the diabolic ethics and erotics of excess—as defined by Georges Bataille, for example?[27] Most importantly, could the ghost be the fictional power that generates the new and the unexpected from the fossilized existence of the real?

It is this context that causes one to pay special attention to the vigorous return of ghosts and fantastic beings to elite and popular Chinese culture in the 1980s. As I have discussed elsewhere,[28] this malady broke out first in Taiwan and Hong Kong and then spread throughout the mainland, thanks to the internet if not the book market. Fantastic and gothic subjects—possession, haunting, exorcism, predestination, retribution, visits to hell, and so on—have been among the favorite subjects of popular media, so much so that the authorities have had to lay down one restriction after another to curtail their circulation. Besides Mo Yan, such well-regarded writers as Yu Hua 余華 (b. 1960), Jia Pingwa 賈平凹 (b. 1952), Su Tong 蘇童 (b. 1962), and Han Shaogong 韓少功 (b. 1956) have made use of uncanny elements, from eerie symbolism to unearthly settings. The landscape of contemporary Chinese fiction is once again haunted by goblins, spirits, apparitions, and phantoms.

One may argue that the recent ghost fever corresponds to the importation of Western fantastic discourse, from gothic romance to magical realism, or more generally that it reflects the global outburst of a fin de siècle imaginary. However, it is not just ghosts but specifically the premodern Chinese fantastic and gothic narrative tradition that has made a comeback in the postmodern literary scene. Take a look at Han Shaogong's acclaimed story "Guiqulai" 歸去來 (Homecoming, 1985). Set some unspecified time after the Cultural Revolution, the story relates a man's visit to a village he believes he has never been to before. Yet the village looks familiar to him: its natural and cultural settings, residents, customs, and even animals remind him of the place where he was exiled as a *zhiqing* 知青 (educated youth) during the revolution. If his name had not been mistaken for some else's, the protagonist might have treated this strange encounter as a homecoming event. A sense of déjà vu abounds. The climax of the story is the protagonist's encounter with a girl who claims to be the sister of his beloved. She tells this man that his old sweetheart passed away long ago.

"Homecoming" has often been discussed either as the climax of scar literature or as the harbinger of root-seeking fiction. What has been ignored is the fact that it is narrated within the conventions of the ghost story. Etymologically, the Chinese word for ghost (*gui* 鬼) is associated with the word for return (*gui* 歸) and hence the interpretation in the ancient Chinese dictionary *Erya* 爾雅: "the meaning of *ghost* is 'that which returns.'"[29] "Return" in this context means a "return home," not to one's human abode but to the site of eternal rest. If life is seen as a temporary sojourn among the living, death represents a return to the source from which all creatures have come.[30]

Moreover, the Chinese title of the story, "Guiqulai," is a pun on the title of the famed poem "Guiqulai ci" 歸去來辭 (Homecoming) by Tao Qian 陶潛 (365–427). But for a writer writing in the aftermath of the Cultural Revolution, "Homecoming" does not evoke the yearning for reclusive withdrawal into domestic refuge but a nightmarish fall into a maze of memory.

In Freudian terms, one may read the story as an uncanny experience, a horrific encounter with something that seems both utterly familiar and utterly strange.[31]

The resurgence of ghostly writing in contemporary Chinese fiction leads us to reconsider the gothic vein of Marxism. This tradition, in Margaret Cohen's words, is "fascinated with the irrational aspects of society's processes and . . . takes seriously a culture's ghosts and phantoms as a significant and rich field of social production rather than a mirage to be expelled."[32] Karl Marx and Friedrich Engels famously begin *The Communist Manifesto* by ironically describing communism as a wandering specter in Europe, an apparitional hope projected from the past onto the future. At the other end of the spectral spectrum, critics such as Walter Benjamin and Theodor Adorno have used the term "phantasmagoria" to critique the representation of ghostly forms in European societies of the mid-nineteenth century.[33] Benjamin sees the Paris of the Second Empire (1852–70) as a "modern" space in which the ordinary is turned into the spectacular and the exterior mixes with the interior, producing a figurative surplus of meaning. This urban civilization is built on a parade of spectral images and illusory sensations that, for Benjamin, may as well be a modern magic lantern show, a phantasmagoria.[34] With Wagner's operas as his cases in point, Adorno criticizes the composer for having turned his works into phantasmagoric ploys by "reproducing the dream world of commodity in the form of myth.[35] Adorno argues that as commodity forms begin to invade all aspects of modern life, all aesthetic appearance is in danger of being transformed into "the illusion of the absolute reality of the unreal."[36]

Jacques Derrida added a polemical twist to this tradition in the 1990s when he noted the "specters of Marx" amid what appeared to be the death of Marxism as a global political force. Derrida holds that traditional scholarship approaches the ghost by ontologizing it, bypassing the issue of spectrality in history: "Haunting is historical . . . but it is not dated, it is never docilely given a date in the chain of precedents . . . according to the instituted order of the calendar."[37] Ghosts—*revenants*, in Derrida's terminology—do not arrive merely from the past but rather anticipate a repeated return in the future. One way to engage with the claims of the death of Marxism, therefore, is to live with the return of the ghosts of Marx. Instead of ontology, one acquires a "hauntology," a ghostly deconstruction of history, identity, and origin. Like a double-edged sword, Derrida's critique helps recall the spirit of Marxism even as it disputes its authenticity.[38]

Within China at the turn of the millennium, phantasms returned not only to fictional narrative but also to political discourse. Wang Hui 汪暉, China's foremost voice of neoleftism, has openly called for a reconjuration of ghosts vis-à-vis Chinese reality. In critiquing the capitalist turn of China, Wang seeks to resurrect revolutionary spirits. For him, the ghost is not so much a supernatural haunting as it is, in Kiyama Hideo's words, "a historical sense that emerges from the piling up of countless dead people."[39] In other words, Wang finds in the summoning of the dead a new possibility of looking forward to the future:

> There are innumerable differences in the ways that ghosts appear, but if one were to abstractly summarize the characteristics of ghosts, the following should not be omitted: 1. ghosts transcend the boundary between humans and things; 2. ghosts transcend the boundary between the inside and the outside; 3. ghosts transcend the boundary between life and death; and 4. with respect to the wandering dead soul, we can sometimes call it a specter as the one described in the beginning of Marx's *Communist Manifesto* in relation to communism which was wandering in Europe.[40]

Wang Hui's case in point is none other than Lu Xun. In Wang's discussion of the master's "The True Story of Ah Q," a satire about a hooligan who lives on the illusory "method of spiritual victory" and dies a laughable scapegoat in a society in drastic changes, he argues that for all his personality defects, Ah Q uses a penitential self-reflection that bursts out at the most unlikely moments of his life, and such a capacity promises the seeds of change in the future. Above all, Wang finds in Ah Q the propensity of "downward transcendence" (*xiangxia chaoyue* 向下超越), the inversion of the upward transcendence stressed by conventional metaphysics. The agent of "downward transcendence" is the ghost, an invisible being that wanders in the liminal zone between the human and the nonhuman and between life and death, ever ready to disturb the stability of the real.[41]

Lu Xun's Ah Q became an iconic figure in modern Chinese literature because of his "method of spiritual victory"—a self-defense mechanism that turns an extreme situation of defeat or humiliation into a victory worthy of rhetorical triumph. In a time when revolution has receded into the remote horizons of socialist China, Wang tries to introduce a new reading of Ah Q's story by seeking out a moment of "transcendence" in the failures of revolution. In contrast to the conventional view that Ah Q's "spiritual victory" is nothing but self-delusion, Wang refers to its inherent revolutionary potential, likening it to a ghost—or, better yet, the wandering "specter" that inaugurates Marx and Engels's *Communist Manifesto*. In other words, insofar as Ah Q's method of "spiritual victory" is in effect one of spectral victory, his habitual self-deception proves to be an unwitting prophecy of future apocalypse.

However, in his allegorical reading, Wang has overlooked the fact that in contemporary China, it is the revolutionary regime itself that is doing everything to forestall any form of social protest, let alone revolution. "Maintaining stability" and "harmonious society" have been the keywords of governance. Moreover, Wang's endeavor to rehabilitate Ah Q, however conscientious, risks erasing the paradoxical implications of Lu Xun's work. Ah Q comes across as a disturbing character precisely because he embodies the murky nature of Chinese reality. Whereas Lu Xun creates a fictional account of Ah Q trapped in reality, Wang strives doggedly to "transcend" it, albeit "downwardly," in terms of theory—and in doing so, he sidesteps Lu Xun's fictitious premise and expels the ghostly force that the master meant to conjure up. Above all, since the regime Wang endorses allows no revolution, his call for a ghostly revolution appears to be a gesture just as empty as Ah Q's exercise of "spiritual victory."

In sum, fiction can be seen as a phantasmal force that propels the dialectic of the revolutionary legacy in socialist China. Insofar as a legacy refers to a palpable or imaginary entity—a gift, artifact, or property, for example—handed down from the past (such as from an ancestor or predecessor), this legacy has a dual significance for contemporary Chinese fiction. On one hand, it points to a revolutionary tradition that is memorable and transmittable, a past that can be rejuvenated and carried on by the generations to come. On the other hand, it points to a revolutionary tradition that is beyond memory and not transmittable, as the past is believed to be long gone and what is left behind amounts to no more than its traces. Both senses of the word entail a politics of posterity.

Becoming Animals

Returning to Mo Yan's *Life and Death Are Wearing Me Out*, we see that change is the leitmotif of Mo's socialist metamorphosis. In the novel, Maoist rural reform is undertaken in such a way as to bring forth a sequence of absurd, gratuitous outcomes. Ximen Nao's continued reincarnations suggest either the lay Buddhist understanding of the karmic cycle or the Nietzschean view of the eternal return. Moreover, by describing Ximen's outrageous adventures in each incarnation, Mo Yan reflects not only on how the socialist agenda has changed the landscape and mindscape of rural China but also on how the agenda has changed, sometimes beyond recognition, when filtered through the layered textures of folk life and imagination. It is through the frictions and fissures between these changes that Mo comes to write his history of the Chinese communist revolution.

Mo Yan's novel is just one of the animalistic allegories that have surfaced in the new millennium. In Jiang Rong's 姜戎 (b. 1946) *Langtuteng* 狼圖騰 (Wolf totem, 2005), the animal allegory is even more direct. A national best seller, the novel relates the story of a sent-down youth's encounter with wolves on the Inner Mongolian prairie during the Cultural Revolution. The wolf is portrayed as a lonely, unscrupulous, and resilient animal to be both feared and emulated by the human. According to the narrator, China has been a meek and submissive sheep culture for too long and can only be reinvigorated by becoming a wolf culture. The novel ignited a national craze for the wolf-like virtues of being wild and unruly. Intriguingly, such a call for the "wolf totem" cuts both ways, suggesting both a nostalgia for the socialist logic of revolution, no matter what the cost, and a yearning for the postsocialist market logic of survival of the fittest.

In the wake of the *Wolf Totem* fever, a series of animal narratives hit the market, including Yang Zhijun's 楊志軍 *Zangao* 藏獒 (Tibetan mastiff, 2005); Li Kewei's 李克威 *Zhongguohu* 中國虎 (China tiger, 2007); and the works of the so-called king of animal fiction, Shen Shixi 沈石溪, such as *Xueshan shenbao* 雪山神豹 (Divine leopard in the snowy mountain, 2015).

However, a quick look at these novels reveals the fact that no matter what animal is invoked, the authors are aiming at an anthropocentric imaginary—the animal merely mimics the virtues or vices of humanity. It is the human, not the animal, that makes the narrative intelligible.

Meanwhile, there have been repeated attempts to break away from the anthropocentric (and Han ethnocentric) inclination of the animal narrative, as evinced by three recent works by Chinese and other Sinophone writers. In "Qingshui li dedaozi" 清水裏的刀子 (Knife in the clear water, 1997), a story by Shi Shuqing 石舒清 (b. 1969), a native of the Ningxia Muslim Autonomous region, the Hui patriarch Ma Zishan finds himself facing a painful dilemma. On the fortieth day after his wife's passing, he is asked to sacrifice his only domestic bull to complete the religious service. While the old man is deep in mourning for his longtime companion, he feels equally sad about parting with the bull, which has worked for the family for many years. The old bull, as if aware of its impending doom, stops eating and drinking three days before its scheduled slaughter. According to traditional belief, when an animal has been marked for sacrifice, it sees the reflection of a knife in the water and reconciles itself with its fate. On the day of slaughter, the old man decides to absent himself from the slaughter, only to be greeted on his return by the severed head of the bull, "a visage of the dead that resembles so vividly the countenance of the living" (*yizhang yanmian ru sheng de sizhe de lian*, 一張顏面如生的死者的臉).[42]

In the Tibetan writer Tsering Norbu's 次仁羅布 (b. 1965) "Fangshengyang" 放生羊 (Sheep of life release, 2009),[43] a Tibetan elder is disturbed by serial dreams of his long-deceased wife who is still being tortured in the underworld. To redeem her suffering and expedite her reincarnation, the old man purchases a sheep that is about to be butchered with the purpose of setting it free as a symbol of atonement. As the old man takes the sheep to attend to the daily routine of circumambulation (Tibetan: *kora*; Chinese: *zhuanjing* 轉經) along the outer pilgrim route enclosing old Lhasa, he develops deeper and deeper emotional ties with the sheep. When he comes down with stomach cancer and can no longer undertake the daily ritual, the sheep seems aware of its master's wish and walks the route on its own.

Like Mo Yan's *Life and Death Are Wearing Me Out*, Shi's and Tsering's stories use the connection between human and animal to explore the meaning of death and transmigration. But the two writers deal with the theme in different ways than Mo does. Whereas Mo lines up the animal figures as a vehicle of human metempsychosis, keeping the struggles of each incarnation distinct from the overarching narrative of the protagonist's transmigration, Shi and Tsering go beyond the comfort zone of anthropocentrism by exploring changing relationships between the human and the animal. In "Knife in the Clear Water," the Muslim elder cannot help being confounded by the bull's mysterious self-abstinence of sorts in the face of its doom. The bull is supposed to be sacrificed to facilitate the family's ritual of mourning, but rather than submit to this instrumental logic, it responds in a way beyond the grasp of the elder's human imagination. The bull's submission and determination in the face of its impending death catalyzes the old man's doubts about the meaning of life and death.

In "A Sheep of Life Release," however, the old Tibetan widower adopts the sheep at first simply because it provides him with much-needed solace. He eventually finds a kindred spirit in the sheep and treats it almost as an embodiment of his wife. But the sheep surprises us by demonstrating a certain "spirituality" (*lingxing* 靈性), as the widower himself suggests.[44] It survives the destined fate of slaughter thanks to the old man's intervention and becomes the caregiver, and even spiritual guide, to him toward the end of the story. Insofar as they both transform from domestic to religious animals, Shi's bull and Tsering's sheep fall into a blurred state in which the human, the animalistic, and the divine are all brought into play—something that is missing in Mo Yan's work and that of the majority of Chinese animal literature writers. The bull and sheep seem to be in a state of existence beyond human intelligibility.

In their study on "becoming animal," Gilles Deleuze and Félix Guattari call attention to "animal" as a process of becoming. Rather than implying a shift from one identity to another or the synthesis of two identities, the authors contend that "there is a reality specific to becoming" and that "becoming is a verb with a consistency all its own."[45] In their framework, "becoming" implies the deconstructing of identity. For the authors, "becoming animal" occurs not through reproduction and hereditary descent but through "contagion," which means deterritorialization—or the breakdown of boundary lines—of multiple species of plants, animals, and humans. They give the example of the orchid and wasp. The orchid, by "appropriating physiological and chemical properties of the female wasp, entices the male wasp to pollinate it," thus transcending the boundaries of classified distinct species.[46] Accordingly, "becoming animal" refers to the process of becoming "anomalous": "neither an individual nor a species . . . but a phenomenon of bordering."[47]

Deleuze and Guattari differentiate in another context between three types of animals. The first type is the Oedipal animal, or the animal domesticated by the human to assume an individualized and sentimentalized identity in alliance with human family life. The second type is the state or archetypal animal, or the animal that has a symbolic presence in the myths, rituals, and spiritual beliefs of human cultures. It is the third type of animal, the demonic animal, that most concerns Deleuze and Guattari. They note that the Latin word *daemon* comes from the Greek word *daimōn* (*δαίμων*), which refers to a lesser deity—namely, a divinity between gods and humans. The word "daimōn" also had the meaning "to divide," and sometimes it could mean the souls or inner selves of men.[48] The authors stress that the "demonic animal" occupies a borderline position that is ever ready to collapse the distinction between the animalistic, the human, the demonic, and the divine.

I will have more to say about daimōn in chapter 5. At stake here is the question of how such a moment of demonic transformation is revealed to the characters and readers alike. Both Shi and Tsering create in their stories a moment when the protagonists encounter the animals' facial expressions. As noted above, "Knife in the Clear Water" culminates with the Muslim patriarch's seeing the lifelike "face" of the severed head of the bull. In "Sheep of Life Release," the elder is compelled to buy the sheep after only a momentary gaze at the sheep's "face": "a sheep faces me bleating, its voice is full of sorrow. I take another look at the fact of the sheep and am struck by a sense of intimacy all over, as if I have known it for a long time."[49] In other words, something unspeakable happens when these two characters meet the animals face to face.

Of course, one can sentimentalize the scenes by reading human sympathy or empathy into the moment of facial encounter. In "Knife in the Clear Water," not only does the old patriarch treat the bull like a family member, but his son even identifies it with his deceased mother. More suggestively, in "Sheep of Life Release," the old man uses the pronoun "you" to refer alternately to both his deceased wife and the sheep. But more significantly, the scenes call for a rethinking of sociality beyond interpersonal relationships. What does the old Muslim see in the empty looks of the dead bull, and what does the old Tibetan man see in the moaning face of the sheep?

The question of the face has been raised by the philosopher Emmanuel Levinas. Levinas uses the word "face" to refer to the living presence of another person that forces us to engage socially and ethically with that person. When someone is exposed to us by being there, existing as an undeniable reality, we cannot reduce the "face" to images or ideas in our head. This impossibility of capturing the other conceptually or otherwise indicates the other's infinity. As Levinas contends, "the face of the Other at each moment destroys and overflows the plastic image it leaves me, the idea existing to my own measure. . . . It expresses itself."[50] Furthermore, "the face opens the primordial discourse whose first word is obligation."[51] With his theory, Levinas lobbies for a radical ethics of reciprocating obligation and love. The human is always another person, and hospitality to the stranger is not merely an exercise in friendship but an unconditional humility achieved through "othering" selfhood.

Despite Levinas's emphasis on the face of the divine "Other," his face still smacks of anthropocentrism. However, Shi's and Tsering's stories about facial encounters take us beyond immediate humanistic engagement. Of course, one can think of the distinct ethnic and religious cultures in which the two writers broach the human-animal interaction. But more pertinent to our concerns is how the two writers tell their stories in such a way as to call forth the sensation of "becoming animal"—that is, both focus on the moment in which the human realizes that he is no more, and no less, than the animal. The sense of affinity thus aroused is nothing if not emotionally charged, a "demonic" affect in Deleuzian terms that is transmitted from one entity to another in the ecological world and beyond.

But the transmigratory process does not even have to involve the reciprocity of human and animal. Take, for example, Syaman Rapongan's 夏曼藍波安 (b. 1957) novel *Tiankong de yanjing* 天空的眼睛 (Eyes in the sky).[52] This is a novel about the life and death of the Tau people, a tribe of Austronesian origin living on Orchid Island southeast of Taiwan. Close to the rich Kuroshio, the so-called black current that runs through the northern Pacific Ocean, Orchid Island has benefited from abundant ecological resources that have shaped the culture of the Tau. Syaman's novel tells how an older fisherman copes with a series of trials, including his declining health, his daughter's untimely death in Taiwan, and the uncertain future of his grandson—who is half Tau and half Han. With these elements, Syaman could have written a sentimental animal fable of the kind often associated with indigenous cultures in the Sinophone imagination. Instead, he simply recounts the old man's life of fishing, boat making, and logging in parallel to the mutations of the world he inhabits. In fact, the novel starts with a lengthy monologue by an old fish about mingling with other schools of fish, encountering human divers, and responding to environmental challenges from changes in the black current to fishing nets.

Involved here is Syaman's effort not to allegorize but instead to approximate the relationships between the human and the fish. If in Shi Shuqing's and Tering Norbu's works, one still discerns the human bond with animals in economic, ethical, and religious terms, Syaman's writing further deterritorializes the anthropomorphic configuration of the world and throws the human into an ecosystem in which life and death take on different dimensions. In the novel, the old man demonstrates an immense capacity to immerse himself and his tribal culture in the unfathomable realm of the ocean, the sky, and the stars. He is taking a deep-sea perspective from which to gauge and survive the world: "Like the dense schools of flying fish, the diverse island inhabitants cross over and pass over the ocean, following the natural rhythm of the Black Current."[53]

One may argue that in the end, Syaman's story is narrated from the human perspective and cannot escape a human-oriented logic. The famous dictum of Zhuangzi comes to mind: "if you are not a fish, how can you know of the happiness of the fish?"[54] But instead of a circular rhetorical question of self-referentiality, Syaman's narrative introduces a new grammar, so to speak, that enables him to decode Han Chinese ecological and ethical knowledge. Critics have repeatedly pointed out that Syaman uses the Chinese language in such a way as to violate received notions of syntactical and semantic structure.[55] He depicts a Pacific perception of place and space through not only an evocative sensibility about the ocean but also a quest for ancestral words passed down as bodily codes, or the memory in the blood. Through describing the old fisherman's daily routines, Syaman demonstrates an extensive knowledge of the stars, ocean, and multispecies world of the Pacific as well as bodily techniques of fishing, canoeing, boat building, and celestial navigation.[56] By extension, through the old fisherman's oceanic perspective, he manages to convey a distinct view of life and the afterlife. Such a view is based on "making kin" with multiple species dwelling on or under the earth—that is, in the world of the "chthulucene."[57]

Returning to the human world of *Eyes in the Sky* that is occupied by death and mourning, we see that Syaman has no intention of tying together the two threads of his novel—the ethical and the environmental—to generate a meaningful humanist reading. Thus, it becomes the reader's responsibility to cross, or crisscross, various territories to make sense of his position of reading. Unlike "Knife in the Clear Water," in which the epiphany of the severed head of the bull reveals to the Hui patriarch the inscrutable meaning of death, or "Sheep of Life Release," in which the Tibetan elder forms an intimate relationship with a seemingly spiritual sheep, *Eyes in the Sky* focuses more on an egalitarianism of affective distribution and environmental governance. It is the "bloc of sensations,"[58] in Deleuzean terms, rather than the organization of relations, that concerns Syaman. He lets his style flow, as it were, from the fish's perspective to the narrator's and ends with a nonending that evokes an amorphous coexistence between the human and fish, as well as the ocean and the sky. As the title of the novel suggests, it is the cosmic "eyes in the sky" that embrace all faces of the earth—the living and the dead.

Enchanted History

Rather than follow the formula mandated by the regime, Mo Yan's *Life and Death Are Wearing Me Out* seeks an alternative method for describing modern Chinese life. Although the plot follows the historical timeline of the PRC from 1949 to the turn of the millennium, it is the alternative history of transmigrations and reincarnations that makes a deeper impression.

Despite the surface progression of socialist time, Mo invites his reader to reflect on history as the gratuitous work of eternal return.

I would call fictional writing along this line enchanted history. I draw my definition from the old Weberian definition of modernity as disenchantment. For Max Weber, the intellectual innovation of modernity consists in the disenchantment with a premodern episteme characterized in particular by theology and the church.[59] To extend Weber's theory to the case of China, the Maoist brand of history can be said to have taken on a dimension of disenchantment. By claiming to exorcise the ghosts of the past, delivering the Chinese people from a state of deadly inertia and restoring them to life, it highlights the agenda of liberated subjectivity and secularized resurrection via revolution.

Such a Maoist vision of disenchantment was turned upside down in the aftermath of the Cultural Revolution. Writers wrote to unleash the power of the immemorial and unspeakable hidden behind the sublime narrative, as well as to summon the afterlives of history in the form of ghosts and goblins. They even ventured to reveal the enchantment inherent in Maoism. That is, at the same time that the ideology enacts (socialist) enlightenment by disenchanting Chinese people from preestablished values and beliefs, it also enchants them, almost in a born-again manner, by calling on the power of political theology—a form of governance based on absolute leadership and solidarity to the exclusion of the designated class enemy.[60] Involved in this dialectic of enchantment is the "fusion of horizons" between iconoclasm and idolatry, socialist mythologies of new manhood and "primitive passions,"[61] rationality and volition. Works such as Lao Gui's 老鬼 (b. 1947) *Xuese huanghun* 血色黄昏 (Bloody sunset, 1987) serve as a good example of the contradictions this ideological operation entailed. The fictional memoir relates Lao Gui's adventures through the Cultural Revolution, his stormy relationship with his parents, his "long march" and experience being sent down, and his repentance when he realizes that all his youthful time and energy have been lost forever to the Maoist cult. Incidentally, the Chinese phrase "lao gui" literally mean "old ghost." Lao Gui's mother was Yang Mo 楊沫 (1914–95), the most popular female author of the early PRC, who is best known for her revolutionary saga *Qingchun zhige* 青春之歌 (Song of the youth, 1958).

In the aftermath of the Tian'anmen incident, however, such an attempt to rewrite history took another twist. At a time when revolution had lost its legitimacy, the discourse of revolutionary history was further deflated. A once emancipatory history has become an emaciated history, as shown in the innuendo of Mo Yan's title *Life and Death Are Wearing Me Out*. But it is writers of the Sinophone world who have offered more powerful interventions, thanks primarily to the freedoms available outside the confines of the PRC. This section focuses on two writers, Chan Koon-chung 陳冠中 (b. 1952) and Ng Kim-chew 黃錦樹 (b. 1967), who strive to reconstruct contemporary Chinese history by conjuring up ghosts and hauntings as well as heterogenous temporalities.

Chan is a renowned Hong Kong writer, critic, and movie producer who has made Beijing his base in recent years, while Ng is a Chinese Malaysian writer residing in Taiwan. In their new works, both start out with counterfactual questions. What if the Nationalists had defeated the Communists in 1949 and continued to rule the mainland up to the present? Or what if the Malayan (later Malaysian, after the founding of Malaysia in 1963) Chinese communists had managed to build their own nation by fending off British colonists and indigenous Malayan nationalists during the Cold War? With these hypothetical questions, the two writers tap into the phantasmal power of fabulation to create a dialectic of time and memory that is an alternative to the one offered by official historiography. Both authors take advantage of a genre that has been rarely adopted by Chinese and other Sinophone writers—uchronia.

As a fictional genre, uchronia refers to a narrative that disrupts the set course of history in such a way as to alter the settled account as to what has happened and become irreversible. Coined by Charles Renouvier (1815–1903) as the title of his 1876 novel *Uchronie: L'Utopie dans l'histoire*, the term is closely related to utopia: utopia refers to "u-topos" in Greek, meaning "no place," while uchronia replaces "topos" with "chronos" to denote "no time." Whereas utopia has been a popular genre in China since the beginning of the twentieth century, uchronias have rarely been written—perhaps for the reason that unlike utopias, which can be far removed from the real world, uchronias build on the past and therefore contest the existing knowledge of history, threatening to reveal the taboos and desires underlying a given historical account. This is precisely the polemical method that Chan and Ng use to engage with Chinese reality.

In 2009, the sixtieth anniversary of the PRC, Chan published *Shengshi* 盛世 (The fat years), a utopia—or dystopia—recounting what would have happened in an alternative China in 2013. The novel starts with a global economic crash in 2011 that paralyzes all the global powers except for China. Thanks to shrewd national leadership, we are told, China was able to take advantage of the crisis and further her economic and social development. As a result, as early as 2013 China can boast the arrival of *shengshi*, a historical epoch of peace and prosperity. While the majority of Chinese citizens welcome the golden times, there are signs—such as a prevailing mood of jubilation called "high lite lite" and massive amnesia—that arouse suspicion among a few nonconformists. To find out the truth, they kidnap a national leader, only to learn something that they never could have imagined.

The Fat Years seemed amazingly prescient to many readers in 2013 when President Xi Jinping launched the "Chinese Dream" campaign, which Chan's 2009 novel prefigured. But this was only the first step of Chan's intervention in contemporary Chinese history. In *Jianfeng ernian: Xinzhongguo wuyoushi* 建豐二年: 新中國烏有史 (The second year of the Jianfeng reign: A uchronia of new China, 2015), Chan looks back at modern Chinese history and asks a thorny question: What would have happened if the Nationalists rather than the Communists had won the 1949 civil war?

As Chan's novel develops, Mao and his colleagues have been exiled by the infuriated Joseph Stalin to the Crimea, while Chiang Kai-shek continues to rule China from the old Nationalist capital of Nanjing. Under Chiang's liberal autocracy, China thrives in the global market economy in the following three decades, but any call for democracy is swiftly suppressed. Chiang Kai-shek passes away in 1975 and is succeeded by his son Chiang Ching-kuo 蔣經國 (1910–88) after a brief transitional period. By 1979, China has already established itself as a supreme global power. This is indeed a Nationalist version of "fat years." However, on the night of December 10, 1979, a group of domestic and overseas dissidents, liberals, and human rights activists secretly gather at Formosa Canteen next to the campus of Beijing University, only to be arrested by Chiang's secret police—their effort to democratize China coming to a sudden halt.

Chan is at his most subversive when mixing historically verifiable data and plausible speculation. After 1949, Chiang Kai-shek created an economic miracle in Taiwan, albeit at the expense of civil liberties, while Maoist China endured one destructive movement after another, culminating in the Cultural Revolution. Looking back from the postsocialist perspective, one cannot resist asking the uncanny question: Would post-1949 China have fared better had Chiang rather than Mao been in power? After all, isn't postsocialist China recapitulating the Nationalist model of a centralized market economy and authoritarian political system perfected by the Chiang regime?

To be sure, these are fantasies based on historical hindsight. But Chan intends to summon forth the ghostly shadows that lurk between the folds of history. For him, history is no more a predetermined plan or a grand narrative than it is a procession of contingencies and speculations from political crises to personal mishaps, all subject to continual reconfiguration. Where historians plough through piles of evidence to explain, sometimes by explaining away, bygone experience, fiction writers can take advantage of their vocation by unearthing the unknown and unknowable, cracking open both the past and the future of "history" and unleashing its potential.

Unlike *The Fat Years*, which takes us to a dystopian future yet to be realized, *The Second Year of the Jianfeng Reign* introduces history as a "double," with the differences and repetitions of bygone events in two timelines working in such a way as to reveal their mutually implicated relations. The title of the novel is symptomatic of this doubled chronology. Although it sounds like a reference to the traditional dating system based on the reign of the emperor, in fact it points to 1979, the second year of the presidency of Chiang Ching-kuo, whose honorific name is Jianfeng. The association of the old imperial system with the Chiang family rule of modern China could not be more ironic. As Chan would have it, in the arena of historical temporality, one can create a pattern of repetition through the operation of displacement and disguise just as easily as one can create a pattern of difference through the operation of divergence and decentering.

Each of the seven chapters of the novel ushers us into the double reading of what history was and what history could have been. For instance, chapter 1 features Zhang Dongsun 張東蓀 (1886–1973), a prominent intellectual and political activist of the Republican era who served as a peacemaker during the 1949 civil war. In Chan's version, Zhang survived Chiang Kai-shek's purge after 1949 and took refuge in Hong Kong, mingling with a group of exiled neo-Confucians. In reality, Zhang remained in China after 1949. For reasons that are still unclear, he was charged with treason by Mao and jailed, eventually dying a pathetic death during the Cultural Revolution. For readers who know Zhang's true story, his fictitious exile in Hong Kong may well represent a better, but still not desirable, end for him and intellectuals like him who suffered terribly under Mao.

Similar counterfactuals are offered in chapters 2 and 4. The former focuses on Sun Li-ren 孫立人 (1900–90), a defiant Nationalist general who was put under house arrest by Chiang after a failed power struggle in 1950s Taiwan. The latter deals with Phuntsok Wangyal 平措汪傑 (1922–2014), a leftist Tibetan who supported Mao's campaign for the self-determination of ethnic minorities during the revolution, only to be put in prison for allegedly promoting Tibetan independence in 1958. In Chan's uchronia, neither Sun's nor Phuntsok's fate would have been better if history could have started all over again. Sun would still have remained under house arrest, only in Fenghua, Chiang's hometown in China, rather than in Taiwan. Phuntsok's Tibetan cause would have proven as offensive to Chiang as it was to Mao, so Phuntsok would have been doomed in this timeline as well.

What is even more challenging is the chapter on literature in Chan's uchronia. We are told that for all of Chiang's hegemonic control, Chinese writers would have enjoyed relatively more freedom to create after 1949: not only would they have been spared (excessive) purges and campaigns, but they also would have served as cultural ambassadors to the world on behalf of China. In this timeline, Lao She 老舍 (1896–1966) wins the Nobel Prize for Literature for his novel on Manchu ethnic life, *Zhenghong qixia* 正紅旗下 (Under the red banner) in 1968, followed by Lin Yutang 林語堂 (1895–1976) in 1975. Meanwhile, writers from all Chinese and Sinophone communities —such as Shen Congwen, Eileen Chang, and Huang Chun-ming 黃春明 (b. 1935)—share the same community. Such a plot cuts against the grain of "true" history. Neither Lao She nor Lin Yutang won the Nobel Prize. Lao committed suicide on August 23, 1966, after being brutally persecuted by the Red Guards, and he never finished *Under the Red Banner*; Lin fled China in 1949 and died in Taipei in 1976; Chang left China in 1952 and spent the rest her life in the diaspora; and Shen gave up his writing career after 1949.

To discern the subtle resonances and discordances between history and its ghostly double, a reader is required to have either solid background knowledge or, more importantly, the capacity to imagine the missing elements so as to gauge the gap between actual and virtual histories. This is where phantasmal creativity triumphs over realism. For Chan, such a counterfactual imagination is not merely one that plays with fantasy but one that has political implications. We thus come to the overarching framework of the novel. On December 10, 1979, we are told that the guests who attend the secret meeting at Formosa Canteen include such figures as Lin Zhao 林昭 (1932–68), Yin Hai-kuang 殷海光 (1919–69), Yu Luoke遇羅克 (1942–70), Lin Xiling 林希翎 (1935–2005), Hu Ping 胡平 (b. 1947), and Gao Ertai高爾泰 (b. 1935). These are all real historical figures, but they came from different locations, political circles, and eras. Yin Hai-kuang was a renowned liberal persecuted by Chiang Kai-shek's regime in Taiwan; Lin Zhao was put to death by Mao for her leftist idealism; and Hu Ping exiled himself to the United States after the Tian'anmen incident. Most intriguingly, many of these figures were already dead by the time of the fictional meeting. In other words, this is a ghostly gathering. Incidentally, the date —December 10, 1979—bears a meaning in its own right. On that day in actual history, a massive demonstration (later named the Formosa incident) against the Nationalist regime broke out in the harbor city of Kao-hsiung, Taiwan. The demonstration ended with a police crackdown: almost all the leaders were arrested and sentenced to jail. It nevertheless ignited the democratic movement in Taiwan, which culminated in the lifting of martial law in 1987, after nearly forty years.

By framing his novel with a ghostly gathering of Chinese political activists, Chan Koon-chung offers a requiem to those who sacrificed themselves for different causes at different moments since the mid-twentieth century, and he expresses a melancholy with respect to the prospects for the Chinese democratic movement in both the past and the present. To those who consider his novel either a nonsensical rewriting of modern Chinese history or a pessimistic overview of the future China, Chan need only point to the famous opening line of Marx and Engels's *Communist Manifesto*: "A specter is haunting in Europe." Not unlike the Marxian specter that roamed nineteenth-century Europe, Chan's ghostly figures may well be messianic messengers from other temporalities to postrevolutionary China. From Chan's uchronic perspective, December 10, 1979, registers not a bygone incident but a literary montage that offers, in Walter Benjamin's words, "the image in the now of its recognizability."[62]

The second case I wish to discuss in this section comes from Southeast Asia. More than thirty million people of Chinese descent live in the area, demonstrating a variety and vitality of Sinophone cultures that can hardly be homogenized by the conventional paradigm of "overseas Chinese heritage." Particularly in Malaysia, Sinophone language and writing have long served as a token of Chinese ethnic solidarity. However, since the 1940s, Malayan Chinese-language authors have had to negotiate between a Chinese identification—nurtured by language and the inevitably powerful influence of the Chinese literary tradition—and a sense of belonging to their local environment.

The southern migration of Chinese writers and intellectuals to Southeast Asia took place between the 1920s and the 1960s. Despite an increasingly oppressive atmosphere, created by the British colonial government and continued by the independent Malayan Federation, Chinese writers played a crucial role in promoting Chinese education and developing the local publishing industry. They established a tradition of Chinese-language literature on the Malay peninsula and Singapore on which younger generations of native-born writers such as Ng Kim-chew drew—and with which they grappled.

As a child, Ng witnessed the ever-tightening control of the Malaysian government on the Chinese community. Ng went to Taiwan in 1986 to study and ended up settling on the island. Nevertheless, one would never guess that Ng had ever left Malaysia based on the course of his career, which has remained oriented toward the land where he grew up. He remains a vehement critic of the culture of Chinese Malaysians. On the one hand, he wants to heighten Chinese Malaysians' vigilance regarding their diasporic position vis-à-vis the hegemony of the local government. On the other hand, he lashes out at their longing for transplanting anything Chinese to a new land, likening their effort to a necrophilic ritual. Between endorsing the complex of the wandering Chinese and disapproving of it, Ng reveals a Sinophone "obsession with China" of the most perplexing kind.

His prizewinning short story "Yuhai" 魚骸 (Fish relics, 1996)[63] builds on the link between the discovery of oracle bones and the birth of Sinophone literary modernity. In 1899, a late Qing official purchased pieces of medicinal dragon bones, only to realize that they were animal bones inscribed with the earliest Chinese characters identifiable to date. But the fact that the bones—as well as the history they represent—were not discovered until the end of the nineteenth century works to synchronize, so to speak, the temporalities of past and present. In Ng's story, a Chinese Malaysian scholar based in Taiwan performs a nocturnal ritual of killing tortoises and producing oracle bones to communicate with the dead and the missing who were lost as a result of colonial rule. The scholar specializes in deciphering the enigmatic signs and languages of ancient Chinese civilizations. In addition to his research, he develops a bizarre hobby of killing turtles and preparing their shells for augury reading, just as his forebears did in the ancient Yin and Shang dynasties. He even discovers that as far back as four thousand years before, turtles available only in the Malay peninsula had been sent to the Middle Kingdom as tribute. When left alone, this sinologist "eats turtle, listens to turtle language, deciphers the oracular messages for familiars in the dark . . . carves out the ancient languages on oracle bones, retrieving the feelings of ancient China."[64]

I have noted above that the Chinese character for ghost, *gui* 鬼, can mean "that which returns [*gui* 歸]."[65] *Gui* 歸 (return) also sounds the same as *gui* 龜 (turtle). When Ng describes the ritual of killing the turtle, he plays out the mysterious phonetic and semantic linkages between these three characters: *gui* 鬼 (ghost), *gui* 歸 (return), and *gui* 龜 (turtle). At every act of augury, apparitions from the past appear to the scholar, including that of his brother—who died in a communist revolution in Malaysia years before. We are compelled to ask: At the end of the twentieth century, can this Chinese Malaysian scholar in Taiwan still return to his imaginary China? Whereas his protagonist carves tortoiseshells in pursuit of a mythical telos, Ng (who also has no home country to return to) inscribes in fiction an oracular message about the nostalgia for a lost promised land. Is such carving or inscribing a gesture of fetishism or a fantastic act of divination?

Through the medium of the oracle bone inscriptions, Ng's story brings together premodern augural technology and postmodern media haunting, late Qing archaeological discovery and fin de siècle diasporic nostalgia. Behind this story is the history of the Malayan Communist Party (MCP). Founded in the early 1930s with the support of Chinese Communist Party and overwhelmingly made up of people of Chinese origin, the MCP gained momentum during the Japanese occupation from 1941 to 1945 and became a strong force in the postwar era, when the British colonial regime returned. The fact that many Chinese immigrants and their descendants joined leftist groups was the result of the unwelcoming cultural atmosphere and oppressive political policies, first implemented by the British colonial government and later expanded by the independent Malayan Federation, that confronted the ever-growing overseas Chinese population. The confrontation culminated in the launch of an insurgency in 1952, followed by the implementation of the Briggs Plan—a British strategy whereby Chinese in Malaya were relocated into so-called new villages so that they and their contacts with MCP insurgents could be monitored.[66]

This story remains untold in Ng's "Fish Relics." Presumably the protagonist's missing brother is among the leftist guerrilla fighters who withdrew into the jungle and died from either colonial gunfire or the daunting environment. When the Malayan Federation was established in 1957, the leftist fighters suffered a loss of political legitimacy because their cause of anticolonialism had been won (at least nominally) by the rightist force. It was also at this juncture that the Chinese members of the MCP were faced with a unique challenge: Should their goal be to clarify their minority status in the revolution and fight for the rights of people of Chinese heritage in Malaysia? Or should they overthrow the newly established authority (dominated by the ethnic Malay majority) by making common cause with the international proletariat? The result was a prolonged losing battle against the increasingly hegemonic Malaysian regime that ended only in 1989.

For Ng, however, the story about thousands of Chinese Malayan youth who joined the communist campaign in its heyday is not over. While many lost their lives, more survived the extreme hardships of jungle guerrilla life, governmental crackdowns, and defection, only to witness the increased dissipation of their dreams and a rapidly changing national ethos even among local Chinese. In his new fiction cycle titled *Nanyang Renmin Gongheguo Beiwanglu* 南洋人民共和國備忘錄 (Memorandum of the People's Republic of South Seas, 2013),[67] Ng sets out to ask a bold question: What if the communist revolution in Malaya had succeeded, and Chinese revolutionaries had established a people's republic on the peninsula?

According to Ng, the People's Republic of the South Seas could have been founded by Chinese communists in Malaya in the 1950s. In reality, it is a phantom polity that was no sooner conceived by Chinese Malayan leftist activists than it vanished from history. All Ng can do is to describe either the prehistory of the republic, when the leftists faced every trial and tribulation in realizing their nation-building dream, or the posthistory, when the leftists were either co-opted by the Malaysian government or simply died off as time passed. What was supposed to take place in history—the founding of the republic—remains an abysmal lacuna, something that can be filled in only by fiction.

We thus come to "Youjian fuyu" 猶見扶餘 (As if seeing Fuyu, 2014), one of the most intriguing of Ng's *People's Republic of South Seas* series. In the story, a Chinese woman is abducted to a mysterious jungle kingdom on the Malay peninsula and made a concubine of the ruler, who sports a red curly beard. Years later, she manages to run away and tell her story to an incredulous audience. The key to deciphering the story lies in its title. Fuyu, or Buyeo, was an ancient kingdom located in northeastern China and northern Korea. In Chinese literature, however, Fuyu is associated with a *Chuanqi* tale of the Tang dynasty (618–907), "Qiuranke Zhuan" 虯髯客傳 (The story of the curly bearded guest), by Du Guangting 杜光庭 (850–933). It is said that after having withdrawn from competing for imperial sovereignty over China in deference to Li Yuan, who eventually became the founder of the Tang dynasty, a legendary hero named the Curly-Bearded Guest sailed overseas and ended up taking over an old kingdom named Fuyu in Southeast Asia. In modern times, the renowned scholar Chen Yinke 陳寅恪 (1890–1969) associated Fuyu with Taiwan, which he saw as the last haven in the midst of the historical turmoil of the communist revolution.

By following the cartographic move of Fuyu from northeastern China to the Malay peninsula by way of Taiwan, Ng tells a story about the dissemination and repetition of history, from an ancient barbarian kingdom to a medieval Chinese tale about the vicissitudes of dynastic transition, and from the Chinese diaspora to the leftist insurgence in Southeast Asia. Moreover, by making his characters unlikely counterparts to the heroic figures of the Tang tale, Ng contemplates both the iterability of memory through fiction and its limitations. Can the aborted cause of the People's Republic of the South Seas really be connected to the epic grandeur of the Curly Bearded Guest's adventure thirteen centuries earlier?

Ng's fictional project brings home the unresolvable paradox of the enchanted histories we have discussed so far. It speaks to both the wildest dreams and the deepest melancholy of overseas Chinese living in the diaspora. More than sixty years after the establishment of the Malayan Federation, Ng's characters are seen as wandering ghosts on the "homeland"—the Malay peninsula that they refuse to call home. They are citizens of the phantom People's Republic of the South Seas or the aborted Malayan People's Republic—both ersatz diasporic versions of the PRC. Nevertheless, at a time when the PRC regime is trying to shed its image as the instigator of leftist insurgencies in Southeast Asia, these characters are destined to be disavowed by their spiritual mother country, too. They are loyalists of the most abject kind because, besides a vague "Chinese dream," they find no political legacy to pledge allegiance to. As Ng's stories become more and more fantastic, his characters' sense of loss becomes more and more poignant.

The Land of Afterlives

Now we move from the phantasmal discourse of skewed temporalities to that of altered topos—that is, spaces in which the subjects find themselves lost chasing an infinitely receding horizon in search of a destination. The sense of gratuitous travel through time and space gives rise to imaginary nostalgia—a homesickness for an object that may very well never have existed—that hovers over the cases introduced below.[68]

In this section, I wish to discuss three writers: Lo Yi-chin 駱以軍 (b. 1967) of Taiwan, Dung Kai-cheung 董啓章 (b. 1967) of Hong Kong, and Yu Hua (b. 1960) of mainland China. They all demonstrate in their works a profound ambivalence about the status of the places they inhabit, which are all—controversially—called China. The government of Nationalist China retreated to Taiwan after the Communist takeover of the mainland in 1949, thus starting a long and slow process of vanishing from the international stage as a phantom China in the diaspora. After 146 years of British colonial rule, Hong Kong returned to the embrace of the motherland in 1997, only for a sense of alienation to build until mass demonstrations broke out in the summer of 2019. Finally, the PRC has supposedly been as strong and prosperous in the past two decades as it has ever been, while behind the facade of prosperity, shadowy lives tell a different story.

All three writers contemplate the fate of these Chinese communities in terms of the politics of afterlives, as either the beginning of an ending, the ending of a beginning, or part of an eternal cycle of transmigration. In extrapolating the meaning of afterlives, the authors seek counterparts in literary history. While their narrative styles show an inclination toward postmodernism, the questions they raise take them to the classical context: loyalism and its negative successor, postloyalism.

Loyalism is a discourse based on the politics of anachrony and displacement. It describes the choice of a premodern political subject to continue to grieve for a fallen dynasty or a lost culture, even at the risk of giving up one's career or even life. However, a paradox underlies loyalism, as it is a sentiment (be it political, cultural, emotional, or ethical) that is legitimized by a reluctant awareness of the demise of that legitimacy: the dynasty must fall before it can be mourned. Loyalism, therefore, gestures toward the belatedness of time and yet gains an unlikely agency from the hope of restoring that which is forever lost. Caught between the desire for the past to be realized in the future and the future to be restored to the past, the loyalist plays out a unique politics of time.

Postloyalism adds yet another twist to this phenomenon. Postloyalism refers to that which happens—in conceptual, affective, and political terms—after loyalism. But insofar as loyalism already implies something that comes after and the resultant sense of mourning and nostalgia, the "post" of postloyalism doubles the temporal and psychological complexity inherent in loyalism. In line with the postmodern subversion of linear chronologies, postloyalism could point to an anticipatory revisioning of the past on behalf of the future, therefore implying a reopening of the pastness of the past. As such, the "post" of postloyalism refers to a desire for a timeline that comes before, rather than after, historical closure: it implies a renewed beginning rather than the ending of a desired history.

With the dialectic of loyalism versus postloyalism in mind, one can see how Lo Yi-chin and Dung Kai-chung cope with the nationalist discourse that has long underlain modern Chinese fiction. Lo is arguably the most important writer of contemporary Taiwan. In his early years, Lo wrote about his parents' generation, people who fled to Taiwan after the national cataclysm of 1949. Despite their varied backgrounds and experiences, these individuals have one thing in common: They cannot let go of the memories of their days on the mainland. As a result, the people in these stories turn their nostalgia into lived reality. Haunted by the past, they become specters, and they transform the city of Taipei into a phantasmal space. As time passes, their children grow up to face a more peculiar dilemma: although born in Taiwan, they feel trapped between the mainland their parents came from and the island they are supposed to call home.

In *Yueqiu xingshi* 月球姓氏 (The moon clan, 2000), Lo tells the tale of a schoolboy who finds his hometown of Taipei turned into a Kafkaesque maze. In the end, the boy comes at night to a place that looks like a huge, haunted ruin. Upon a closer look, the ruin turns out to be the construction site of the Chiang Kai-shek Memorial Hall. In *Yuanfang* 遠方 (Faraway, 2003), Lo writes about a mainland émigré's Taiwan-born son, who rushes to the mainland to look after his father—who had fallen into coma on a homecoming trip. In a noisy, dirty hospital, the son and his long-lost brothers (from his father's first marriage, before 1949) are reunited, and they take care of their father together while savoring the tragicomic sensations of kinship and alienation. In the end, the Taiwan-born son transports his dying father back to Taiwan, a symbolic gesture of farewell to the homeland.

Ng Kim-chew has used the word "abandoned" (*qi* 棄) to describe Lo's aesthetics of storytelling.[69] He notes that Lo's writing hinges on nearly indescribable acts of effacement, followed by a fixation on loss. Ng contends that Lo's writings emerge from his adherence to "ontological abandonment," an existential state caused by disavowal of the self.[70] Lo speaks directly to this "ontological abandonment" in a poem titled "Qi de gushi"

棄的故事 (The story of Qi [or abandonment]).The poem takes on a mythological dimension as it narrates the birth of the founder of the Zhou dynasty (1046–256 BCE)—the longest dynasty in the history of China—whose name is Qi. As legend goes, Qi's mother conceived him after stepping in the footprints of the god Shangdi. The child survived being abandoned three times by his mother and was therefore named Qi, "the abandoned one." Lo describes in his poem the condition of desertion and abandonment as a "gesture predestined when I was curling myself up in my mother's womb" before being "deserted/lost on the way" to the world. Abandonment is not only a gesture but also a trace of destiny—a historical line registering the imprints of loss, deprivation, and forfeiture.

For Lo, writing is nothing if not a venue in which loss and abandonment manifest themselves. This stance finds its most provocative expression in *Xixia lüguan* 西夏旅館 (Western Xia Hotel, 2008). In almost half a million Chinese characters, the novel parades an endless string of bizarre encounters that occur within the insular space of the hotel. Each of its rooms opens to a story (a story within a story), from a necrophilic romance to a phantasmal manhunt, and from a burlesque intrigue to a nightmarish carnival. With this kaleidoscopic sequence of unlikely stories, Lo seeks to illuminate the ontology—or rather the hauntology—of *qi*, an experience of being both abandoned and possessed, both lost and haunted.

More significantly, Lo's novel draws a parallel between a postmodern haunted hotel and a premodern barbarian regime. The hotel name is a reference to the Western Xia dynasty (1038–1227; also known as Tangut Empire), which was ruled by the non-Han Tangut people and fostered a thriving hybrid civilization of Han and non-Han origins. The dynasty was overthrown by the Mongols, and its short-lived cultural splendor was thrown into oblivion in subsequent centuries. More intriguingly, the Western Xia people were forced into a diaspora and completely disappeared from history. Did they fall victim to natural disasters or genocide? Did they integrate with other Han or non-Han cultures? Or did they travel somewhere else? Struck by the enigma of the Western Xia people, Lo relates their history to the diasporic experience of those who emigrated to Taiwan from mainland China after 1949, a culture he believes is destined to soon disappear. He makes his protagonist a wanderer in the city who is purportedly the last descendant of the Western Xia people, but the man might as well be any intruder from another time and space.

One leitmotif of the novel is the mingling and segregation between the Han and the Hu (non-Han barbarian) cultures throughout history. For Lo, such a fact suggests that Taiwan is a political entity existing in a state of exception with respect to China and the rest of the world. As nativist voices urging a declaration of Taiwanese independence grow ever more strident, Taiwan has had to negotiate its dubious status as both part of China and an independent state, both the bearer of the torch of Chinese civilization and a force for indigenous identity. As Lo would have it, the politics of exclusion and inclusion were as precarious in the Western Xia era as they are now in Taiwan. Both regimes are seen as sandwiched between the Han orthodoxy and non-Han heterogeneities and, as a result, trapped in multiple temporalities—or multiple states of exception. At a time when Taiwan nativists are trying to sever all ties to China, Lo remains anxious about the island's fate. He conjures up the specter of the Western Xia and hosts it in the transitory space of a hotel. Hovering over the Hotel Western Xia is the question: In the face of both self-desinicization and Chinese political encroachment, will Taiwan become another Western Xia, which enjoyed short-lived glory and then disappeared into the storm of history?

Whereas Lo seeks to find in Taiwan the remains of the Western Xia kingdom, the Hong Kong writer Dung Kai-cheung strives to chronicle the past and future of Hong Kong by revisiting the ancient capitals of the Song dynasty, Bianliang 汴涼 (of the Northern Song, 960–1127—present-day Kaifeng) and Hangzhou 杭州 (of the Southern Song, 1127–1279).[71] Since the mid-1990s, Dung has created a series of works about the mysterious V (for Victoria) City. Instead of indulging in nationalist hopes for the restoration of the past, his narrator observes the rise and the fall of the metropolis from the perspective of a postapocalyptic future. He recollects its grandeur in the same mode that ancient dynastic capitals such as Chang'an 長安 (Xi'an), Bianliang, and Hangzhou were often eulogized, pondering the illusory and ephemeral nature of all cities in world history. Underneath his text lies the question: Why, more than twenty years after the 1997 handover, are Hong Kong citizens struggling more than ever to negotiate their identities?

In novels such as *Menghualu* 夢華錄 (Dream of splendor) and *Fanshenglu*

繁勝錄 (Account of prosperity), Dung relates in the future perfect tense the splendor and prosperity of V City that will have been ruined by a certain point of time. The titles of the two novels are of special historical significance. *Dream of Splendor* brings to mind Meng Yuanlao's 孟元老 (dates unknown) *Dongjing menghualu* 東京夢華錄 (East capital dream of splendor), arguably the most famous loyalist account of everyday life in classical Chinese literature. When Bianliang, the thriving capital of the Northern Song, fell into the hands of Jurchen barbarians in 1126, Meng fled into exile. In a quasi-encyclopedic manner, his book catalogues the old capital's commercial life, seasonal products, and festivals, as well as its foods, customs, and traditions—all of which had evaporated like a dream. Likewise, *Account of Prosperity* is influenced by *Xihulaoren fanshenglu* 西湖老人繁勝錄 (Account of prosperity by a senior gentleman on the West Lake; author's name unknown), a book recollecting the bygone urban life of Hangzhou, where the Song dynasty built its new capital after the fall of Bianliang. By copying the style and structure of the two Song works, Dung's novels about life in Hong Kong generate the sensation of a ghostly déjà vu, while the sense of pastness of Hong Kong is projected into the time after 2046, fifty years after her return to Chinese sovereignty.[72]

Chinese nationalists expected that the people of Hong Kong would welcome the restoration of Chinese sovereignty after 156 years of colonial rule, but Dung's fiction invalidates such an assumption. On the eve of the return, according to Dung, Hong Kong was experiencing not wish fulfillment but rather a deep sense of loss. By anticipating that Hong Kong will one day become a ruined city like Bianliang and Hangzhong, Dung preemptively enacts a historical melancholia, one that speaks to the eternal return of a fallen city. Nevertheless, since both Bianliang and Hangzhou were Song capitals, Dung's analogy between Hong Kong and the two ancient cities insinuates that Hong Kong, though a postcolonial metropolis, might enjoy a postloyalist independence—from both British and Chinese rule.

In his study of Hong Kong and 1997, Ackbar Abbas describes the city as thriving on "the politics of disappearance."[73] Hong Kong's peculiar lack of identity is due to its status as "not so much a place as a space of transit," whose residents think of themselves as transients and migrants on their way from China to somewhere else. Abbas invokes "déjà disparu" to describe the sentiment in Hong Kong, "the feeling that what is new and unique about the situation is always already gone, and we are left holding a handful of clichés, or a cluster of memories of what has never been."[74] Thus, Abbas contemplates the inevitable fall of the colonial city in the postcolonial period.

By making Hong Kong a site of phantasmal nostalgia, Dung's novels at first seem to fit Abbas's theory. However, Dung strives to depict a Hong Kong that is not necessarily as transient as Abbas would have his reader believe it is. Dung sees the fate of Hong Kong as parallel to that of the great cities of premodern China, thereby sharing with us something genealogically traceable: a history composed of multiple varieties of the urban politics of disappearance. In other words, Hong Kong need not be trapped in postcolonial vacuity of disappearance once and for all; rather, it is a site that generates postloyalist yearnings as do other ancient cities of China. It is in the continuum of constructions, ruinations, and reconstructions of the city that Dung defines the fate of Hong Kong independently from that of China.

Thus, the city—be it Bianliang, Hangzhou, or Hong Kong—constitutes a stage within a process of continual re-creation, and this is exactly what fiction is all about:

> "Dreamlike splendor" is the final destination of all cities in the world that have enjoyed their due moment of glory. It seems to be an eternal law that one is bound to awaken from a dream, and that splendor is destined to decline. But insofar as writing is an action that takes place perennially in the flux of time, the significance of past and future can be realized in the here and now. A dream need not always be illusory, and splendor need not be doomed to vanish. All experience, all existence, once collected, recorded, and inscribed, can escape monodimensional space and time, becoming a world that expends and generates [its past and future] ad infinitum.[75]

Above all, Dung contends, "fiction is the nature of not only V City but all cities. The mapping of a city has to be a piece of fiction of self-expanding, modifying, concealing, and overthrowing."[76]

Finally, we return to mainland China. In Yu Hua's *Diqitian* 第七天 (The seventh day), Yang Fei, a forty-one-year-old divorced man, is killed suddenly due to a gas explosion at a restaurant in which he is dining. Lacking the money for an on-schedule cremation, he must roam the afterlife aimlessly until his turn for cremation comes. Over the course of seven days, he runs into the souls of his deceased family members, his foster father, his ex wife, and his neighbors who perished in the demolition of their homes. It turns out that Yang was born and lost on a moving train and was discovered and raised by a railroad switchman. Traveling on, Yang runs into many others who are also died recently of unnatural causes—poisoned babies, organ sellers, young suicides, innocent convicts, and numerous innocent casualties as a result of civil mismanagement. Like Yang, they are waiting in the long line to be cremated.

Yu Hua, perhaps the most globally renowned contemporary Chinese author after Mo Yan, is known for such epic works as *Huozhe* 活著 (To live, 1993) and *Xiongdi* 兄弟 (Brothers, 2007). He emerged in the mid-1980s with works identified with the avant-garde school. With cold, clinical precision, he introduces a series of Kafkaesque scenes in these early works: a callous crowd watches a man who mutilates himself in a public space ("1986" [1986], 1987); two brothers are sentenced to kill each other as a result of an accidental death in the family ("One Kind of Reality" [*Xianshi yizhong* 現實一種], 1987); and a seemingly elegant classical love story culminates in cannibalism ("Classical Romance" [*Gudian aiqing* 古典愛情] 1988). These stories challenge the realist formula of describing trauma and testimony, pondering the limitations of poetic justice, and thus subverting the Maoist discourse of the sublime.

Despite its biblical allusion, *The Seventh Day* promises neither eternal rest nor salvation. As Yu indicates, the dead in his novel are victims of the twin monsters of postcapitalism and postsocialism in contemporary China. They are ordinary men and women thrown into a world full of failed promises and wasted expectations, and even after their untimely deaths, they remain impoverished and underprivileged. At the beginning of the novel, the spirit of Yang Fei is running late for his own funeral appointment at the local crematorium. He barely makes it, only to be told that more important and wealthier guests are already waiting in the VIP lounge and will enjoy priority service. These privileged dead are showing off each other's ocean-view burial plots and organic headstones, while Yang comes to realize that he does not even have adequate funerary garments or an urn for his ashes.

Wandering in the postmortem world, Yang is reunited with his foster father; learns more about his life as a foundling; and reconciles with his ex wife, who has just committed suicide. He meets other wandering souls who offer horror stories of legal injustice, state violence, consumerist mania, and massive demolition projects. As critics have noted, some of the stories appear to be drawn from news reports or, more conveniently, social media, and there arises an uncanny sensation that Yu is writing a superrealist account or even plagiarizing the viral stories of the day. The boundary line between fiction and reality becomes more ambiguous than ever, just like that between life and death as depicted by Yu.

Yu is not a newcomer when it comes to writing stories of eerie duplications and revenants. Here I trace a genealogy by looking at "Classical Romance" and the abovementioned *To Live* and *Brothers*. As its title suggests, "Classical Romance" was inspired by the classical genre of talent and beauty (*caizi jiaren* 才子佳人) fiction, and Yu is lavish with the clichés one expects to find in the genre: a chance encounter between a talented scholar and a beautiful girl, a nocturnal liaison, and a romance that seems to promise a happy ending. But what happens next is anything but a faithful imitation of convention. Three years after their separation, the scholar is reunited with his beauty in the midst of a famine. The beauty is found in a tavern, not as a guest to be served but as a dish to be prepared, her limbs being chopped off to order. No sooner does the scholar purchase the dying beauty than she asks him to terminate her existence: their romance is consummated in a mercy killing.

Yu Hua parodies the talent and beauty convention by literally mutilating its idealized characters and conventions.[77] Through such a radical appropriation, he may intend to indicate that gruesome violence can erupt at any time and that it is futile to try to make sense of such an eruption. The ultimate violence in his story derives not from the presentation of the ghoulish action as such but from the lack of any affective response to the action. Yu is said to have been fascinated with the concept of eroticism in Georges Bataille's *The Tears of Eros* (*Les larmes d'Eros*), particularly the part pertaining to the tie between eroticism and violence that culminates in death.[78] While

Yu Hua may reveal his indebtedness to the French writer with the Grand Guignol of the scholar's killing of the beauty, such a bloody scene does not generate any lasting shocking power but rather leaves the reader with a sense of placid irony.

Yu Hua's best seller *To Live* describes the trials of a man named Fugui through the first decades of the new China. The son of a wealthy landlord, Fugui led a wanton life before the revolution. After the new China was founded, he became the target of condemnation in the incessant movements that followed: from the land reform to the three-anti and five-anti campaigns, the collectivization drive of the people's communes, the Great Famine, the Cultural Revolution, and the postrevolutionary era. Fugui loses his property, status, and loved ones, leaving him, at the end, with the realization that all he has is his capacity to live.

A heart-wrenching story about the making of a socialist new man through the history of the PRC, *To Live* has been hailed as a landmark about-face from avant-gardism to new realism. Despite its description of the sorrows and pains that a generation of Chinese were made to endure, it ends with a reconciliation, however implicitly ironic, between a humble citizen and history as overseen by the party. For this reason, the novel was endorsed by the literary authorities even in the wake of the Tian'anmen incident. It was not until the publication of *The Seventh Day* that the critical thrust Yu embedded in *To Live* and other works became legible: if, as *The Seventh Day* proposes, the afterlives of the Chinese people are as boringly absurd and petty as their lives, *To Live* may as well mean to live like the living dead, or to barely survive.

If "Classical Romance" and *To Live* are still couched in the radical logic of love, life, and death of the past and present, *Brothers* presents Chinese society as an entropic vortex devouring whatever values remain. The two-part novel depicts the fate of two "brothers"—who in fact have no blood kinship—from the Cultural Revolution to the beginning of the twenty-first century. Part 1 is a sentimental exposé of the revolution reminiscent of scar literature, and part 2 is a farcical parade of contemporary absurdities à la late Qing exposé fiction. The drastic emotional and thematic swing between the two parts is disturbing to many readers. But insofar as excess defines the rhetorical and thematic mode of his novel, Yu can be pardoned for his hyperbole and cynicism. Indeed, his novel raises a series of questions: Are the Cultural Revolution and the postsocialist market discrete and opposed phenomena? Or are they indicators of a causal linkage, or even a ghostly isomorphism, of the two apparently antagonistic ideologies of leftism and liberalism? What is the prospect of the Red legacy if Mao and Mammon prove to be interchangeable icons in the service of a new hybrid party line? Finally, in light of the fact that *Brothers* became a best seller thanks to its unabashedly bad taste and a massive publicity stunt, has Yu not become what he sets out to ridicule—that is, an inciter and instigator of socialist or capitalist degeneracy?

To return to *The Seventh Day*, I suggest that the novel represents Yu Hua's latest and darkest attempt to imagine an individual's fate in relation to his family, society, and nation. This is where we see the most nihilist turn of postloyalism. Unlike Lo Yi-chin and Dung Kai-cheung, who try to delineate in their works the politics of attachment to a marginalized community, a vanishing city, or a lost regime, Yu guides us in *The Seventh Day* to a world in which nothing any longer matters for good or ill.

While postloyalism presupposes one's capacity to remember and mourn, however disoriented one might be, *The Seventh Day* simply erases that capacity. The dead cannot die again. As temporalities are flattened out, a warp in time emerges in Yu's postmodern, and postmortem, narrative. Writing can no longer be seen as an affirmation of progress and plenitude, as conventional Maoist realism would have it. Instead, it is but an elegiac anticipation or haunted mimicry of a desired nullification. As Xiaobin Yang has put it, in Yu's world, "all the past events are dispersed as ruins, discontinuities or collages in an instant. . . . There is no temporal duration in this moment, no rational development of history; everything is conjured up in the Now."[79]

To conclude, whereas in *Life and Death Are Wearing Me Out* Mo Yan blends the lay Buddhist belief in karma and the socialist mythology of reincarnation as one way to reconstitute the meaning of history, Yu Hua's *The Seventh Day* points to a different if not more pessimistic view of reality, one that promises no retribution or transmigration but only the total dissipation of values and desires. Both novels touch on the ethics of corporeality and the politics of the legacy on which the conventional mimetic realism is based, and both take issue with the narratology of the Maoist sublime. The famous line referring to *White-Haired Girl* comes to mind here: "The old society turns a human into a ghost; the new society turns a ghost into a human." As the two authors insinuate in their novels, the grand plan of socialist resurrection has had not a few hiccups. Perhaps the dog, the ox, the donkey, and the pig as described by Mo Yan are lucky beings after all, as they still may once again spin the wheel of fortune and be reincarnated again. For Yu Hua, to live in contemporary China is to wait for the seventh day, all the while knowing that there will never be any kind of resurrection.

4

"The Beam of Darkness"

Fiction as Transillumination

The dark night gave me black eyes,
I use them nonetheless seeking for the light.
GU CHENG, *Selected Poems*

Those two lines are the entirety of Gu Cheng's 顧城 (1959–93) 1979 short poem "Yidairen" 一代人 (One generation of people), arguably the most cited poetic work written in the aftermath of the Cultural Revolution.[1] With three intertwined images (dark night, black eyes, and light), the poet conveys the perplexing sentiments of one generation of Chinese youth. Although "dark night" symbolizes obscurity and mystery, the person is given "black eyes" with which to search for "light." Here, "black" may refer to the eye color of the majority of Chinese people, shadowy prospects as seen from Chinese eyes, or especially blindness. More intriguingly, as the person uses his black eyes to seek for the light in the dark night, one wonders: Whence comes the light? Does it come from within or beyond the darkness of night? Is the light an optical illusion, an astrophysical marvel, or a metaphor for something else entirely?

One of the most popular poets of the so-called new era, Gu Cheng was one of the founders of *Jintian* 今天 (Today), the first and most famous independent avant-garde literary magazine in China in the late 1970s. Gu had no formal education beyond primary school, due to the outbreak of the Cultural Revolution as well as his extremely withdrawn nature. But he demonstrated talent as early as age six, and he continued to write even at the height of the Cultural Revolution, when his family was viciously persecuted. In the late 1970s, together with other poets such as Bei Dao 北島, Mang Ke 芒克, Duo Duo 多多, and Yang Lian 楊煉, Gu helped create the school of misty poetry (*menglong shi* 朦朧詩). The poets called for enlivening the poetic language that had been ossified by Maoist discourse and experimented with themes and images that would have been unthinkable just a few years before.

Although light versus darkness is among the most familiar motifs of world literature, Gu Cheng's use of it was groundbreaking in his time. In his analysis of literary and artistic symbolism during the Maoist era, Lowell Dittmer points out that the contrast between light and darkness was used not only as part of socialist aesthetics, but also of moral schemes and ideological mandates. This contrast was implanted into every layer of life, with light suggesting divine ascendance to virtue and truth, and darkness the hellish fall into vice and secrecy.[2] Gu's poem upsets this dichotomy with a series of oxymoronic expressions: the darkness of night as he sees it may give rise to a vision that is both invisible and luminous. Moreover, the light that one generation of people is seeking may mean either the shining from beyond the horizon or a flash of lightning in the darkest part of the night.

Gu Cheng's poem helped inaugurate a new paradigm of literary optics in the postrevolutionary age. Despite continual governmental intervention, literature through the 1980s sought to test the party line with equivocal allusions, circuitous imageries, or simply minimizing any direct relevance to life. Narrative fiction best demonstrated the tendency of re-vision. For instance, Wang Meng wrote *Ye de yan* 夜的眼 (The eyes of night, 1979) with Gu's poem in mind:

> Eyes are supposed to fail to see things clearly at night. But the night also let many see things that look unclear at daytime. I cannot help thinking of Gu Cheng's poem "The dark night gave me black eyes / I use them nonetheless seeking for the light." There are things that can be better discerned in the darkness than in the light.[3]

As discussed in chapter 2, Wang Meng was once hailed as the most promising writer of the 1950s. Nevertheless, he was exiled to Xinjiang in the early 1960s, and was not rehabilitated until after the Cultural Revolution. "The Eyes of Night" is a mildly modernist piece that signaled his cautious comeback. Written from the perspective of a young country writer, the story relates the bizarre sensation of a world turned upside down in the wake of the Cultural Revolution.

In "Mingruo qinxian" 命若琴絃 (Life like a fiddle string, 1985), a story by Shi Tiesheng 史鐵生 (1953–2010), a sent-down youth, a blind young itinerant fiddler is promised by his master, who is also blind, a remedy for curing his blindness once he has broken a thousand strings of the fiddle he uses for performance. The young man achieves the goal after many trials, only to be told that the actual count of broken strings for regaining his eyesight has been reset to twelve hundred. As the young man is playing "in the dark," his master ponders: "Although the goal is illusory, it is a necessity. Otherwise, the string won't be tightened up by the player, and no sound can be played at all."[4] Equally intriguing is Bi Feiyu's 畢飛宇 (b. 1964) *Tuina* 推拿 (The masseur, 2012), a prizewinning novel about a group of blind masseurs in a massage clinic—their lives, desires, fears, ambitions, and sorrows. Partially inspired by José Saramago's *Blindness*, Bi's novel develops its own allegory for the body politics of clairvoyance versus blindness, as China undergoes a drastic transformation at the turn of the new millennium.

Inspiring as they are, these examples are couched in a neat dialectic of vision and blindness, light and dark, and knowledge and ignorance and are thus susceptible to ready interpretations. But recent years have seen an increasing number of fictional works that either break away from or add unexpected twists to such a dialectic. These works cast multiple shadows behind revolutionary lights and discern new sources of light where they are least expected. As the following sections will discuss, at their most provocative, contemporary Chinese and other Sinophone fiction writers take us into a dark space rarely explored by their predecessors. Whereas Lo Yi-chin describes the mysterious link between the black hole billions of light years away from the earth and a black hole that opens between his legs, Yan Lianke 閻連科 (b. 1958) gives a surrealistic portrait of "the day the sun died" in central China,[5] causing thousands of Chinese citizens to lose themselves in a hypnotic delirium. These works perplex readers in such a way that they undermine not only the leftist solar semiotics but also the larger rationale of modern enlightenment.

I use the term "transillumination" to describe contemporary Chinese and other Sinophone fiction writers' ocular poetics and politics of envisioning China. My use of this term is intended to resonate with Walter Benjamin's call for "profane illumination," a surrealist experience opposed to the sacred and moralistic illumination found in religion.[6] According to Margaret Cohen, Benjamin finds in surrealism a "materialistic, anthropological inspiration" for teasing out the revolutionary constellations hidden in the untimely and outmoded.[7] My way of using "transillumination" takes us beyond the dialectic of critical materialism underlying the Benjaminian discourse. If "profane illumination" derives its power from the anthropological invocation of the material world as well as a yearning for revolution as a messianic revelation, transillumination looks deeper into the blind spot (so to speak) that is embedded in such a paradigm, searching for additional light sources from both the human and the posthuman domains.

As noted above, "transillumination"—a term borrowed from medical examination—refers to the shining of a light through an area of the body to check for abnormalities. When used as a metaphor, transillumination may at first simply suggest literature's power of illumination that pierces through surface reality. Indeed, it has become a cliché to associate the enlightening power of literature with the providers of light and optical media, such as a torch, lightbulb, camera, or even an x-ray. In Chinese socialist optics, the revolutionary and divine aspects of literature are supposed to shed light on external and internal malaise.

Nevertheless, I call attention to the negative dialectic of illumination inherent in the optical technology of transillumination, something that violates the conventional division between light and darkness. I am thinking of the light that shines so brightly as to blind the eyes or travels so fast and so far as to appear invisible, as well as of the darkness that contains so many different shades as to project a spectrum of luminary obscurities or that is so unfathomably deep that it cannot be penetrated by human vision.

I examine writings that explore subjects so dark as to preclude any clear explanation. Yet I observe the way in which, paradoxically enough, they create a source of illumination in the darkness. The writers discussed below ask questions about the epistemology of light and dark and the body politics of blindness and insight in a way rarely seen in twentieth-century Chinese fiction. Can there be a light that is invisible to our eyes? Is there a light that originates in the darkest corners of the mind yet emits an unsolicited glow over the world? Is there a light from outer space, or even the realm of divinity, that is beyond the reach of human perception and comprehension?

These questions bring to mind Lu Xun, the arch-connoisseur of transillumination. I argue that at the beginning of modern Chinese literature, the master was already contemplating the light that blinds and the darkness that shines through the invisible spaces of humanity, as well as the kind of art that would engage with such a light and project an excess of the profane and the sacred. Lu Xun cast a long shadow over the modernity project of enlightenment, which hinges on dissipating the obscurity of the Chinese condition and illuminating the Chinese people.

This chapter will start with a critical review of the imaginary of illumination from the literary revolution of May Fourth to the Cultural Revolution. I will then describe the "dark consciousness" that arose almost at the same time but that has been obscured by the mainstream call for light, heat, and power. In the remainder of the chapter, I will focus on contemporary Chinese and other Sinophone fiction, reflecting on how writers imagine the transilluminating force of light within and beyond darkness and contemplating the ethical and political meaning of such a new literary optics with respect to Chinese reality.

Darkness at Noon

Modern Chinese fiction began with a call for a light that would reveal the darkness of the status quo. Xu Nianci, writing under the pseudonym Donghai Juewo 東海覺我, published "Xin faluo xiansheng tan" 新法螺先生譚 (A new account of Mr. Windbag, 1905),[8] a story about a Chinese scientist's one-man voyage to outer space that culminates in an aborted attempt to fly to the sun. Mr. Windbag is a scholar inclined toward iconoclasm. To break away from modern epistemological constraints, he spends day and night in deep contemplation of the most complex and profound questions, until he reaches a point where "his mind goes deranged and forgets everything."[9] Driven by a mysterious force, Mr. Windbag runs up to the top of a mountain that is 360,000 feet high, stumbling onto the peak where he is subject to the gravitational pull of all the planets of the solar system. Trapped in the vortex engendered by this collision, Mr. Windbag is so shaken that his body and soul are separated from each other.

While the shell of his body descends all the way to the center of the earth, Mr. Windbag finds his soul an "incredible source of thermal and luminescent radiation,"[10] whose power is ten thousand times stronger than that of the sun. Lit up like a huge lightbulb, the soul of Mr. Windbag flies around the globe. When it passes over European countries, its light dazzles scientists and the general public alike. Mr. Windbag then flies over China, but nobody there pays any attention to this unidentified flying object. Even though it is high noon, the majority of Chinese remain in bed, sound asleep. As if the sun were not bright enough, Mr. Windbag exerts the full amount of his power to illuminate the land, but he still fails to awaken the Chinese people from their deep slumber. More to his chagrin, even the very few who are already awake stay in their beds, smoking opium and caressing their concubines' bound feet.

Although the imagery in "A New Account of Mr. Windbag" may not appear unconventional to readers of our generation, Xu should be seen as a groundbreaking writer who invoked the sun at a time when China was darkened by defeatism and ineptitude. The tropes of light versus darkness, sobriety versus slumber, and planetary vision versus parochialism all anticipate the symbolism of the enlightenment campaign that took place a decade later. Borrowing Benjamin Schwartz's description of Yan Fu, Xu's contemporary, one may say that Mr. Windbag embodies the two archetypal modes shared by late Qing intellectuals: the Faustian desire for knowledge at the risk of transgressing established boundaries, and the Promethean passion that calls for dedication and self-sacrifice for the welfare of humanity as a whole.[11]

As the story develops, Mr. Windbag flies at such speed that he runs into the moon and is bounced into the trajectories of other planets. He visits Mercury, where elderly human beings are being reprocessed and made anew, and stops on Venus, where the ground is made of jewels and gold and the sky is covered by a dome of paper-thin air. In the last part of the story, one finds Mr. Windbag launching a journey to the sun, so that he can collect sunbeams to light up (or enlighten) China. But a mile before he could land, his trajectory carries him past the sun because his speed exceeds orbital velocity. As a result, he is hurled back to earth and crashes into the Mediterranean Sea like a comet.

While Mr. Windbag's ideas of revolutionizing China end up becoming mere empty talk, the four basic elements he explores on this cosmic voyage—sound, light, heat, and power—nevertheless become the overriding images that preoccupy Chinese intellectuals in subsequent decades. During the May Fourth era, intellectuals and political activists all aspired to acquire an illuminating power of new knowledge and agency that could enlighten the Chinese people. Regardless of their epistemological, emotive, or political agendas, supporters of the May Fourth movement all harbored an optimism (perhaps with a degree of self-aggrandizement) that had been rarely seen in previous decades. Two examples can serve to illustrate how bright the future appeared to them. Hu Shi, arguably the embodiment of May Fourth liberal humanism, wrote:

> I laugh at the earth
> That revolves around the sun,
> Making only one circle each day and night;
> I laugh at the moon
> That cannot be full forever.
> I laugh at the hundreds and thousands of planets,
> Which can never move out of their orbits.
> I laugh at the electric power,
> Which travels half a million miles in an hour,
> And yet cannot catch up
> With the flash of an idea in my mind![12]

At the other end of the political spectrum was Guo Moruo 郭沫若 (1892–1978), who eventually joined the communist cause. Driven by romantic solipsism in his early days, he wrote that "we want to serve as the sun, giving light on our own, and generate our own galaxy."[13] In "Tiangou" 天狗 (Heavenly dog, 1920), the poet likens himself to a mythological creature called the Heavenly Dog that, according to legend, devoured the sun and other planets:

> Ya, I am a sky dog!
> I have swallowed the moon,

I have swallowed the sun.
I have swallowed all the planets,
I have swallowed the entire universe.
I am I!
I am the light of the moon,
I am the light of the sun.
I am the light of all the planets,
I am the light of x-ray,
I am the total energy of the entire universe.[14]

Notice the way in which Guo identifies himself not only with the luminous planets but also with an x-ray beaming through the entire universe. Immersed in multiple light sources, the poet becomes a godlike figure descending into the human world of darkness on a mission of deliverance. This symbolism of light took on an ideological dimension in the mid-1920s, when the Chinese leftist movement began to sound its call to arms. By way of contrast with the darkness of the status quo, revolution was said to be the source of light and heat.

This mixture of images drawn from the lived experience and fantastic imagination is encapsulated by the famous opening scene of Mao Dun's 茅盾 (1896–1981) *Ziye* 子夜 (Midnight, 1933), an exposé of capitalist corruption and a document of leftist underground engagement in 1930s Shanghai. The novel opens with a scene in which a neon sign of three English words—"Light, Heat, Power"—glares down from atop a warehouse in one of the foreign concessions.[15] Light, heat, and power are the elements in the material infrastructure that will ensure the strength of China. They are also moral imperatives—associated with enlightened thought, principles, and action—that are necessary for the success of China's struggle for a better future.

The symbolism of light versus darkness was soon incorporated into explicitly revolutionary writing. In his famous treatise "Shijianlun" 實踐論 (On practice), first published in 1935, Mao Zedong upholds the principle of "practice" to change the world, arguing that "China has already reached a historic moment in the world and in China, a great moment unprecedented in human history, that is, the moment for completely banishing darkness from the world and from China and for changing the world into a world of light such as never previously existed."[16] In 1945, Mao delivered a speech titled "Liangge zhongguo zhi mingyun" 兩個中國之命運 (Two fates of China) to repudiate Chiang Kai-shek's *Zhongguo zhi mingyun* 中國之命運 (The fate of China, 1943). In the speech, Mao declared that "we should strive in every possible way to fight for a bright future and bright fate, and oppose the other kind of dark future and dark fate."[17]

What follows is a now familiar story. The symbol of the sun was at the center of both literary and artistic articulations in the first three decades of the People's Republic of China (PRC), culminating in the Cultural Revolution. "The East Is Red" (*Dongfanghong* 東方紅), arguably the most popular propaganda hymn derived from a folk song, moved the Chinese people through sound, while red, glossy, and bright (*hong guang liang* 紅光亮) became prescribed principles of aesthetic and cultural production. Chinese youth were compared by Mao to "the morning sun at eight and nine o'clock,"[18] and Mao was hailed as the brightest sun shining over China and the whole globe. The titles of two popular novels by Haoran 浩然 (1932–2008), the leading novelist of the Cultural Revolution, *Yanyangtian* 豔陽天 (Bright sunny days, 1964) and *Jinguang dadao* 金光大道 (The golden road, 1970), speak to the yearning for and mandate of solar imagery at that time. To use Ban Wang's terminology, this is the "sublime figure of history" at its most exuberant.[19]

It is in the context of such a powerful discourse of light, radiation, clairvoyance, and super-vision throughout modern China that the rise of literary works in the 1980s that dwelled on blindness, such as Gu Cheng's poems and Wang Meng's and Shi Tiesheng's fiction, became most provocative. These works provided a new way of debating and describing the poetics of luminary inscription at a time when a once bright solar discourse revealed the black hole at its center and the dark side of history demanded a second look at its hidden truth.

As it happens, there has been a counter discourse to China's search for light and enlightenment since the May Fourth era. Lu Xun was one of the most eloquent interpreters of the poetics of darkness in modern times, declaring that "if there should be no more torches [lighting up the world], I would be the only light."[20] In an essay written five months after the beginning of the May Fourth movement titled "Women xianzai zenyang zuofuqin" 我們現在怎樣做父親 (What is required of us as fathers today, 1919). Lu Xun wrote: "Let the awakened man burden himself with the weight of tradition and shoulder the gate of darkness. Let him give unimpeded passage to the children so that they may rush to the bright, wide open spaces and lead happy lives henceforward as rational human beings."[21] As T. A. Hsia has suggested, Lu Xun was fascinated by the destructive and seductive power of darkness. As much as he might have wished to strike an unequivocally progressive image, Lu Xun impresses us as someone on the threshold between life and death, awakening and slumber, hope and despair, and enlightenment and madness.[22] He was extremely comfortable with the dark domain of funeral rites, graves, executions, ghosts, demons, and death wishes.[23]

Lu Xun's obsession with ghosts reaches its apex in *Yecao* 野草 (Wild grass, 1927), a prose poetry collection filled with surreal settings, nightmarish encounters, and lost souls (*youhun* 游魂). Likewise, in *Zhaohua xishi* 朝花夕拾 (Morning flowers plucked at the sunset, 1927), a collection of essays about his memories from childhood, Lu Xun spares no effort in describing the ghostly ambiance in which he grew up. He acknowledges the terror and beauty of death and the mystery of life embodied by the ghost figures. He started his career with the hope of expelling these ghosts, only to fall so spellbound by them that, with his pen, "he has recreated them, and they have lived a charmed life ever since."[24]

Lu Xun is not the only modern writer to be so enchanted with the shadow of darkness. Thanks to her troubled family background and personal inclinations, Eileen Chang, considered to be a priestess of the cult of Shanghai decadence in the 1940s, was at her best when telling stories about romantic depravity and moral aberration. These stories, though rendered in realistic style, constantly suggest a gothic world:

> People only sense, to the point of terror, that things are not quite right in all aspects of their daily lives. People live in an era, but this era sinks like a shadow and they feel they have been abandoned. In order to prove their existence and grasp a bit of something real and quite elemental, they have no choice but to draw from their ancient memories for help,

memories lived by all humanity in all eras. . . . Thus a strange feeling toward surrounding reality emerges, a suspicion that this is an absurd, ancient world, dark and shadowy, and yet bright and clear.[25]

When Lu Xun took up such subjects as dead fire (*sihuo* 死火) and pale light (*baiguang* 白光), and when Chang portrayed those who walk "one step after another, to where there was no light,"[26] they were gesturing against the modern agenda of writing as revelation. Both authors were acute observers of the skewed manners and morals of the Chinese people on the threshold of enlightenment, and more importantly, both sought to explore the other side of mimetic realism. They understood that although realism incited calls to arms, it was always ready to silence any rebellious echoes, and although it promised light, at the same time it projected darkness. But it was not until they engaged with a dark consciousness that they came to terms with the paradox of transillumination.

"The Beam of Darkness": From Lu Xun to Giorgio Agamben

My use of the term "dark consciousness" is inspired by, but not limited to, the scholar Chang Hao's 張灝 (b. 1937) use of it (*youan yishi* 幽暗意識) to describe the polemics of crisis and contingency ingrained in Chinese thought.[27] Specifically, for Chang, "dark consciousness" refers to "an attention to and critical reflection on the inherent dark side of humanity as well as the dark forces deeply rooted in the human society."[28] Chang emphasizes the distinction between his "dark consciousness" and "crisis consciousness" (*youhuan yishi* 憂患意識), a term coined and made popular by the neo-Confucianist scholar Xu Fuguan 徐復觀 (1904–82). If "crisis consciousness" points to the human awareness of the perils of historical contingency, "dark consciousness" reminds us that there is something more ominous lurking behind intelligible historical experience, something that is "born with human nature and has ever loomed in human civilization."[29] In other words, "crisis consciousness" serves only as a prelude to "dark consciousness" which refers to the ontological untenability of the human good.

Trained in the tradition of classical liberalism and Max Weber's thought, Chang derives his "dark consciousness" from his Calvinist understanding of original sin. In a Weberian manner, he contends that such an awareness of human fallibility propelled the communal effort to curb individual vice so as to facilitate the general good, thus giving rise to liberal democracy.[30] As Chang argues, although lacking the notion of original sin, the Chinese intellectual tradition has its own legacy of "dark consciousness," represented by the Han epistemology of the fusion between heaven and the human, Confucian ruminations on humanity (Mencius's belief in human perfectibility versus Xunzi's 荀子 notion of human susceptibility to evil), and the Mahayana Buddhist doctrine of *fuxing* 復性 (restoring essence or nature), among other traditions of thought. The neo-Confucian engagement with the gap between humanity and its animal nature is an especially striking case.[31]

Looking back at the political turmoil of modern China, which resulted in the Maoist regime, Chang cautions against the optimistic tenor of Chinese political thought, urging a critical reappraisal of not merely the "crisis consciousness" but also the "dark consciousness" so as to foster a more nuanced analysis of Chinese modernity. Chang suggests that Chinese (political) thought has yet to make a break with the "sage-king paradigm," a benign autocracy of both moral superiority and political efficacy. This paradigm, Chang claims, has fostered an "ultimately optimistic" (*zhongji leguan* 終極樂觀) mode of thinking that favors the ideas of human perfectibility and the ability for the human and heaven to communicate. It also provides the rationale for a theocracy (*zhengjiao heyi* 政教合一) that conflates human rulership with theological or ideological legitimacy. Most importantly, these factors help produce a strong inclination toward utopianism, often in the form of anticipatory nostalgia for the return of a bygone paradise. As Chang puts it, "No one can deny the fact that modern political culture has been characterized by the tendencies of political authoritarianism, utopian mentality, and the concept of theocracy. And no one can deny the fact that these tendencies are rooted in the concept of sage-kingship, a residue of Chinese tradition."[32]

However, critics have pointed out the shortcomings of Chang's theory of "dark consciousness." The renowned Kantian and Confucian scholar

Lee Ming-hui 李明輝, for instance, questions the applicability of Chang's Weberian model to the Chinese context, and Hu Ping takes issue with his overarching critique of Confucianism and autocracy at the cost of historical specificity.[33] From a different perspective, scholars have already noticed that late Ming intellectuals' conviction of the attainability of the good by ordinary people created an unexpected moral anxiety.[34] That is, insofar as people are endowed with an immense capacity to achieve virtue and expected to do so, they are left with little room to make mistakes in pursuit of this goal.[35] People are thrown into a never-ending test of their moral integrity, in which any slight misstep might be an irredeemable fall. Ironically, the apparently free-spirited call for self-betterment is at the same time a strict demand for self-rectification.[36] For a late Ming or early Qing scholar such as Chen Que 陳確 (1604–77), humans are faced with an almost existential challenge of becoming "either saint or beast" (*rufei shengren, jishi qinshou* 如非聖人, 即是禽獸).[37]

One may conclude that Chang Hao's and his critics' concerns about "dark consciousness" are based on the moralistic schema of good versus evil or its symbolism of light versus dark. But as scholars have observed, in both Daoism and the Wang Yangming 王陽明 school of Confucianism, the dialogue between light and darkness contains layers of nuanced interplay. For Wang Yangming, the innate consciousness of epiphany is comparable to a flash of spiritual light (*lingming* 靈明) that illuminates even the darkest area of the world: "even in the middle of dark night, one can vaguely discern the distinction of light versus dark."[38] Such an epiphanic experience finds a different manifestation in Daoist discourse. For instance, Zhuangzi describes "celestial light" (*tianguang* 天光) as that which unveils the essence of virtue, even though the Way resides ultimately in the immensity of darkness: "The essence of the Perfect Way is deep and darkly shrouded; the extreme of the Perfect Way is mysterious and hushed in silence."[39] Moreover, Laozi famously states that "he who knows his brightness veils himself in darkness" (*zhibai shouhei* 知白守黑).[40]

Therefore, darkness need not be associated merely with the moral degeneracy of the human condition. In addition, it refers to either the immanent depths of the human heart or mind or the transcendental otherness responsible for the fecundity of the Way and the unknown. It should be noted that Laozi's dialectics of light and darkness inspired Martin Heidegger. In his 1957 lecture "Basic Principles of Thinking," Heidegger criticizes the Western philosophical tradition as one in search of pure brightness at the expense of sophistication. He contends that the true light lies "concealed in the darkness that is both the origin of the basic principles of thinking and the place of thinking these principles. Similarly, true darkness is not complete darkness without any light at all. It is pregnant with profound light."[41] Using a poem by Friedrich Hölderlin as a case in point, Heidegger talks about "dark light" as that which informs the human encounter with the world.[42] For Heidegger, poetical vision helps reveal the world as mystery and shed light on the finitude of human existence. Heidegger directly cites Laozi's *Daodejing (Tao Te Ching)*:

> Laozi says: "Who knows his light, will remain covered in his darkness." To this we add the truth which we all know but few are capable of: mortal thinking has to go into the depth of a well in order to see the stars. This is difficult. It is even more difficult to protect the purity of darkness, which is being interfered with by a light that will only shine. That which only shines, does not give light. The scholastic presentation of the doctrine of laws of thinking just shines in such a way, as if the content of these laws and their absolute validity become clear at once to everyone.[43]

Conversely, "light" can suggest the shining of either transcendental grace or human wisdom or their implosion. When light is taken to mean excessive exploitation of reason and optimism, it may bring devastating darkness, as exemplified by the explosion of the atomic bomb—which, in Heidegger's words, amounted to "a thousand suns."[44]

The above summary of philosophical ruminations on darkness is oversimplified, to say the least, but I simply wish to point out the rich potential of Chang's concept of "dark consciousness." That concept seems to arise merely from the loose definition of human nature as consisting of a moral bearing or a political engagement. Building on Chang's premise, I would like to take "dark consciousness" not as a moralistic state of mind but as a critical protocol, one that deemphasizes the logic of idealism in deference to skeptical, speculative thinking. Accordingly, "dark consciousness" drives us to ponder what Emmanuel Levinas calls the "otherwise than being," those potentialities that exist beyond the reach of the rational.[45] Precisely because "dark consciousness" evokes what is beyond what can be perceived, it is also beyond the scope of what can be accounted for in cognitive, psychic, or transcendental terms. "Dark consciousness" may indicate original sin, the real of Freudian or Lacanian unconscious, or even the "obsession with China,"[46] but it points more to the fault line between and beyond these known realms.

Let us approach the issue from yet another perspective. Giorgio Agamben has called on the polemics of darkness in answering the question: "What is contemporary?" In an essay by that title, Agamben describes the contemporary, citing Friedrich Nietzsche and Roland Barthes, as "the untimely." The contemporary is someone who refuses to conform to social norms, someone who straddles multiple temporalities—either too soon or too late, either already or not yet—yet is able to "see the obscurity" arising from the folds of time. In other words, contemporaries truly belong to their time yet appear to neither fully coincide with it nor adjust themselves to its demands. It is paradoxically that "relationship with time that adheres to it through a disjunction and an anachronism" that gives rise to a special vision. Agamben concludes that "the contemporary is he who firmly holds his gaze on his own time so as to perceive not its light, but rather its darkness."[47] The "contemporary is the one whose eyes are struck by the beam of darkness that comes from his own time."[48]

Agamben offers a series of examples to illustrate this "beam of darkness," two of which are relevant to our concerns. One comes from the neurophysiology of vision: "The absence of light activates a series of peripheral cells in the retina called 'off cells.' When activated, these cells produce the particular kind of vision that we call darkness. Darkness is not, therefore, a privative notion (the simple absence of light . . .) but rather the result of the activity of the 'off cells,' a product of our own retina."[49] More inspiring is the analogy Agamben draws from astrophysics. Since the number of galaxies and luminous bodies in the universe is almost infinite, Agamben tells us, "the darkness that we see in the sky is something that, according to the scientists, demands an explanation. . . . In an expanding universe, the most remote galaxies move away from us at a speed so great that their light is never able to reach us. What we perceive as the darkness of the heavens is the light that, though traveling toward us, cannot reach us, since the galaxies from which the light originates move away from us at a velocity greater than the speed of light."[50]

Agamben's contemplation is further enriched by contemporary anthropologists' and cosmologists' observations of dark matter. For Daniel Everett, an anthropologist in social linguistics, dark matter refers to the tacit competence inherent in the human faculty to generate sensorial and cognitive meanings in response to environmental and cultural stimuli. Based on years of field research among the Amazonian people of the Pirahã, Everett observes the multiple forms of human adaptability to a given ecology of living and ends with a Buddhist-like conception of the cultural self as a set of reflexive experiences of changing values and perceptions, nonmonic episodes, and psychological configurations—anything but biological instinct or the vague concept of human nature. The result is what he calls "the dark matter of the mind."[51] For James Peebles, winner of the 2019 Nobel Prize in Physics, dark matter refers to the hypothetical invisible mass that constitutes the majority of matter in the universe. As Peebles tells us, the universe evolved after the Big Bang when light rays started to shoot outward into space, and dark matter exerted its influence in a way yet to be grasped by human knowledge. Dark matter is called dark because it does not appear to interact with observable electromagnetic radiation such as light, and so it is undetectable by existing astronomical instruments. But astrophysicists can gauge its energy by measuring the gap between the temperature of the radiation emitted after the Big Bang and the amount of matter it created.[52] The visible matter of stars and planets that human beings can currently perceive or detect amounts to only 5 percent of the universe. It should remind us of the infinity of the universe evoked by Liu Cixin's *Three-Body Problem* trilogy discussed in chapter 2. As one of his characters says when first entering a four-dimensional bubble in outer space, "even a little tiny part of it is unfathomable."[53]

Returning to the Chinese context, I argue that "dark consciousness" finds its most enchanting manifestation in the form of literature. In sharp contrast with the extant paradigm of enlightenment, literature that truly sheds light on the syndrome of Chinese modernity is that which engages not light but darkness. It ushers one into the terra incognita, where enlightenment surfaces only insofar as it is underwritten by the latitude of the unknown and the occult, and as a result the boundary line between enchantment and disenchantment becomes murky. To be sure, "dark consciousness" may arise from the exposure of the negative aspects of reality, an encounter with that which has been eclipsed, or one's discernment of the shady corners of the individual psyche or social ethos. But "dark consciousness" also compels us to look into the flux of latent propensities, circulatory affects, and speculative processes of becoming that enact the human imagination of infinitude.

Accordingly, I stress the literary capacity that is embedded in "dark consciousness." Literature facilitates the imaginary thrust from within and beyond human values and beliefs, a disruption where it is least expected. At its most polemical, it exerts the abysmal force that voids established values as much as it begets "anticipation"—which, in Paola Iovene's words, "involves the fears and aspirations that shape lives and narratives in their very unfolding, and the perception of the possibilities and limits that inform human actions and are often mediated by literary texts."[54]

Of all modern Chinese writers, Lu Xun depicts the relationship between enlightenment and dark consciousness in the most precarious terms, and of his numerous writings about darkness, the trauma, spectrality, and cannibalism inherent in the Confucian edifice, his essay "Yesong" 夜頌 (Ode to night, 1933) is the most succinct statement of his concerns. Lu Xun starts with an ambiguous reference to "those who like night are not necessarily loners, idlers, invalids, or afraid of the light" and then describes the type of people who are especially fond of the virtues of night:

> People's words and deeds tend to appear different in daytime or at night, under the sun or under the lamp. The night is the mysterious celestial attire woven by Nature, embracing everyone, giving them warmth and comfort, such that they shed off artificial masks and clothes, nakedly enclosed by the dark domain of infinitude.
>
> In the night as it is, there are shades of darkness and light. There is twilight and dusk, darkness that fails sensibilities and the pitch-black state that blurs everything into a mess.[55]

Notice how Lu Xun starts with a conventional idea of night in moral and psychological terms and moves to indicate the sensory and conceptual nuances within the infinitude of night. He then proposes a connoisseurship of night informed by metaphysical thought. A "lover of night," he muses, "is the one who has ears to hear the night and eyes to see the night." More importantly, the "lover of night" is someone dedicated to "being in the darkness and seeing all the darkness." The "lover of night" is one who "seizes the light bestowed by night."[56]

Lu Xun's "lover of night" is someone gifted with an extraordinary capacity of discernment—a gift Lu Xun claimed for himself. His wife, Xu Guangping 許廣平 (1927–68), has called attention to the fact that Lu Xun used a pseudonym Youguang 游光—literally meaning wandering or transient light—for the essay under discussion and others related to night. The pseudonym has the ominous connotation of a baneful spirit in a graveyard.[57] In other words, Lu Xun was suggesting a "posthuman" look at the human condition. The transient light he identifies with is an emission not from moral interiority, but from the ethereal terrain of the unknown. Still, the idea of "the light bestowed by night" raises many questions. How would one trace the source of the light from the night? Why does such a light, transient as it may be, function to illuminate an opaque reality?

Revisiting Gu Cheng's poem ("The dark night gave me black eyes / I use them nonetheless seeking for the light"), we may better understand why "the dark night" may generate the "beam of darkness." As if echoing Lu Xun's lines, Gu situates himself in the darkness, but he is able to see everything. In Lu Xun's words, "a gentleman walks into the dark room and stretches into laziness; lovers move from the moonlight into shady bushes, casting knowing glances at each other. The night falls, smearing all writers' and scholars' lofty, natural, awakened, indignant, or bright manners under the beaming sunshine or on the glossy paper, exposing instead their nightly sentiments of begging, cowering, cheating, bragging, and trickery."[58] In the meantime, with his black eyes, the poet keeps looking for the esoteric light within and beyond darkness. The shining may be coming so fast that it enters and passes through the world in the very same moment; it is a "too soon" that is also a "too late" of an "already" that is also "not yet." It allows us to recognize in the obscurity of the present the light that, without ever being able to reach us, is perpetually traveling toward us.

The Day the Sun Died: Yan Lianke and the Mythopoetics of Darkness

In the midst of the twin campaigns of the "Chinese Dream" and "Tell the Good China Story," contemporary Chinese writers are encouraged to develop a narrative that reflects the bright side of the socialist past and present, thus generating positive energy in anticipation of the future. But for a writer such as Yan Lianke, it is the untold part of the China story and the repressed side of the Chinese Dream that concern him. In his recent novel *Rixi* 日熄 (The day the sun died, 2015), Yan relates a chilling story of one night in a small city in central China called Gaotian. Instead of settling down for the night, the citizens of the city roam the streets and nearby fields. Like automatons set in motion, they senselessly mingle and collide with each other. As more and more people swarm onto the streets and engage in violent deeds, the city quickly descends into bloody chaos until corpses are "blanketing the ground like fallen fruit."[59]

The story is narrated by a teenager, Li Niannian, whose parents run the New World funerary shop that sells "everything dead people might need" —from wreaths to paper ornaments and burial clothes. The town's nocturnal carnival brings unexpected business to the Li family. As the novel develops, the funerary shop turns out to be only a front for the true Li family business: Niannian's parents are actually running a secret trade in "corpse oil," the oil that drains from the burning of bodies in the town crematorium. The infamous practice of cannibalism in Chinese society as described in Lu Xun's "Diary of a Madman" thus takes a new twist.

Yan Lianke is one of the most controversial figures in contemporary Chinese literature. The winner of the Kafka Prize in 2014, Yan has a unique background: he joined the People's Liberation Army in 1978 at the age of twenty and remained in the service until 2004. In his early days he was known for drawing on his professional background to depict military life. Then in the mid-1990s his style underwent a drastic change. Eschewing the conventions of realism prescribed by the authorities, he began to explore the absurd and uncanny aspects of the lower strata of Chinese society. The result is a series of eerie caricatures of and critical reflections on contemporary China, from the AIDS epidemic to the absurdities of the education system, and from moral bankruptcy in rural life to socialist and capitalist excess in the city. His works provide an overarching look at China at its most grotesque.

Yan has a keen, journalistic sensibility with regard to social events and is capable of turning anything he touches into a dark carnival. For example, *Shouhuo* 受活 (Lenin's kisses, 2004) tells of a group of poor, disabled peasants who follow the plan of their village's party leader to purchase Lenin's embalmed body from the bankrupt Soviet Union and make it the main attraction of a Red version of Disneyland; they seek to raise money by performing the acrobatic marvels their disabled bodies are capable of. *Sishu* 四書 (Four books, 2011) takes us to a concentration camp during the Great Famine, when starvation and coercion induce betrayal and complicity, culminating in self-cannibalism—all framed within the Confucian and biblical themes of benevolence and propriety, belief and salvation. Underlining Yan's writing is a haunting—and ghoulishly humorous—exposé of the insulted and the wounded of socialist China.

Yan has described his writing as an exercise of "mythic realism" (*shenshi zhuyi* 神實主義),[60] a radical mixture of various brands of realism, from socialist to magical realism. In contrast with socialist realism, mythic realism lays bare, distorts, and even exaggerates the Maoist mandate to represent what the people should believe to be true, so much so that it becomes not merely a parody of realism but a fantastic invention itself. One such example is his novel *Jianying rushui* 堅硬如水 (As hard as water, 2000), which chronicles the ups and downs of a pair of male and female radicals during the Cultural Revolution. Despite their cruelty in leading brutal campaigns, the two turn out to love each other tenderly. They betray their respective spouses, carrying on their affair literally underground—in a tunnel dug by them for the purpose of their nocturnal trysts. Nevertheless, they find themselves unable to consummate their intercourse without listening to propaganda songs and shouting Maoist slogans. While Yan sets out to satirize communist body politics, he renders an intriguing story of true love between two adulterous villains. One wonders whether his novel is about a socialist comradeship turned into an erotic fantasia or a surreal celebration of revolutionary libido.

The Day the Sun Died is Yan's most recent engagement with his mythopoetics of darkness. Indeed, each section of the novel is marked by the progression of time into night. No sooner is one dark moment displayed than the next, even darker, one comes up, and even the much-anticipated sunrise turns out to be a moment of eclipse. As Niannian tells us, at sunset in late June, the residents of Gaotian suddenly start "dream-walking" like zombies. Instead of sleepwalking, "dream-walking" is "a result of the way in which whatever you are thinking about during the day becomes engraved in your bones, so that after you go to sleep at night you continue your thoughts from when you were awake, and try to carry out those thoughts in your dreams."[61] As if carrying out whatever is repressed in the daytime, Gaotian citizens stage a parade of revenge, vandalism, looting, and murder. Their behavior escalates into group revelry and hysteria as the night goes on, to the point at which depravity becomes despair, and frenzy generates horror.

According to Yan, in postsocialist China no one can survive with clean hands and a pure heart. Hence, he says, "I am one of those people who is fated to experience the darkness."[62] Therefore, "when I look at contemporary China, I see a nation that is thriving yet distorted, developing yet mutated. I see corruption, absurdity, disorder, and chaos. Every day, something occurs that lies outside ordinary reason and logic."[63] As a result, "I came up with a new form of writing that is premised on a conviction that the darker it is, the brighter it becomes; and the colder it is, the warmer it becomes."[64]

Insofar as he writes to parody a China under hypnosis, Yan was anticipated by Han Song, who wrote "Wode zuguo buzuomeng" 我的祖國不作夢 (My nation does not dream, 2003; unpublished). In that story, China appears to be so productive and prosperous that there is no longer any need to differentiate the daytime from the nighttime. Unlike the Chinese characters in Yan's novel who let loose their repressed impulses in dream-walking at night, their counterparts in Han's story are said to be working happily around the clock so that there is no time left for even an outburst of repressed energy. As the story develops, it turns out that all of the Chinese people have been programed by "the communal microwave" of the "Committee of Darkness" (Heian weiyuanhui 黑暗委員會) to be in a deep state of slumber, one that makes them believe they are awake and deliberately carrying out governmental assignments.

Han Song's story and Yan Lianke's novel bring us back to the two examples of early modern Chinese literature we discussed above in this chapter. In Xu Nianci's "A New Account of Mr. Windbag," Mr. Windbag flies over China at noon, only to see the majority of Chinese still sound asleep, and even the very few who are awake choosing to stay in bed and smoke opium. Assuming that the sun is not bright enough to wake up his compatriots, Mr. Windbag makes a futile attempt to illuminate China with his own shining power. One may recast Lu Xun's famous question about the "iron house"[65]: if one finds an iron house with no exits that has caught fire, should one wake up those who are sound asleep inside, causing them to panic and giving them futile hopes of escape, or simply let them die in their sleep? Han's story offers a third possible option: under the control of the "Committee of Darkness," Chinese people dream in such a way as to believe they are awake, thereby inhabiting a society free of the distinction between sleep and consciousness. In the story, there is no distinction between the iron house and the world outside its walls.

Moreover, literature, as Lu Xun would have it, engages the reader not only with social and political virtue versus evil, or utopia versus dystopia, but also with the stratagem of unnamable entities (*wuwu zhizhen* 無物之陣)—the paradox of the amorphous existence of nothingness. For Lu Xun in the 1920s as for Han Song in the twenty-first century, revolutionary zeal generates as much iconoclastic momentum as the involutionary tendency to return and turn inward, enlightenment gives rise to entropic desire and self-reflexive ambivalence, and the dream threatens to become a nightmare at any moment. Speaking of Chinese dreams, Lu Xun had his own interpretation of dreams as early as 1933:

> To dream means freedom,
> To talk about a dream means no freedom.
> To dream is to dream of something real,
> To talk about a dream is inevitably to lie.[66]

But is there any way out? If there is, it may be revealed by Yan's critique of darkness and light in contemporary China. In his acceptance speech for the Kafka Prize, Yan related a story about a blind old man in his home village: "Every morning when the sun came up, he would turn to the Eastern mountains and, facing the rising sun, would say to himself, 'It turns out that sunlight is actually black—but that is good!' Even in winter, when the blind man was warming himself under in the sunlight, he would always say with a broad smile, 'The darker it gets, the warmer it becomes!'"[67] As Yan recalls, this blind man had several flashlights, and whenever he went out at night he would take one with him. The darker it got, the longer and brighter the beam from his flashlight would become. As a result, as he was walking through the village streets in the middle of the night, people would be able to see him coming and wouldn't run into him. Furthermore, when people encountered him, he would use his flashlight to illuminate the road in front of them. According to Yan, "in order to commemorate this blind man after his death, when his family and the other villagers went to pay their respects and offer gifts, they all offered flashlights full of fresh batteries. As a result, his coffin was filled with flashlights."[68]

Yan indicated that his philosophy of writing has been inspired by the blind man's story: "I came up with a new form of writing that is premised on a conviction that the darker it is, the brighter it becomes; and the colder it is, the warmer it becomes. The entire significance of this writing lies in permitting people to avoid its existence. My writing, in other words, is like the blind man with the flashlight who shines his light into the darkness to help others glimpse their goal and destination."[69] It takes a blind man to find the blind spot embedded in ordinary vision. There is an immense realm of darkness to be explored beyond the knowledge granted by conventional vision.

In his fiction, Yan has experimented with a new logic of blindness and insight. This dialectic does not merely recapitulate the dialectic of vision and darkness. As his Kafka Prize speech indicates, although the blind man has never seen either the sun or the light, that does not mean that he is incapable of imagining it through his mind's eye. Furthermore, this blind person is capable of perceiving multiple, nuanced sensations of light and darkness that are obscured for a visually normal person.

In *Memoirs of the Blind*, Jacques Derrida comments on the intriguing dialogue between visibility and invisibility, blindness and vision, and suggests that "in order to be absolutely foreign to the visible and even to . . . the possibility of the visible, this invisibility would still inhabit the visible, or rather it would come to haunt it to the point of being confused with it."[70]

Derrida questions the premise of the metaphysics of optical vision and *ratio* (knowledge and rationality). He contends that it is the blind or the visually challenged who discern the "ruin of vision." Derrida critiques the discourse of the Enlightenment for being centered on the looking subject and placing sight at the top of a perceptive hierarchy. The eye of enlightenment is supposed to be the agency that exhausts the field of the visible, but Derrida instead argues for a hypervisuality that is so detailed and acute "that the viewed object itself becomes strangely opaque": "The visible as such should be invisible, not as visibility, the phenomenality or the essence of the visible, but as the singular body of the visible itself, right on the visible—so that, by emanation, and as if it were searching its own medium, the visible would produce blindness."[71]

The climax of *The Day the Sun Died* is an apocalyptic moment in which human and inhuman impulses mix together and the world becomes hell. What makes Yan's novel different from the conventional doomsday narrative is that he is aware of his own inability to see through the chaos. He creates a character like himself and makes him undergo writer's block. As a result, this fictional counterpart fails not only to solve the mystery of the dream-walking mania but also to pin down its moral implications. Thus, the novel prods the reader to imagine the "ruin of vision," so to speak, to readjust the spectrum of light and darkness and ask darkness, at a time when the sun has died, to reopen the tension between the unthinkable and the detestable.

All Nights in the World: *Chi Zijian and Necropolitics*

In Chi Zijian's 遲子建 (b. 1964) novella *Shijieshang suoyou deyewan* 世界上所有的夜晚 (All nights in the world, 2005), the first-person narrator is a woman writer and folklorist who has recently lost her husband, a magician by profession, in an accident. To cope with her bereavement, she takes a trip to a hot spring, only to be stranded in a small coal-mining town called Black Pond (Wutang 烏塘) when her train breaks down. Wandering through the town, she is stunned by its sullen, suffocating atmosphere. Black Pond is a place polluted not only by toxic air due to overmining but also by the omnipresent sentiment of mourning. Mining accidents happen so frequently that women come from everywhere to seek marriages with local miners—in the hope of quickly becoming widows with a right to claim compensation from the government. This is only the beginning of the mysteries and sordid dealings in which our protagonist will find herself entangled.

A leading woman author in contemporary China, Chi comes from Mohe Country in Heilongjiang. Mohe is the northernmost county of China, on the Sino-Soviet border. Chi first won attention for a series of lyrical portraits of her native region, the best of which are collected in *Beijicun tonghua* 北極村童話 (Tales from an arctic village, 1986). But Chi's talent is not limited to documenting her local culture, and she has since written about the saga of Harbin in the plague of 1910 (*Baixue wuya*, 白雪烏鴉 [Snow and raven, 2010]); the rise and fall of Manchukuo, the puppet regime created by Japanese imperialists in the 1930s (*Manzhouguo* 滿洲國 [Manchukuo, 2000]); and, in particular, the lives of indigenous peoples such as the reindeer-herding Evenki of the Greater Khingan Mountains (*E'erguna he youan* 額爾古納河右岸 [Last quarter of the moon, 2005]). Whatever subject she works on, Chi distinguishes herself by soberly reflecting on individuals' confrontation with changes in the ecological environment and the historical contingencies that arise in both public and private spheres. *All Nights in the World* (hereafter referred to as *All Nights*) is a case in point.

At the beginning of the story, the narrator is so engrossed in grief that she hopes to "smear herself with nothing but mud" in the hot spring.[72] However, she learns something unexpected during her accidental stay in Black Pond. She encounters a series of bizarre, gratuitous deaths, including those of a woman losing her life by treating her dysentery at a veterinary clinic; a dirge-singing painter accidentally hit and killed by a framed painting he made for a customer's birthday party; and a woman barber who dies from rabies as a result of being scratched by her client's dog. Driven by professional curiosity, the narrator starts to collect stories and dirges about the accidents as if creating a vicarious outlet for her own sorrow. Moreover, she finds herself increasingly drawn to a woman of dubious reputation known simply as "Jiang Bai's wife." Jiang Bai was a miner who mysteriously disappeared after a mine accident, and his wife has since become a hard drinker and a promiscuous woman. Rumor has it that Jiang Bai may have run away with another woman. Soon after, the narrator invites herself to Jiang Bai's wife's home and they develop a guarded friendship. Jiang Bai's wife always looks bitter and irritable and vigilantly guards one padlocked room. One night, after Jiang Bai's wife passes out from drink, the narrator steals her keys and opens the locked door. She finds in the room a freezer with an incense altar atop it, and inside the freezer is the frozen corpse of Jiang Bai.

Just as it seems that Chi is relating a story of necrophilia, she unveils more details. It turns out that Jiang Bai had been one of ten to die in a mining accident. But since an accident with a death toll of fewer than ten does not need to be reported to the higher authorities, local officers have cut a deal with Jiang Bai's wife to keep her husband's body hidden and classify him as "missing."

Lurking behind Jiang Bai's frozen corpse and his wife's alcoholism and promiscuity are the chilling facts of governmental corruption and a conspiracy verging on collective neurosis. Instead of necrophilia, Chi tells us a story of necropolitics—the systematic manipulation of individuals' lives and even deaths in the interest of governance.[73] Thus, the core of *All Nights* points to something horrible looming behind the realization of socialist utopia.

As one mystery leads to another, the plot of Chi's novella unfolds like a series of black boxes within other black boxes, each containing something more inscrutable than the next. The novella culminates in the unveiling of the secret of Jiang Bai's wife, which seems to answer the questions raised at the novella's beginning. Nevertheless, there is another story that exists not within but outside of the novella. An informed reader will understand that *All Nights* is referring to an open secret from Chi's own life. In 1998, Chi married Huang Shijun (黄世君), a local official of Tahe County. However, their happy marriage ended far too soon when Huang died in a car accident in May 2002. Though devastated by the tragedy, Chi managed to eventually resume writing, and *All Nights* is one of the two pieces she wrote in commemoration of her husband. In other words, the novella is an elegiac work occasioned by the author's own bereavement. Although Chi harbors a deep sympathy for Jiang Bai's wife, the female narrator who wants to "smear up her own face with mud" out of grief may well be the author's fictional counterpart.

To be sure, one need not know Chi's personal story to appreciate her work, and we should not fall into the biographical fallacy of conflating the writer's life with her work. Still, insofar as trauma has so profoundly affected Chi's life and career and shaped the image readers have of her, one may understand *All Nights* as a unique example of a writer's deepening engagement with the condition of art and life—and death. *All Nights* is first and foremost an inquiry into the art of dramatizing trauma so as to survive it.

To explore the dialogue between mortality and narrativity implied in *All Nights*, let us take a detour back to two stories of the May Fourth era. The female character Jiang Bai's wife reminds us of the character Xianglin's wife in Lu Xun's famous story "Zhufu" 祝福 (New year's sacrifice, 1924). In that story, the ill-starred Xianglin's wife is driven by sadness to share her suffering with the townsfolk. Her story first draws sympathetic listeners and induces tears, but as she repeats the story again and again, people start to lose patience and eventually treat her as a nuisance. Even the sympathetic narrator fails to answer her question, "Is there a soul that remains after one's death?" when encountering her by chance on his homecoming trip. The question looms mysteriously even after Xianglin's wife dies a beggar on the eve of the Chinese New Year.

Chi's story can also be read in light of "Ye" 夜 (Night, 1933) by Shen Congwen. In that story a group of young soldiers take shelter at an old man's mountain hut one night after getting lost on a mission. To kill time, they take turns telling tall tales while their host sits quietly and watches them. As the night wears on, the soldiers become more lively, and each story becomes increasingly creepier. Once the soldiers have exhausted their imaginations, they ask the old man to tell his story. The old man has no story to share. Instead, he opens the door of one room and shows the soldiers a dead, dry body lying in bed—his late wife.

Storytelling has been regarded by promoters of Chinese modernity from the time of Liang Qichao to the present as that which helps illuminate the human condition and restructure the world. But with their stories, both Lu Xun and Shen Congwen appear to have complicated that vision. In "New Year's Sacrifice," Lu Xun creates an unaccountable storyteller who fails to rescue Xianglin's wife from her predicament, consequently throwing into question his own identity as a so-called new youth. Meanwhile, Xianglin's wife turns out to be an inefficient storyteller. Her heartrending confession quickly becomes repellent to her audience, who are perpetually looking for newer and sadder stories for sentimental consumption. In contrast, Shen's narrator ends his story with the exposure of a corpse, which silences everyone. At the same time that the display of the dead appears to have terminated the whole storytelling sequence, it implies an open ending. The corpse, though incapable of utterance, compels us to ask who she was and how she died. Instead of telling, it embodies the story of the unknown destiny that befalls all human beings.

Two critical perspectives can be cited to help explain the connection between narrative and mortality. Walter Benjamin famously differentiates storytelling from information conveyed through narrative forms such as the news media and the novel. He suggests that unlike information, the story is a symbolic operation vital to human sociality. It draws its power not from external verification but from the awareness of death. One's wisdom and real life, the essence of stories, become transmissible on the condition of death: "Death is the sanction of everything that the storyteller can tell. He has borrowed his authority from death. In other words, it is natural history to which his stories refer back."[74] In contrast, Hannah Arendt has contended that the human condition can be defined as narrativity. For her, utterance in the form of storytelling in public space is the genesis of communication and sociality, which in turn constitutes the meaning of life. Through storytelling, the past is remembered in such a way as to form communal history, while the future is being projected onto the horizon.[75]

Arendt and Benjamin thus seem to address the tangibility of storytelling from the opposite ends of the human condition: the close versus the beginning of life. A closer look indicates that for all their conceptual differences, both are concerned about the existential fate of the human, and both seek to break open such a precarious closure through the communal bonding of storytelling. Whereas Benjamin claims that the raison d'être of storytelling lies in the shared fate of death, Arendt highlights its generative power as the only way to sustain a society's lineage and solidarity.

With these two critical perspectives in mind, one can better see how Lu Xun and Shen Congwen have problematized the paradigm of narrating Chinese modernity. Lu Xun questions the moral qualms of his narrator and implied audience by describing Xianglin's wife as trapped in the limbo between life and death. In contrast, by laying bare the deceased body that silences all utterances, Shen enquires into the paradoxical relations between eternal silence (death) and storytelling. If Benjamin and Arendt have argued that storytelling is an instrument for communal cohesion, the two Chinese writers suggest that the primal scene of storytelling is always already truncated, and that full-fledged communication between the storyteller and the audience is untenable. Still, even if it does not promise to remedy the circumstances it describes, the story must still be told.

It is in this context that we return to Chi's *All Nights* and ask how her work forms a dialogue with that of the two writers of the May Fourth generation, a dialogue that illuminates the dark domain of mortality. As mentioned above, midway through the novella, the narrator is shocked to discover Jiang Bai's frozen body stored in a locked room. Nevertheless, it quickly becomes clear that the apparently necrophilic deed of Jiang Bai's wife is motivated by not her passion for the deceased but by her forced complicity with the local government. She has accepted the officials' compensation money in exchange for keeping quiet about her husband's death in the mining accident. Her neurotic and licentious behavior afterward are symptoms of both her bereavement and guilty conscience. In view of the fact that Black Pond is known for so-called professional widows who capitalize on their husbands' untimely deaths, Jiang Bai's wife comes across as an accomplice, however reluctant, of the collective crime.

Unlike Xianglin's wife, who tells her sad story to all and obsesses over the question of the afterlife, Jiang Bai's wife is denied the chance even to mourn publicly, since her husband is legally listed as missing—much less to consider the whereabouts of his soul. Nor is she able to disclose her secret like the old man in Shen's "Night," who literally displays his wife's body to the soldiers to tell her story by showing what is unspeakable. Stunned by Jiang Bai's eternal oblivion, a liminal case of neither death nor life, Chi's narrator cannot help but reflect on her own position as a widow. She wonders if there is a place even darker than the "dark night of death."[76] Chi does not stop her narrative here, however. Instead, she keeps raising questions about "death under erasure" and ponders the impossibility of redemption. Her questions bring us to the last part of the novella.

With the multiple stories about death in mind, Chi's narrator leaves Black Pond to resume her trip to the hot spring resort. There she comes across a child who has recently lost his mother and maimed father. She teaches the child a few magic tricks she learned from her husband, in the hope of cheering the child up. One night, the narrator walks to the riverbank near her quarters and sends her husband's old razor, which she has carried since his death, away on a floating lantern. As she opens his shaving box, she witnesses a butterfly fly out.

The novella ends in a ritualistic gesture by the narrator of bidding farewell to her beloved. The figure of an ascending butterfly reminds us of Zhuangzi's famous fable of dreaming that he was a butterfly and then waking up and wondering if he was simply a butterfly dreaming of being Zhuangzi. But I doubt that Chi would be content with such an easy interpretation for a story loaded with so many layers of narratives about death. Nor do I think that the ending can be explained by resorting merely to the Freudian definition of "mourning" as an affective ritual of severance from the dead. I argue that through her novella, Chi is accomplishing a much more nuanced agenda, something I will call a radical compassion for the dark matter of the human condition. By compassion, I mean Chi's capacity to extend her sympathy for their loss to all of those that undergo similar or worse fates. And by radical, I mean her willingness to explore—by listening to and narrating—stories about the unfathomable abyss of death and to venture to represent the unrepresentable.

In her refusal to singularize her sorrow, Chi dramatizes the dark, fecund domain of the dead. Each of the stories points her to a different dimension of a domain that seems to be endlessly expanding—hence the novella's title, *All Nights in the World*. Here Chi appears to part ways with Benjamin in that she does not see death as the all-embracing whole necessary for the human condition to be intelligible, nor does she seem to agree with Arendt, as she is less optimistic than Arendt about storytelling being the sole force capable of giving life to humanity. Storytelling, as Chi would have it, is neither a ritual that instantaneously unravels the mystery of life nor a ploy to survive the threat of death. Rather, it serves as the point of departure for a venture into the darkness of "all nights," a venture that promises no safe return.

If Lu Xun and Shen Congwen appear to have intensified the May Fourth paradigm of narrativity in different directions, Chi comes across as coping with something that is more menacing. According to socialist biopolitics, death is supposedly well under control and darkness completely excluded. Chi has nevertheless produced a novella that goes beyond the two May Fourth writers' engagements and, more significantly, confronts the socialist projects of managing life and death. And she does so by teasing out rather than turning away from the immense horizons of darkness:

> Are there are any places where we can truly see darkness? In this sleepless world, the soul of darkness has been torn asunder and lost by man-made brightness. . . . Did God not give us darkness to serve as a hotbed for our dreams?[77]

The Black Hole: Lo Yi-chin and His Superman with Broken Balls

The mystery of Lo Yi-chin's *Kuang Chaoren* 匡超人 (Superman Kuang, 2018) starts with the novel's title. Kuang Chaoren is supposed to be the name of a character in the eighteenth-century novel *Rulin waishi* 儒林外史 (The scholars, 1750) by Wu Jingzi 吳敬梓 (1701–54). Lo takes this appellation out of its original context to serve as a euphemism for his novel's original title, *Pojiji chaoren* 破雞雞超人 (Superman with broken balls). What is the significance of this obscene image? What does the eighteenth-century classic have to do with Lo's novel about the genital ailments of a contemporary Taiwanese man?

It all starts, Lo's first-person narrator tells us, with a small hole he discovers right behind his scrotum. He does not take the hole seriously until it has already expanded and begun to ooze pus and give off an awful odor. The situation quickly worsens so much that Lo finds it difficult to move around, let alone rest properly at night. However, the infection becomes an unthinkable source of inspiration, driving Lo to create a novel that covers topics from castration complex to sadomasochistic mania; from the metaphor of illness to the typology of enigmas; and, even more amazingly, from the myth of the goddess Nüwa mending the cracks of heaven to the astrophysics of the black hole.

Kuang Chaoren is the last volume in a trilogy by Lo, the first two being *Hotel Western Xia*, which I discussed in chapter 3, and *Nüer* 女兒 (Daughter, 2013). While we can find in the novel trademarks of Lo's style, such as a tell-all confessional impulse; litany-like free associations on anything from urban trivia to trepidation; a fragmentary structure; decadent imagery; and, most importantly, dark humor, it impresses us with something else. *Hotel Western Xia* creates an epic pathos out of the mysterious extinction of a minority civilization in Chinese history, while *Daughter* turns its attention to the domestic sphere, embarking on a wild, postmodernist escapade involving gender ethics. Compared with these two novels, *Kuang Chaoren* appears to take an inward turn, ruminating on the meaning of "the hole." Lo seeks to write about the metaphysics of the body—or, more outrageously, the cosmos—by targeting the opening between his legs.

The hole in *Kuang Chaoren* manifests itself first in the darkness of corporeality. As Lo describes it, when he first discovers the area, it is "a big hole breaking out under my testis . . . something like a canker sore that keeps opening up and smells odorous. It does not look like a symptom of venereal disease, but rather like some stubborn fungal infection."[78] Meanwhile he develops other symptoms, such as fatigue and high blood pressure. Although Lo has long enjoyed fame (or notoriety) for the heavily confessional inclination of his writing, one may still hesitate to read *Kuang Chaoren* as a true story. Lo is pushing the mode of confessional narrative to such an extreme that he challenges one's taste for realism. His description of his "hole"—its size, color, smell, feel, treatment, and daily development—is so meticulous as to become surreal. The hole even has a character of its own: menacing, corrupt, and morbidly seductive.

Male genital ailments have all too often been associated with clichés from phallic anxiety to the castration complex, but Lo seems determined to prove himself more imaginative (or morbid). As if discovering a literary bonanza in this hole, he piles up literary allusions, medical jargon, and pseudo philosophical queries to the point of crossing all boundaries of decency. At one point he asks: "What does it mean to be a superman with broken balls? Just imagine, the Superman is wounded in the bulging area of his crotch, the most vulnerable cavity, an entry point of harm, an obsession with pain."[79] The fear of castration looms ever larger as the novel develops.

In one of the most striking moments of his self-debasement, Lo's narrator fears that "someone may humiliate me, using pornographic language: 'You have got a cunt in your cock!'"[80]

As the novel progresses, Lo's hole becomes the mouth to a tunnel through time and space. Through this tunnel he not only participates in the weird private moments of the celebrities of Taipei but embarks on a space odyssey in a remote cosmic age. All adventures, however incredible, come down to expressions of pain, shame, and an unfathomable fall into vacuity prompted by the hole in question. As discussed in chapter 3, almost all of Lo's stories tend to circle around his anxiety about being trapped in a state of disgrace and abjection as a cuckolded husband, a son failing to meet his father's expectations, a social outcast, or a loser. If *Hotel Western Xia* deals with the motifs of loss and abandonment in time, *Kuang Chaoren* reinforces this by adding the spatial dimension that is the hole—the dark, deep space that threatens to devour everything in physiological, geographical, and even astronomical terms.

Thus, Lo presents a saga in search of the meaning of the hole. His narrative shuttles back and forth between his investigation of the infected area under his penis and the exposure of social absurdities that threaten to suck everything into the hollow space of boredom, hypocrisy, or mere nonsense. It also presents conceptual and moral dilemmas in the human condition that have been transformed into unresolvable aporias. Ultimately, it maneuvers us into considering the astrophysical symbolism of the black hole. An invisible, extremely massive area of space-time in the galaxy, a black hole is a gravitational field so intense that no matter or radiation can escape from it—not even light, which is why black holes cannot be seen. Scientists can detect a black hole only by gauging the effects of its gravity on the stars and gases orbiting it. When a black hole and a star are close together, matter that falls into the black hole can form an external accretion disk heated by friction to such high energy levels that the resulting light can paradoxically make the accretion disk one of the brightest objects in the universe. This kind of light cannot be seen with human eyes: a blackout of sorts is created as a result of excessive exposure to light.[81]

Lo has taken great interest in astrophysics and related scientific discoveries in recent years. *Daughter* was his first attempt to bring human ethical dilemmas to bear on, among other topics, relativity, the uncertainty principle, quantum physics, and molecular orbital theory. References to Erwin Schrödinger's cat, the Möbius strip, Max Planck's quantum mechanics, and Niels Bohr's atomic theory permeate his otherwise bizarre, episodic narrative. His knowledge of modern scientific discoveries notwithstanding, Lo has entered a field that few fiction writers have stepped into. No longer is he content with the conceptual dance or language play associated with postmodernism. Rather, he tries to go beyond human knowledge and explore the fabric of the cosmos, as epitomized by the black hole.

Lo indulges his fantasy regarding the black hole behind his testis and dramatizes his shame and fear on a cosmic scale. As he suggests, disgrace, like a suppurating wound that has not been treated, generates a metaphysics of the darkest kind. At its most outrageous, the hole seems to have a life and technologies of its own that are "like legions of invisible metal insects digging laboriously like miners in the hole, deeper and deeper."[82] The hole is not only an inscrutable viral attack on the body but also the symbolic genesis of malevolence beyond one's discernment and control:

> There is a deep cavity in the center of my body. It is not the same as a sense of disability, amputation, phantom limb, a shift in the body's center of gravity; or the penetrating melancholy the eunuchs of ancient times felt after the excision of the hormone secretion center. . . . The hole in the balls, like a lively creature, running vigorously into the space beyond your knowledge—antimatter, or dark universe, or another dimension—is getting bigger and bigger, deeper and deeper.[83]

At the other end of the spectrum of his physiological and astronomical inquiries, Lo means to explore the heart of darkness. One needs to revisit the allegorical dimension of Lo's novel. As noted above, the title of the novel, *Kuang Chaoren*, is derived from the eighteenth-century magnum opus *The Scholars* by Wu Jingzi. Throughout the novel Lo also makes numerous references to another premodern Chinese fictional masterpiece, *Journey to the West*, mentioned in chapter 2.

Kuang Chaoren is one of the most unforgettable characters of *The Scholars*, an episodic novel about a group of scholars trying to survive at a time when the literati circle was already overpopulated and passing the civil service examination no longer guaranteed bureaucratic advancement. A young scholar from a humble background, Kuang is at first known for his diligence, humility, and filial piety, thereby winning everyone's favor. But once he joins the elite class, Kuang quickly reveals his true nature. Not only does he betray his mentors, friends, and wife for his own advancement, but he also thrives on brokering legal suits and engaging in bureaucratic machinations. Shrewd as he is, Kuang goes through ups and downs in the treacherous world of officialdom. He is a survivor, and we last see him scheming about a new deal, looking as genteel and conscientious as ever.

As Shang Wei points out in his study of *The Scholars*, Kuang Chaoren embodies the spiritual bankruptcy of the intellectuals of Wu Jingzi's time.[84] But our question is, why does Lo pick Kuang Chaoren's name for the title of a novel that otherwise seems to have little to do with *The Scholars*? Although the novel never tells us explicitly, Lo hints more than once that he intends to highlight the *habitus*—the habits, skills, and dispositions of a given community—of the world of belles lettres of both the mid-eighteenth century and his own time. That is, the manners and morals that once made Kuang Chaoren a hypocrite are still integral to the literary and intellectual circles of contemporary Shanghai, Beijing, Hong Kong, and Taipei. However original, independent, or even eccentric they claim to be, Lo contends, the literati and scholars of our time are no more than "faltering shadows from the slide shows of hundreds of years ago."[85] In a civilization entrenched in imposture and masquerading, everyone walks around like apparitions, using their "gills" and "tentacles" to breathe and probe ways to survive the vanity fair.[86] Lo envisions society as a black hole that draws anyone near it into its dark, yawning depths.

On the other hand, the black hole lies nowhere but in Kuang Chaoren's own heart. Lo notes that the world of imposture and hypocrisy Kuang inhabits turns out to be fearsomely competitive and demanding. To achieve his ambition, Kuang must work hard day and night, and he is just one of the many "robotic puppets bouncing erratically at the joint of the annular gear of *hengtianyi* [the seismograph of ancient China] in a heterogeneous dimension."[87] Lo questions whether he is not a robot like Kuang in contemporary Taipei and asks if the hole behind his testis is not a secret entry into his inner mechanism.

Since the literal meaning of Kuang's given name, Chaoren, is "surpassing the human" or "superman," what Lo has done with his I-narrator is to reveal his equivocal human qualities. That is, aside from his identities (from thug to invalid), Lo likens him to a robot, an insect, a ghost, a thing, or merely an inscrutable hole. While Lo is known for self-deprecation, in *Kuang Chaoren* he may wittingly or unwittingly have entered the domain of the posthuman. Instead of looking at the world from a universal humanist viewpoint, he is more willing than ever to explore the darkest potential of the human for good and ill, and play with its amorphous representations to the point of dehumanization. Lo's speculative daring enables him to collapse multiple genres—from confessional realism to magic realism, and from metafiction to science fiction—into a hybrid sequence. By traversing the boundary lines of narrativity, he is able to invoke the posthuman conditions of disease and artificial intelligence, animalistic habitus, and the cosmic prehistory of the Big Bang.

Therefore, it may not be coincidence that along with *The Scholars*, Lo seeks to engage with the classical novel *Journey to the West*. As mentioned in chapter 2, the novel chronicles the pilgrimage of the monk Tripitaka, with the assistance of a trio of monsters turned disciples (including one called Monkey), to the West in a search for Buddhist scriptures. It has been popular for centuries thanks to its fantastic use of supernatural elements and figures and presentation of a Buddhist enlightenment comprehensible to the lay reader. However, Lo's reading (or rewriting) turns the novel upside down. He envisions the journey as a gratuitous trial preprogramed by Buddha, a test that turns out to reveal the illusory adventures of the heart. Even the promised moment of enlightenment comes only as a signal of the immense vacuity that further perplexes the pilgrims. In other words, what concerns Lo is the dark matter (so to speak) that permeates the journey, something that cannot be understood within a secular humanist schema:

> The holy scripture that takes thousands of miles to obtain teaches nothing but the meaning of nothingness. It is like a world of the dead, expanding immensely, ornamented in color and painted gold, an eternal two-dimensional space . . . befuddled, drifting with the wind, finding no form to embody in the next incarnation. What a gratuitous turnaround it

is to credit one's misery on the empty account of someone else's dreamscape or even to slumber without dreaming! How long does the wandering take? One thousand years, two thousand years?[88]

Lo's Monkey is a creature trapped between superhuman and subhuman agencies. Monkey is a superman, "more than a man, capable of a power that ignites gigantic horror and creates awesome marvels."[89] Monkey is particularly known for his ability to transform himself into multiple forms. Yet at the same time, Monkey's bestial nature can never be fully human. Monkey is tamed by Buddha and made to escort Tripitaka on the pilgrimage to the West—a mission that, in Lo's words, "belies" (*gufu* 辜負) its own immanent power. Through Monkey's adventures on the road, Lo witnesses not so much triumphant conquests of monsters but mystical encounters with the invisible forces embodied by the caves the monsters inhabit—Yellow Wind Cave, Black Wind Cave, Bottomless Cave, Spider Web Cave, and so on —all enticing the pilgrims to pay them a visit, and all exuding dark forces that threaten to devour the pilgrims.

It is at this point that Lo lets his Monkey take a great leap forward, traveling from the supernatural world of divinities and monsters to the mysterious sphere of astronomical mutations. Monkey's bitterest trial, Lo tells us, lies not in the monstrous caves of earth but in the caves found in the dark space-time of the galaxies—that is, the black hole. "The black hole is just too huge," being a hole within a hole and thus that defies any concept of matter, something whose sense of brokenness, fragmentation, annulation, and agony in the midst of dark vacuity, gives rise to "a hole within a hole."[90] Thus, Lo makes his Monkey an absurd hero in a new millennium, a lonely creature traveling in the unknown extraterrestrial domain:

> Can you tell if, in its continual transformation between identities, [Monkey] would go over the brink at any moment and suffer an eternal fall? Perhaps the havoc will happen somewhere between his sixty-ninth and seventieth transformation? All gods who are watching Monkey's adventure are covering their faces with their hands, crying, "Don't!" "One more somersault and you will end up becoming nothing." But we are all trapped in the storm which twists our faces and tears apart our bodies

> like a spin dryer, turning us into that antimatter, that antispace, that conceptually reversed dimension.[91]

This is the extravagant, mercurial style that makes Lo one of the most provocative writers in the Chinese language. Whether he is relating the viral infection of his genitals to the viral havoc of the cybernetic world or rereading the mythological pilgrimage of Monkey into the astronomical quest for infinity, Lo has blazed a new trail for contemporary Chinese literature. It is hard to identify generic attributes in his work, as each episode of his novels is presented as though all of them would soon be sucked into the obscure vortex generated from within. Wavering between nihilist simulacrum and existential implosion, he has succeeded in creating a black hole, or a space-time of eternal loss and abandonment, where plenitude and reality should be.

We have so far discussed three approaches to the poetics of darkness in contemporary Chinese fiction. Yan Lianke creates a cannibalistic carnival on "the day the sun died," a political satire of the socialist symbol of the sun; Chi Zijian seeks to embrace "all dark nights of the world" to redeem human imperfections, from personal tragedy to bureaucratic corruption and ecological crisis; and Lo Yi-chin breaks away with the physical and epistemological limits of anthropocentrism and asks about the posthuman conditions of being human. These writers have adopted the symbolism of night, darkness, blindness, secrecy, death, and the black hole to engage with what I call the epistemological occult that informs Chinese postmodernity. They have come a long way from Xu Nianci's legend of Mr. Windbag or Lu Xun's melancholy contemplation of a society in demise. Most importantly, as the capturers of the "beam of darkness," these contemporary Chinese writers discern in the immense domain of darkness what has long been buried as a result of cognitive complacency, cryptocracy, or psychological repression. They treat the depiction of darkness as a beginning rather than an ending to their narratives, therefore opening up multiple dimensions of the invisible.

5

The Monster That Is Fiction

In the preceding chapters I have described narrative fiction, or *xiaoshuo*, as one of the most polemical ways to engage with Chinese postmodernity at the turn of the millennium. Throughout the twentieth century *xiaoshuo* has been regarded as the main literary vehicle for enlightenment and revolution, facilitating both social critique and socialist enchantment, personal expression and political propaganda. The genre faced multiple challenges in the last decade of the twentieth century amid the media market boom on the one hand and the shake-up of cultural politics on the other hand.

However, narrative fiction has never lost its momentum. Instead, it has morphed into a number of exciting new forms. In a reality permeated with "strange things,"[1] storytelling is more in demand than ever. For this reason, the president of the People's Republic of China has launched a campaign to "tell the good China story," and the vast need for "good stories" in industries from computer games to moviemaking is evinced by the ever growing market for intellectual property. In the meantime, contrary to the conventional wisdom that reading novels has gone out of fashion, megafiction—novels that are millions of characters in length—has enjoyed phenomenal popularity on the internet.[2]

Against this background, this book asks why fiction matters in China, not only at the beginning of the modern period but also in the contemporary era. To better address this question, I have introduced a series of discourses of narrativity by critics from within China (such as Liang Qichao, Lu Xun, and Shen Congwen) and from the West (such as Hannah Arendt, Walter Benjamin, and Gilles Deleuze). These critics have tried to explain the fictional turn of modern narrativity from ethical, political, and affective perspectives and have offered their observations of its agency and consequences—or the lack thereof. I have focused my discussion on printed narrative fiction in contemporary China, not only because fiction remains most inextricably intertwined with current Chinese cultural politics but also because it serves as the intermediary between the modern boom in fiction that began in the late imperial era and the proliferation of countless media variations in the foreseeable future.

I have introduced three thematic threads that best demonstrate the vitality and variety of contemporary Chinese fiction. Transgression identifies the deviant subjects and voices that contest the legal, ethical, and cognitive boundaries related to reading and writing fiction. Transmigration calls attention to the cycles of life and death that lie beneath and beyond anthropomorphic horizons, questioning the tenability of humanism when encountered by multiple forms of being in time and space. Transillumination takes issue with the extant paradigm of realism as characterized by luminosity and enlightenment, seeking instead to engage with "the beam of darkness"[3] that sheds light on the invisible and unthinkable.

Based on these three threads, I offer my own theoretical take on contemporary Chinese fiction as a way to conclude my survey. I propose to look at the dynamics of Chinese fiction since 2000 in terms of the monster that is fiction. This intervention is derived from a framework I explored in my 2004 book, *The Monster That Is History*. In that book, I examined the ethics and politics of fiction from the late Qing to the end of the twentieth century in relation to representations of violence and its reverse, the violence of representation. I argued that where history fails to address man-made and natural atrocities, fiction arises to bear witness to the immemorial and unthinkable. With this book, I further argue that it is fiction that is capable of facilitating history's power of imagination and judgment and fabulating its view of the past and future.

Taowu *Revisited*

I draw my concept of fiction as monster from the late Qing critic Tao Youzeng 陶佑曾 (1886–1927), who in "Lun xiaoshuo zhi shili jiqi yingxiang" 論小說之勢力及其影響 (On the power of fiction and its impact, 1907) conceives of narrative fiction as *guaiwu* 怪物 (monster):

> At the center of the twentieth century there is a huge monster. It walks without feet, flies without wings, screams without being prompted; it pricks one's brain cells, shocks one's eyes, stimulates one's thoughts, enhances one's intelligence. It is now solemn, now humorous, now singing, now weeping, now provoking, now persuading, now satirizing, now teasing. Prevailing and permeating, indulgent and immersive, when the heat within it builds to an extreme, it emits a burst of lightning and an immensity of magic power. It has huge strength of unthinkable magnitude, and it miraculously lights up the literary world. What is it? It is fiction.[4]

Here Tao describes fiction as an amorphous, menacing creature, capable of exerting enormous power over the human. Not only can fiction manipulate its readers' affective faculties, but it also embodies a "huge strength of unthinkable magnitude" that can change the status quo and mold reality. To be sure, Tao's assessment of *xiaoshuo* reminds us of Liang Qichao's famous statement in 1902, which inaugurated the discourse of modern Chinese narrative fiction:

> To renovate the people of a nation, the traditional literature of that nation must first be renovated. Thus to renovate morality, we must first renovate fiction; to renovate religion, we must first renovate fiction; to renovate manners, we must first renovate fiction; to renovate learning and the arts, we must first renovate fiction; and even to renew people's hearts and remold their character, we must first renovate fiction. Why? It is because fiction exercises a power of incalculable magnitude over mankind.[5]

What distinguishes the two lies in the fact that Liang concentrates on the unmediated relationship between fiction and politics (*qunzhi* 群治) while Tao goes one step further to describe the "assemblage," in Deleuzian terms, of fiction as a "bloc of sensations."[6] In other words, although like Liang, Tao promotes fiction with an eye on its political and pedagogical impact on the Chinese people, he is more ready than Liang to spell out the protean power of becoming that is its secret. Where Liang stresses the effect of fiction, Tao stresses its affect.

In *The Monster That Is History*, I approached modern Chinese historical violence by looking at the symbiosis of monstrosity and modernity reflected by narrative fiction. In light of the incessant turmoil in twentieth-century China, I proposed that when history and historiography fail to articulate the atrocities and absurdities that most Chinese people suffered, fiction serves as a more powerful testimony.

The figure I use to explain this relationship between fiction and history is the ancient monster *taowu* 檮杌 and its changes in connotation over time. *Taowu* was initially known both for its ferocious nature and its divinatory power. In classics such as the *Shenyi jing* 神異經 (The classic of the fantastic and the strange), *taowu* is described as a creature that has "a human's face, a tiger's feet, a pig's teeth, and a tail as long as eighteen feet."[7] The historian Tu Cheng-sheng argues that the imagination, invocation, and categorization of monsters (*wuguai* 物怪) are the first markers of civilization in ancient China. According to Tu, the naming of a monster is crucial to the formation of tribal and state identity. Moreover, the knowledge system associated with the worship, deciphering, and institutionalization of *wuguai* leads to the formation of the ritual, bureaucratic, and legal systems of a state. As late as the Zhou dynasty (1046–256 BCE), Tu claims, *wuguai* were still referred to as an externalization of the virtue (*de* 德)—or "humor" of the social body—of a state. Above all, *wuguai* serve a crucial role in the rise of ancient historiography.[8]

Taowu underwent numerous transformations over the centuries, to the point where it became identified with humans of evil inclination—as seen in accounts in the ancient histories *Zuozhuan* 左傳, *Shangshu* 尚書, and *Shiji* 史記. It is said that Prince Zhuanxu's son, Guen, was of such a wayward nature that he earned himself the monstrous name of *taowu*. As Sima Qian 司馬遷 (145–86? BCE) writes in *Shiji*, this "wayward son . . . turns his back on any moral teachings and is incorrigible. This son is called *taowu* by the world."[9] Together with three other evils of the time, this human *taowu* was tamed and exiled to the frontiers, where he would scare away the baneful mountain spirits of the *chimei* 魑魅 (demon)—that is, evil beings were used to ward off other evil beings.

Somewhere along the way *taowu* became identified with history itself. Thus, the people of the ancient state of Chu believed that "*taowu* is an animal that can foresee the future, so it can always run away before the hunters arrive. Since history reveals both past and future, it is referred to as *taowu*."[10] One finds the following statement in *Mencius*:

> The *Sheng* of the Chin [Jin], the *T'ao U* [Taowu] of Ch'u [Chu], and the *Spring and Autumn Annals* of Lu are the same kind of work . . . and the style is that of official historian.[11]

The metamorphosis of *taowu* from monster to historical account, while indicative of the flexibility of the ancient Chinese imaginary, points to one way in which Chinese history took shape. Thanks to its fiendish nature, *taowu* compels the ancients to "remember and recount its wickedness so as to take precautions."[12] In other words, the monster was invoked as an objective correlative, so to speak, of bygone human experience, registering that which is immemorial and yet unforgettable in the Chinese collective memory, and cautioning against any similar mishaps in the future.

Relevant to our concerns is the revival of *taowu* in the early seventeenth century, a time that saw the downturn and collapse of the Ming dynasty. In 1629, Li Qing 李清 (1602–1683) wrote a roman à clef titled *Taowu xianping* 檮杌閑評 (An idle commentary on monsters) to expose the evil perpetrated by the eunuch Wei Zhongxian 魏忠賢 (1568–1627) and his cronies. In the novel, *taowu* is invoked to register not only contemporary absurdities but also the moral urgency of making sense of the times. Li's fictional effort was replicated by two other novels produced at moments of historical crisis: *Taowu cuibian* 檮杌萃編 (A compendium of monsters, circa 1905), by Qian Xibao 錢錫寶 (1865–?), and *Jin taowu zhuan* 今檮杌傳 (A history of *taowu* of modern times, 1951) by Jiang Gui 姜貴 (1908–81). The former presents a cavalcade of imposters and shams during the last days of the Qing dynasty, while the latter portrays the chaos in a town in Shangdong Province on the eve of the Chinese communist revolution.[13]

In their efforts to construe and configure the irrationalities of these moments, all three writers call on the ancient monster *taowu*. By conjuring up *taowu* anew to serve their own eras, these writers renew the haunting question of the ambiguous power of fiction with regard to the barbarism of history. Thus, for Jiang, the function of conjuring up *taowu*, or history in fictional form, is to "record evil so as to admonish."[14] The evil human looks and acts much the same way as an evil monster would, an overlap that blurs the cultural and moral boundaries that humanity would like to draw around itself.

However, insofar as *The Monster That Is History* highlighted the analogical relations between history and monster, my observation in that book addressed only the mediating role of fiction as a narrative form. When fiction takes the place of history, it is simply an inscription of the acts and consequences of evildoers, meant to recount the past in such a way as to caution subsequent generations against immorality and aberration. Here I would like to expand that argument by foregrounding the way in which the mechanism of *taowu* is constitutive of fiction. Even when it is given a moralistic rationale, fiction can be "monstrous" in its own right. I contend that although modern Chinese fiction is often promoted as a way of praising the good and excoriating the evil, the act of writing fiction ironically relies on the continued accumulation and inclusion of that which is immoral and supposed to be excluded. Fiction generates its own antithesis: even if its moral telos holds true and valid in the long run, fiction—as a narrated account of and remonstration with wayward histories—nevertheless reveals, and even inhabits, vice, waste, and anomaly.

I take issue with the conventional wisdom that at a time when history has failed to convey the moral meaning of the past in the present, fiction becomes its substitute. I ask insofar as it is an amorphous, "rootless" representation of human experience, can fiction transcribe and impeach evil and violence without betraying its own suspect, malleable nature? When fiction is written under the name of *taowu*, hasn't it already intimated the subversion of civilization by its own discontents? Evil has continued to proliferate from one generation to another despite the supposed power of history to hold it to account—so much so that, with a twist of logic, one may even ponder whether evil and the violence it entails have not become part of the raison d'être of fiction. More disturbing are the moments when the act of writing fiction in and of itself seems to flirt with violence.

Perhaps for this reason, Liang Qichao and Lu Xun, the two pioneers of modern Chinese fiction, expressed their misgivings even at the beginning of modern Chinese fiction. As discussed in chapter 2, Liang was disappointed by the fact that for every piece of new fiction published to narrate the new China, many more works catering to the general public's low taste were produced. Lu Xun found an even more menacing paradox in his work. The more his fiction exposed the dire circumstances of reality, the more it belied the hope that reform and revolution would alter the status quo. Perhaps for this reason too, Mao Zedong and his followers set out to head off the unintended consequences of fiction by regulating how it should be conceived of, produced, and circulated.

Ambiguity abounds when one looks into how *taowu* the monster was translated into *taowu* the diviner, and how *taowu* as history is folded into *taowu* as fiction. In view of the incessant outbursts of violence and brutality across generations, one must ask: Could fiction be regarded as both an embodiment and an indictment of monstrosity? If so, to what extent has the promotion and circulation of fiction provided insights and to what extent has it nurtured indifference? This paradox becomes all the more poignant in modern times that are characterized by an unimaginable spectrum of monstrosity. Particularly in view of the massive scale of violence and pain that the Chinese subjected themselves to in the name of enlightenment, rationality, revolution, and utopian plenitude, one senses that the line between understanding and complicity has never been so difficult to discern.

But fiction cannot be reined in by the harness of history. With the anomalous and polymorphous mediation of *taowu*—as monster, outcast, historical account of evil, and fictional representation—we may find ourselves imagining past inhumanity in the hope of achieving a future in which such inhumanity can scarcely be imagined. We may come to realize that without the imagination of the inhumanity of the past and future, we are unprepared to recognize it in its next incarnation. For this reason all modernities bear the imprints of primitive savagery. A monster haunts the human struggle for self-recognition and betterment. How to come to terms with this monstrosity by way of teasing out its hidden divinatory power remains a task as urgent in our millennium as it was in ancient times.

Fiction and Daimōn

Considering the connection between monstrosity and fictionality opens another intriguing theoretical path for analyzing contemporary Chinese fiction—namely, rethinking the demonic nature of fiction. The Chinese critic Chen Sihe 陳思和 has called attention to the "demonic elements" in Yan Lianke's writing in recent years.[15] With Yan's *As Hard as Water* as his focus, Chen borrows Wolfgang M. Zucker's theory of "the demonic" to analyze the villainous figures' frantic deeds during the Cultural Revolution, pondering the extent to which Yan's fiction shakes up the conventional paradigm of socialist literature. For Chen, the demonic refers not to villainy but to the mercurial human nature that responds alternately to the calling of the divine and the temptation of evil. Granting its threat to human well-being, Chen finds in the demonic the potential of the religious sublime: it arouses both pity and horror in such a way as to point to the entwined horizons of downfall and salvation. Whereas one finds in Western literature a gallery of demonic figures (from Johann Goethe's Faust to Fyodor Dostoevsky's Karamazov brothers), Lu Xun's Mara Poet, a poet endowed with the satanic spirit to destroy the status quo, is the archetype of the Chinese demonic.

Chen's "demon" or "the demonic" is even more ambivalent than it initially appears. As noted in chapter 3, "demon" is derived from the Greek "daimōn," which originally referred to a lesser deity—namely, a divinity between the gods and humans. Extant fragments by Heraclitus suggest that the word "daimōn" means "to divide" and sometimes also referred to the souls or inner selves of men: "man's character is his daimōn."[16] Zucker points out that the original Greek word did not have negative implications and was used interchangeably with *theos* up to the fifth century. Then in the New Testament, it took on the modern connotation of "demon," an evil spirit inferior to God, and of the manifestations of everything evil or detrimental to demons' human victims.[17] Whatever is possessed by demons also becomes demonic. However, no matter whether the demonic has the neutral meaning of a deity ranked between god and human or the negative meaning of an evil spirit or a person possessed by it, the term always seems to entail a state of being human and nonhuman at the same time.

What concerns us is the way in which the demon manifests itself in art and literature. In Greek tragedy, the daimōn is associated with the inevitable fate of destruction. The hero of a tragedy is seen as possessed by his demonic nature in such a way that he can never be reconciled with the divine order, no matter how hard he tries.[18] As elaborated by Zucker in the case of

Heraclitus's writing, "The demonic element, which determines man's fate and from the viewpoint of the tragedy leads to the inevitable catastrophe, is founded in man's own, always mysterious self. . . . [T]his self always remains hidden in the darkness and silence of its ultimate meaning; it cannot be elucidated by the logos, but is presented in the twilight of doxa, in the mythos."[19]

Gilles Deleuze and Félix Guattari have taken a different approach to the daimōn, including the multiple implications of the figure in their inquiry into the posthuman condition. For these critics, the process of becoming animal is only one becoming among others in the multitude of species in the world. Of the three types of animals—the Oedipal, the state, and the demonic—identified by their study, they call attention to the "demonic animals"[20] that traverse the boundaries between the animal and the divine, the human and the inhuman. Deleuze and Guattari stress the original Greek sense of daimōn: situated in between the world of the living (states of beings) and a suprasensible world made up of inorganic life, affects, and impersonal forces. It is in relation to demonic animals that becoming animal takes place.[21]

Zucker, Deleuze, and Guattari all note the protean, anomalous, and transitory characteristics of the daimōn. If Zucker places more emphasis on the inborn demonic inclination of the human and its cognitive capacity to divide against itself, Deleuze and Guattari uphold affect as something transmitted by the daimōn in the value-free; minute; and most importantly, personal form. In Francis Bacon's paintings of slaughterhouses, Deleuze sees the expression of the human being's becoming animal. It is not that Bacon intends to evoke a sentimental identification with the dismembered animalistic state, but instead that "every man who suffers is a piece of meat. Meat is the common zone of man and the beast, their zone of indiscernibility."[22]

At the same time that the daimōn represents the blurred lines between man and animal, it can also represent the eerie combination of man and machine. Ever since the publication of Mary Shelley's *Frankenstein*, the machine turned human or monster has been used as an intervention in the Western fantastic tradition. The technological turn of the modern has been associated with the positive, rational claims of the cognitive paradigm since the Renaissance, as well as the mass management of the human being in both capitalist and totalitarian forms of governance. Modern society betrays its Leviathan nature when humans are turned into "a cog and screw" in either the Fordist production line or the Leninist hegemony. But both the capitalist and socialist systems appear to be overwhelmed by new machinery as humans find themselves turned into posthuman, in N. Katherine Hayles's words, by the end of the twentieth century.[23] For Hayles and other critics from Donna Haraway to Cary Wolfe, in the context of this cybernetic revolution—with computers integrated into our daily lives, inscrutable algorithms that govern the information we receive, and ever more sophisticated methods of managing data that describe billions of people—the question of what is the human must be asked again. The human is no longer limited to flesh and blood but is instead conceived of as a prosthetic assembly powered by built-in programs and artificial intelligence. In that sense, we are all Frankenstein's descendants.

Jacques Derrida has proposed what he calls "a politics of the virtual" in commenting on postmodern technology. He asks, "how is one to reconcile, on the one hand, a thinking of the event, which I propose withdrawing, despite the apparent paradox, from an ontology or a metaphysics of presence . . . and, on the other hand, a certain concept of machineness?"[24] For Derrida, an "event" manifests itself first and foremost in singular terms: it happens "to someone, some living being who is thus affected by it." In contrast, the machine "reproduce[s] impassively, imperceptibly, without organ or organicity, received commands"; it obeys "a calculable program without affect or auto-affection."[25] Derrida imagines that if one day, "with one and the same concept, these two incompatible concepts, the event and the machine, were to be thought together, you can bet that not only . . . will one have produced a new logic, an unheard-of conceptual form. In truth against the background and horizon of our present possibilities, this new figure would resemble a monster."[26]

In the context of our discussion, the "monster" of the virtual as described by Derrida may represent the latest incarnation of fiction. This is where event and machine meet to generate an immense web of cybernetics and informatics, one that assimilates fabrication into fabulation. The ancient monster, be it called *taowu* or daimōn, has assumed a new facade and system in remolding the way we (as posthumans?) perceive and interact with the world. Fiction may well be the "place of a thinking that ought to be devoted to the virtualization of the event by the machine, to a virtuality that, in exceeding the philosophical determination of the possible . . . exceeds by the same token the classical opposition of the possible and the impossible."[27]

It is at this juncture that we may reconsider Tao Youzeng's description of fiction as a monster that "has huge strength of unthinkable magnitude, and it miraculously lights up the literary world." To be sure, Tao was promoting the monstrous entity of fiction to facilitate his own agenda at the beginning of the twentieth century, but his description may still apply in the new millennium, as we seek a venue where the fantastic and the verifiable, the contingent and the repeatable, and *taowu* and artificial intelligence can interact with each other.

Returning to the thesis of this book that fiction matters in contemporary China, I argue that in the "new era" in which biopolitics, cyberpolitics, primitive passions, and political theology are intertwined in a manner unimaginable in the previous century, fiction has become an apparatus more instrumental than the one that in Tao's time served to "prick one's brain cells, shock one's eyes, stimulate one's thoughts, enhance one's intelligence." One learns to harness the "monster's" divinatory power through playing with the virtual in multimedial forms, while remaining alert to the monster's potential to turn into something beyond recognition.

The Scientific and the Divine

I started this book by discussing Lu Xun's "The Diary of a Madman" as an origin story for modern Chinese fiction. By way of concluding this book, I take another look at Lu Xun, digging into two less explored aspects of his fictional discourse and contemplating how they have been turned into new sources of inspiration for two recent novels, Ma Jian's 馬建 (b. 1953) *Rouzhitu* 肉之土 (Fleshy earth, 2008; translated as *Beijing Coma*) and Han Song's *Yiyuan sanbuqu* 醫院三部曲 (The hospital, a trilogy, 2018). Whereas the former was published overseas and remains banned in China, the latter was published in China on the eve of the centennial anniversary of Lu

Xun's "Diary of a Madman." Both help shed light on the demonic power of fiction today, thereby delimiting the literary and political imaginary—from monstrous *taowu* to artificial intelligence—in the age of "telling the good China story."

Fifteen years before writing "The Diary of a Madman," Lu Xun, then still a medical student in Japan, became interested in science fiction and translated Jules Verne's (1828–1905) *De la terre à la lune trajet en 97 heures et 20 minutes* (Ninety-seven hours and twenty minutes from the earth to the moon, 1865) into *Yuejie lüxing* 月界旅行 (A trip to the moon, 1903).This interest was clearly fostered by the growing popularity of science fiction in Japan and later in China, as promoted by Liang Qichao and other literati. As Lu Xun states in his preface to *A Trip to the Moon*:

> All changes start with an ideal, followed by putting the ideal into practice. . . . Colonizing the stars and traveling to the moon will become such a common thing that even ordinary adults will take it for granted. . . . Since people have searched in vain on earth for Johnson's paradise and Milton's Eden, it is now time for the Chinese people to rise up [and find their own extraterritorial paradise].[28]

Here Lu Xun presents Samuel Johnson's paradise and John Milton's Eden as two utopias to serve as models for Chinese reform and calls for extraterrestrial adventures so as to discover paradise in outer space. In doing so, he echoes the calls of Liang Qichao and other late Qing writers to modernize literature by conjuring up utopian fiction.

More striking than even this voyage to the stars is Lu Xun's translation or re-creation of a short story titled "Zaoren shu" 造人術 (The art of creating humanity) in 1905.[29] His work is based on a version by the Japanese writer Hara Hôitsu-an (1866–1904) of a work by the American author Louise Jackson Strong.[30] The story centers on a scientist's discovery of a "life-germ" crucial for cloning creatures and his subsequent success in creating a microscopic "sprout of humanity" (*renya* 人芽).[31] Lu Xun's translation is loosely based on the beginning of Strong's original story, and it remains unclear as to whether he was aware of its ending—in which the "sprout of humanity" has multiplied so much as to threaten the scientist's well-being, and the "monsters who would prey on human flesh" finally even exterminate themselves.[32] Perhaps the cannibalistic impulse of Lu Xun's "Art of Creating Humanity" is projected into "The Diary of a Madman."

Carlos Rojas has noted that Lu Xun's interpretation of the "sprout of humanity" emphasizes the sprout germinating into a living organism less than the protagonist's capacity to create a new creature. By eliding the "sprout" part of the medical discovery and titling his story "The Art of Creating Humanity," Lu Xun has shifted his story to the subtle connection between medical technology and literary expertise, as well as that between biological testing and psychological input.[33]

However, at almost the same time as he was promoting science fiction, Lu Xun was already questioning the assumption that science was the panacea to the malaise of China. In a series of essays, he pointed to *shensi* 神思 (divine thought) as an alternative. A concept that originated in *Wenxin diaolong* 文心雕龍 (Literary mind and the carving of dragons), a famous work of medieval Chinese literary criticism, *shensi* was adopted by Lu Xun (and possibly contemporary Japanese scholars as well) as a euphemism for the imagination. According to Lu Xun, "divine thought" arises from the primordial impulses of humanity, and it is best manifested in the form of literature. In modern times, the "new school of divine thought" (*xinshensizong* 新神思宗) is to be found nowhere but in the Mara Poet—the poet with the demonic power.[34] The term "divine thought" appears eleven times in his literary manifesto "Moluo shili shuo" 摩羅詩力說 (A treatise on the Mara Poet, 1908).

As he asserts that "divine thought" provides the quintessential momentum behind human creativity, Lu Xun casts doubt on the efficacy of modern science, particularly its positivism and reliance on deduction. He argues for recovering human imagination, the wellspring of scientific knowledge, and he locates the origin of human imagination in the mythology of ancient times. He pays tribute to ancient Greek thinkers who, in their inquiry into nature, found the "true roots" of science in the conception of myth, and he lashes out at those who consider science to be the only source of truth and debunk mythology as superstition.[35] In "Kexueshi jiaopian" 科學史教篇 (Lessons from the history of science, 1907), Lu Xun traces out the genealogy of Western science as well as the symbiotic development of science and mythology in human history. He contends that mythology originated with people in ancient times who witnessed the marvels of the world and employed the concept of "divine thought" to humanize them. In doing so, he questions the universal applicability of modern Western scientific discourse. At his most provocative, Lu Xun states:

> Human beings, in their observation of phenomena and in their investigation of the material world, felt as though everything embodied some mysterious inspiration from which we derive poetry and song as well as everything that is beautiful or ingenious. Those with an understanding of spiritual matters still return to this point today, yet people in China had already arrived at such an understanding some four thousand years ago. If these things are to be denounced as superstition, then what constitutes the "true" faith? Our gentry, at a time when the country is on the decline, have become spiritually blocked and interested only in petty gain. Though they are alive physically, they are dead spiritually. Thus, they are ignorant of the mysteries and curiosities of life, as well as indifferent to the appeal of nature, bowing only before the emoluments of office. . . . Thus, the most urgent task before us today is to rid ourselves of this hypocritical gentry; "superstition" itself may remain![36]

At stake here is Lu Xun's paradoxical narratology, one that links "divine thought" with demonic (Mara) poetics, and science with mythology. In a sharp contrast with the standard interpretation of his enlightenment project, Lu Xun undertakes a radical intervention that challenges any easy antithesis of modernity versus tradition, or enlightenment versus enchantment. Accordingly, the new literature Lu Xun pursued must be understood in the same dialogic terms. He was after all nurtured in both the newest form of scientific education and the time-honored storytelling ambience of myths, tales, and superstitions.

This leads to our reassessment of the other origin of Lu Xun's fictional project: the legacy of Chinese mythology. In *Zhaohua xishi* 朝花夕拾 (Morning flowers plucked at sunset, 1927), a collection of reminisces about his childhood, Lu Xun writes fondly about his initiation into the world of the *Shanhai jing* 山海經 (Classic of mountains and seas)—a stupendous compilation of geographical and cultural information on pre-Qin China. We are told that he first heard about the classic from a family friend and then became increasingly curious about its content. One day, much to his pleasant surprise, his nanny, Ah Chang, got a copy for him. It became "his most favorite reading" (*zuiwei xinai de baoshu* 最爲心愛的寶書).[37] Human-faced monsters, nine-headed snakes, a one-legged ox, and a bag-shaped creature named Dijiang 帝江—all are said to have enlivened his world, which was otherwise characterized by estrangement and misfortune. In particular, Xingtian 刑天, the beheaded deity who fights against the supreme gods with a shield in one hand and a battle axe in the other, using his nipples as eyes and his belly button as a mouth, would become a haunting motif in Lu Xun's literary and political works.

The *Classic of Mountains and Seas* can be traced back to the fourth century BCE, and its extant version came into being around the beginning of the Han dynasty. In eighteen sections, it describes over 550 mountains and 300 rivers, presenting an immense landscape in great geological and botanical detail and including topographical curiosities and spectacles. But this is not a geography book in the conventional sense. Rather, it presents monstrous creatures, invincible animals, weird immortals, and enchanted figures in contestation on the land that is now China. In other words, the *Classic of Mountains and Seas* has stood out in ancient Chinese literature, clearly distinguished from the Confucian works that would form the more orthodox tradition by its primitive fantasies and uninhibited account of nonhuman and inhuman forces and the appeal of its tales of grotesquery and changeability.

Lu Xun calls the *Classic of Mountains and Seas* a "book of shamanism in ancient times" (古之巫書) that introduces both a world of wizardry and mythology and the practice of communicating with the unknown world.[38] Relevant to our discussion, Lu Xun's appreciation of the text reflects his deep-seated fascination with the outlandish and the otherworldly despite his commitment to enlightenment and scientific knowledge. In *Morning Flowers Plucked at Sunset* and *Wild Grass*, one finds goblins, spirits, ghosts, and phantoms haunting the environment in which Lu Xun grew up. In T. A. Hsia's opinion, Lu Xun remained enchanted by them throughout his life.[39]

Shuttling between science fiction and mythology—as well as between the "art of creating humanity" and his engagement with demons, ghosts, and monsters—Lu Xun's literary adventures went far beyond the realism and humanism for which he has been hailed as the paramount model. This is why I argue that more than a hundred years after the publication of "The Diary of a Madman," Lu Xun still stands as the greatest source of inspiration for Chinese fiction in the new millennium.

Tell the Good Hospital Story

Two contemporary novels offer responses to Lu Xun's imaginary of China. The first is Ma Jian's *Beijing Coma*. Arguably the only full-length novel about the Tian'anmen incident to date, the novel depicts in minute detail the rapid cycling between excitement and dejection of the activists at Tian'anmen Square in the spring of 1989 and the military crackdown on the morning of June 4. But what the novel really means to talk about is the delayed consequences of the incident and the "slow violence"[40]—and its disavowal—that befell the Chinese people long after the bloodshed on that early June morning.

At the center is Dai Wai, a medical school student who before the incident had a bright future ahead of him. But like many other students, Dai was involved in the demonstrations, and he was gunned down by People's Liberation Army forces milling about the square on June 4. A stray bullet went through his head, paralyzing him forever and placing him in a prolonged coma. Ten years after the incident, Dai begins to regain his consciousness though he remains bedridden. He is blind and mute, but capable of hearing and thinking. As his old wounds heal, fragmentary thoughts about the incident return in fits. Ma Jian starts his story from Stephen Dedalus's dictum: "History is a nightmare from which I am trying to awake."[41]

Ma first gained attention in the mid-1980s as an avant-gardist, and he won notoriety for a series of fictionalized reports about his trip to Tibet. In particular, "Liangchu ni deshetai huo kongkong dangdang" 亮出你的舌苔或空空蕩蕩 (Stick out your furred tongue or otherwise, 1987), scandalized readers for its explicit portrait of sexual customs and the Tibetan ritual of sky burial, in which a corpse is laid out in the mountains for wild animals to devour. By then, Ma had already moved to Hong Kong. The outbreak of the student demonstrations in the spring of 1989 drew him back to Beijing, and he became a fervent participant in them, together with thousands of like-minded youths at that time. Ma exiled himself after the events of June 4, eventually settling in England in 1998. During his years in the diaspora, he continued to write and experiment with new styles, as evinced by *Lamianzhe* 拉麵者 (The noodle maker, 2004), a novel in which all the organs of the (imaginarily) dismembered protagonist are independently profiled to constitute a grotesque, surreal portrait of a late socialist Chinese subjectivity.

It took Ma Jian ten years to finish *Beijing Coma*, a novel inspired not only by the massacre at Tian'anmen Square but also by a family misfortune—his brother was paralyzed as a result of an accident. The allegory at the heart of the novel is fairly obvious. Dai Wei's pathetic semblance of living suggests a nation existing in a state of Agambenian bare life (*homo sacer*) or, worse, a state of collective inertia.[42] A sense of urgency abounds as Dai Wei gradually remembers bits and pieces of the Tian'anmen incident while, thanks to both government censorship and consumerist mania, Chinese society is sinking deeper and deeper into amnesia. This irony prompts a Lu Xunesque question: is not every citizen of a nation that is suffering from a spiritual state of paralysis somewhat comatose?

But *Beijing Coma* is more than the protest novel one might expect from a dissident. Instead, it surpasses our expectations by pointing to two opposite ends of a literary typology. On the one hand, it provides a detailed account of life on Tian'anmen Square and in the sickbed, so meticulous as to raise questions about the limits of realism. On the other hand, it interpolates into the narrative a series of interludes of monstrous creatures and outlandish landscapes, which are drawn from none other than the *Classic of Mountain and Seas*.

With respect to life on Tian'anmen Square, Ma Jian applies an almost anthropological curiosity to the student protesters' everyday practices during the demonstration. By way of contrast with the familiar heroic narrative, Ma depicts a group of young people who are as revolutionary as they are egotistical and whimsical, quarreling over tactics and money and indulging in sexual escapades whenever possible. As the crisis on the square intensifies, they blame each other, and their community falls into anarchy after a series of schisms. What is puzzling is the fact that Ma describes the episodes in such a detailed manner, even to the point of boring the reader. How mimetic must a novelistic account of history be to achieve the effect of the real?

The question becomes more perplexing as Ma describes Dai Wei's life as a bedridden patient. Confined to a sickbed for years, Dai watches helplessly as his body decays and transforms itself into a "fleshy tomb." Worse, his body is exploited for multiple purposes. His urine is sold to quacks for quirky medical purposes, his penis is aroused by a nymphomaniac, and one of his kidneys is put up for sale by his mother so as to make ends meet. Ma foregrounds Dai's mother, who has tirelessly taken care of her son for years against all odds, while coping with her own bitter memories of the past and aging body. As the novel comes to an end, the cramped bungalow that has housed Dai for years is demolished by a Hong Kong developer brought in to help beautify Beijing before the Olympic Games. A bulldozer is positioned over Dai's home, in an incident that is poignantly juxtaposed with flashes of memories of the tanks that ran over the students' bodies on Tian'anmen Square. As Belinda Kong points out, *Beijing Coma* presents a powerful indictment of the biopolitical and capitalist cannibalism of a contemporary Chinese society that thrives on "self-injury."[43]

Nevertheless, beyond his painstaking testimony about life during the student demonstrations and his exposé of complete abjection, Ma Jian has something else to offer. Let us return to the novel's interludes derived from the *Classic of Mountains and Seas*. In this desolate, mysterious land of China, supernatural creatures roam and strange phenomena lurk: "on the Mountain of the Empty Mulberry two hundred *li* north lives a wild beast that resembles an ox but has the markings of a tiger. Its roar sounds like a human groaning in pain. Whenever this beast appears, a disaster will befall the land."[44] In addition, "three hundred *li* further south is Mount Luminous. There are crystals and snakes on its slope. A wild beast that looks like a fox lives on the mountain. It cries out its own name. Whenever it appears a panic will engulf the land."[45] And "on Fajiu Mountain lives a bird with a white beak and red claws. It is the reincarnation of Emperor Yandi's daughter who drowned in the East Sea. It cries out 'Jingwei, Jingwei,' so people call it the jingwei bird. Every day, it picks up twigs and stones from the mountain and drops then into the East Sea, trying in vain to fill it up."[46]

Ma Jian indicates at the beginning of his novel that Dai Wei is an avid reader of the *Classic of Mountains and Seas*. His multiple references to the classic can therefore be understood either as Dai's unconscious adventure into the supernatural world, where his body and mind are transformed—or liberated—in such a way as to flirt with the forbidden and the unthinkable. Or one can argue that Ma is setting up a parallel between the world of the *Classic of Mountains and Seas* and contemporary China: both are inhabited by raw brute forces of the unknown, and both thrive on grotesquery and violence. I would suggest instead that Ma's continued interpolation of mythological accounts into the guiding narrative generates a lyrical overtone in a novel otherwise loaded with realist details. The accounts, mostly direct quotes from the ancient text, function like a series of incantations ushering the reader into another time and space. They constitute a subterranean voice, an apostrophe of sorts, that addresses the missing and the dead—or the void.

At a time when eyewitness accounts, on-site audiovisual reports, underground testimonies, casualty data, and theoretical analyses regarding the Tian'anmen incident have proven useless in the face of total, authoritarian denial, Ma Jian seems to contend that only through calling on primal mythmaking power can one engage reality anew. This brings to mind Lu Xun's famous endorsement of superstition over knowledge and his call for "divine thought" to overcome the fraudulence of reason and reasoning. Or, to use his metaphor of the Mara Poet, a post-Tian'anmen writer is supposed to exert his or her demonic power so as to unveil the invisible of the real.

Finally, let me add a few words about the Chinese title of *Beijing Coma*, *Rouzhitu* 肉之土. *Rou* means flesh or meat; *tu* means land, soil, or earth and sometimes connotes tomb; and *zhi* is a possessive particle. The two characters *rou* and *tu* together can be literally translated as, for example, "meat earth," "fleshy tomb," and "land of flesh," all of which sound awkward. It is not difficult to see why Ma's English-language publisher chose *Beijing Coma* as the title instead. To be sure, the Chinese title vividly conveys the image of protesters' bodies flattened on location by the tanks, as well as the comalike inertia of the afterlives of the incident. Still, one tends to overlook the fact that *rou (zhi) tu* is also related to the *Classic of Mountains and Seas*. Also called *taisui* 太歲, *rouyuan* 肉芫, *shirou*, 視肉, or *turou* 土肉, *routu* refers to a fungus (*ganoderma lucidum*) with a texture resembling that of both meat and vegetable. In Guo Pu's 郭璞 annotated version of the *Classic of Mountains and Seas*, it is described as having "eyes but no stomach, flesh shaped like an ox liver, capable of reproducing itself and therefore staying generative forever."[47] In other words, it is something between the human and the posthuman. Ma thus drives home the afterlife of—and the life after—the Tian'anmen incident.

Compare Ma Jian's novel to Han Song's *Hospital*, a trilogy about a medical dystopia turned into a cosmic nightmare. The three parts of the trilogy are *Yiyuan* 醫院 (Hospital, 2016), *Qumo* 驅魔 (Exorcism, 2017) and *Wangling* 亡靈 (Dead souls, 2018), each focusing on a space where the topos of the hospital metamorphoses into something unexpected. Han has described the themes of the three parts as a progressive sequence of human civilization, from the "drug era" (*yaoshidai* 藥時代) to the "drug battle" (*yaozhanzheng* 藥戰爭) and then the "drug empire" (*yaodiguo* 藥帝國).

In the first volume of the trilogy, the protagonist Yang Wei 楊偉 (whose name sounds like yangwei 陽痿 [impotence]), a middle-aged reporter and poet, goes on a business trip to C City. Falling sick after drinking a bottle of mineral water, he goes to see a doctor at a local hospital. What is supposed to be a minor case quickly turns into a Kafkaesque nightmare. Yang travels from one department to another and is ordered to take all sorts of tests, but he can never receive a clear diagnosis. He ends up staying in the dirty, crowded hospital day after day, finding no way out. As a matter of fact, he appears to be trapped in the hospital forever. Meanwhile, he has one strange encounter after another, including an unlikely romance and a brush with a malicious mass murder conspiracy.

In *Exorcism*, Yang Wei appears to be still hospitalized, only eventually coming to realize that the hospital is actually on a ship floating in the "red sea"—while everything, including the sea, turns out to be controlled by algorithms. At the mercy of an invisible artificial intelligence, the patients and doctors are set in motion by various programs, and no one is exempt from the eternal cycle of disease and treatment. The hospital is nothing but a huge simulacrum. As Han puts it, this is a "drug era": everyone is born to be sick and therefore subject to repetitive medical care—and medical abuse—ad infinitum. As a matter of fact, the hospital has proven to be the reality of human existence:

> Doctors create the next universe by prescribing and disseminating medicine, and cultivating patients. . . . The eternal hospital is neither hell nor

heaven. Lonely, ultimately lonely . . . but the Captain believes the other shore will suddenly rise up, just like bubbles amid a deluge of sterilizing fluid.[48]

Han's trilogy culminates in *Dead Souls*, in which a huge hospital is established on Mars thirty thousand years after the extinction of civilization on earth. The title *Dead Souls* is naturally a reference Nikolai Gogol's *Dead Souls*, which Lu Xun translated as *Sihunling* 死魂靈 (Dead souls, 1935–36). Thanks to the remarkable technology of the Martian hospital, the dead are continuously resurrected and the ruined reborn. Once death and life have become a programable and repeatable part of a huge mechanism, a posthuman kind of transmigration—"meta-death" and "meta-life," in Han's words—becomes the nature of existence. Through the microcosm of an infinite hospital, Han drives home the message that appears in almost all his works: we live and die in a doomed eternity. The critic Zhang Fan urges us to imagine the scene: "The cosmos has become a field of life and death, a gigantic hospital. On Mars, thirty thousand years from now, a hospital is erected amid mist and dust. The hospital has internalized and eternalized productivity and technology, replacing family, the nation, distribution, and labor, to become the sole superstructure, infrastructure and form of existence. Medical AI [artificial intelligence] controls human life and death, health and disease; gender rights have been abolished; traditional morality demolished. Human society boils down to the relationship between doctors and patients; the human gains immortality while yearning for death."[49]

The above summary cannot do justice to the stupendous trilogy, which is filled with a seemingly inexhaustible series of ghoulish episodes, grotesque figures, and sublime scenes of the wildest kind. Known for his engagement with the "the fear of seeing,"[50] Han has created in his previous works various liminal and transitory spaces—from subways to high-speed railroads, and from the "cosmic tomb" to the "red ocean"—in which the human is forced into endless hallucinatory trials while suffering "realistic" horror and pain. Michel Foucault would have welcomed Han Song as a Chinese interpreter of heterotopia. Han's transient spaces are always under some conspiratorial spell, and his promised horizons and destinations all prove to be euphemisms for yet another dimension of closure and incarceration.

The hospital represents the epitome of his ontological claustrophobia, a space-time that annuls the past and future of not only mankind but also the universe.

Like Ma Jian's *Beijing Coma*, Han Song's trilogy easily suggests a political allegory. Haunted by the image of the so-called sick man of Asia, forerunners of modern Chinese writers from Liu E 劉鶚 to Lu Xun and Chen Duxiu 陳獨秀 (1879–1942) were obsessed with disease as a metaphor of China in crisis. In subsequent decades diseases such as leukemia, tuberculosis, syphilis, and AIDS were cited to symbolize Chinese malaises from individual ennui to bureaucratic corruption, and from medical malfunction to political tyranny. It is leftist literature, nevertheless, that spells out the hospital as the venue in which all the above syndromes are confronted. Ding Ling's story "Zai yiyuan zhong" 在醫院中 (In the hospital, 1941), an exposé of the dark side of a hospital and a reflection on the terms of self-sacrifice in Yan'an, is arguably the most provocative confrontation of the party line written during that era. In the wake of his Yan'an talks on literature and art in May 1942, Mao Zedong launched a rectification campaign, pushing the therapeutic symbolism of party politics to the extreme under the slogan "fix the past mistakes so as to forestall the future ones, cure the sick so as to save the people" (*chengxian bihou, zhibing jiuren* 懲先毖後, 治病救人).[51]

When Han Song likens Chinese society to a monstrous hospital, he envisions at the same time a "drug empire" ruled by the Maoist laboratory. This is not only a political allegory but a medical punk fiction, a form that mixes posthuman technological vision with an exposé of the most vicious crimes. In *Exorcism*, Han introduces the doctors and directors in charge of the hospital, revealing bit by bit that they are all part of an artificial intelligence running amok. They are on a mission to kill patients so as to resurrect them, or to infect them with incurable viruses so as to treat them. Most intriguingly, Han tells us that the overarching mechanism by which the artificial intelligence operates the hospital is literature: only literature has the power to create and destroy anything as efficiently as the hospital.

In the middle of *Exorcism*, the patients launch a mutiny on the medical ship, and they send Yang Wei to discover the secrets of the hospital administration. This investigation leads to one of the most chilling dialogues in modern Chinese literature. Yang Wei runs into Dr. Immortality—who, though he is nicknamed "the sower of evil," turns out to be a literature lover. Dr. Immortality states, "a doctor cannot understand the entirety of life even if he has dissected thousands of dead bodies . . . fortunately, we have literature." From Shakespeare to Cao Xueqin 曹雪琴, from Tolstoy to Su Dongpo 蘇東坡, literature contains the full spectrum of sickness and health, a fact that leads Dr. Immortality to the conclusion that "the essence of everything is nothing but literature."[52] He therefore oversees two programs that have been implanted into patients' bodies, one controlling lived selfhood and the other narrated selfhood. He then monitors—really, manipulates—the narrative mechanism so as to modify the patients' records and memories and modulate their pain. He comments, "Medical treatment is first and foremost a matter of belief; life may as well be a menu of assorted treatments." Of all advanced medical technologies, Dr. Immortality declares, "the most important is to tell the good hospital story."[53]

Thus, Han Song has provided an intriguing response to President Xi's 2013 dictum "tell the good China story," a response that has become downright uncanny as, in the midst of the coronavirus outbreak in 2020, Xi called on Chinese citizens to "tell the good China story of fighting the epidemic." Some did not need Xi's prompting. Li Wenliang 李文亮 (1986–2020), a medical whistle-blower, attempted to warn the authorities about the coming crisis in late 2019 and was punished for spreading what was called a rumor. Li contracted the virus from a patient and died three days after Xi's call for a good story; he was later officially honored as a "martyr." Was Li's a good story?

But instead of just poking fun at the Chinese president, Han Song prods us to think more about the quintessential dilemma present since the genesis of modern Chinese literature, as dramatized by Lu Xun's decision to drop medicine in favor of literature in 1906. Let us revisit Lu Xun's statement:

> The people of a weak, backward country, even though they may enjoy sturdy health, can only serve as the senseless material of an audience for public executions. . . . Our first task was surely to transform their spirits, and I thought at that time that literature could best meet the task of spiritual transformation. I then began to think about promoting literary activities.[54]

If, with this statement, Lu Xun made a career decision that helped give rise to modern Chinese literature, Han Song has rebutted the master's logic by giving it an ironic twist. For Dr. Immortality, literature need not provide merely a spiritual cure for sick people; rather, it is the programed language that underlies the paradigm of the medical operation. But insofar as post-socialist or postcapitalist medicine works like a double-edged sword to cure and kill the patient at the same time, literature is performing a parallel function to simultaneously enlighten and enchant the reader as patient. Or, judging by the way in which Lu Xun continuously questioned the validity of literature, perhaps Han has not rebutted the master's argument but reiterated his misgivings.

Thus, a hundred years after Lu Xun's "Diary of a Madman," Han Song wrote *Hospital* to recapitulate and even deepen some of the themes inherent in modern Chinese literature: the illusory line between disease and medicine; the tension between claustrophobia and agoraphobia; the fear and temptation of cannibalism; and, above all, literature as both a symptom of and a cure for Chinese spiritual malaise. More significantly, Han has echoed the master's twin engagement with both science and mythology, or both enlightenment and "divine thought." In the *Hospital* trilogy, while the technology of reproducing and controlling human life and death reminds one of "The Art of Creating Humanity," in which the human sprout is processed to become a specimen for scientific experimentation, the voyage of the hospital on the "red sea" and through outer space comes across like a posthuman version of the *Classic of Mountains and Seas*—an endless parade of extraterrestrial monsters and cybernetic phantoms.

The *Hospital* trilogy starts with a mysterious spaceship operated by two monks and a nun heading toward the immense darkness of the galaxy—on a mission in search of Buddha. Toward the end of *Dead Souls*, we see that the patients and doctors are trapped in yet another cycle of transmigration in the hospital on Mars, while destroying each other under the gaze of Avalokitesvara or Guanyin, the goddess of mercy. Are they robotic phantasms or dead souls? Can the goddess of mercy offer salvation? With these questions, Han Song seems to be projecting a postapocalyptic vision in seeking the source of transillumination, and casting an equivocal look at divinity, or "divine thought," as the last hope of redeeming the monster that is fiction.

Notes

Chapter 1

1. Xi said: "對世界形勢發展變化, 對世界上出現的新事物新情況, 對各國出現的新思想新觀點新知識, 我們要加強宣傳報道, 以利於積極借鑒人類文明創造的有益成果。要精心做好對外宣傳工作, 創新對外宣傳方式, 著力打造融通中外的新概念新范疇新表述, 講好中國故事, 傳播好中國聲音." See "Xi Jinping zhongyao jianghua shujuku" 習近平重要講話數據庫 Digital library of important talks by Xi Jinping), accessed February 15, 2020, http://theory.people.com.cn/BIG5/n1/2019/0222/c40531-30897581.html. Unless otherwise noted, all translations from the Chinese are mine.

2. The Chinese title for the campaign 講好中國故事 has also been translated as "tell the China story well."

3. Xi said: "生動講述防疫抗疫一線的感人事蹟，講好中國抗擊疫情故事." See Xi Jinping's talk to the Standing Committee of the Political Bureau, accessed February 20, 2020, http://www.moe.gov.cn/jyb_xwfb/s6052/moe_838/202002/t20200203_417633.html.

4. Zhao Yanjing 趙燕菁, "Jinkua jianli zhongguo hexin kangji xushi 儘快建立中國核心抗疫敘事 (Expedite the making of the core narrative of combating coronavirus)," http://www.aisixiang.com/data/120808.html; Li Yongjin 李咏瑾, "Ganzhi zhenshi kelidu" 感知真實顆粒度 (Feel the graininess of truth), accessed April 16, 2020, http://www.bjd.com.cn/a/202004/16/WS5e97356be4b0df866aa95a7a.html.

5. Wang Hui 汪暉, "Gemingzhe renge yu shengli zhexue: jinian Liening danchen 150 zhounian" 革命者人格與勝利的哲學: 紀念列寧誕辰150周年 (Revolutionary personality and the philosophy of triumph: Commemorating the 150th anniversary of Lenin), accessed April 26, 2020, https://www.guancha.cn/wang-hui/2020_04_22_547798_6.shtml.

6. The anonymous editor wrote: "善講故事是古今中外著名政治家、思想家的共同特點, 更是中國共產黨領袖的過人本領" (Xi Jinping, *Xi Jinping jiang gushi*, 1).

7. Mao told the story on June 11, 1945. See Alan Lawrance, *China since 1919, Revolution and Reform*, 103–4; David E. Apter and Tony Saich, *Revolutionary Discourse in Mao's Republic*, 77–78.

8. Mao Zedong, "Jiangeming jinxing daodi" 將革命進行到底 (Carry on the revolution to the end), in Mao Zedong, *Zhongwen makesizhuyi wenku* 中文馬克思主義文庫 (Library of Marxist thought in Chinese), accessed February 14, 2020, https://www.marxists.org/chinese/maozedong/marxist.org-chinese-mao-19481230.htm.

9. President Donald Trump is also fond of a version of this parable. See Dara Lind, "'The Snake': Donald Trump Brings Back His Favorite Anti-Immigrant Fable at CPAC," *Vox*, February 23, 2018, https://www.vox.com/policy-and-politics/2018/2/23/17044744/trump-snake-speech-cpac.

10. Michel Foucault's "regime of truth" refers to "the types of discourse which it accepts and makes function as true; the mechanisms and instances which enable one to distinguish true and false statements, the means by which each is sanctioned; the techniques and procedures accorded value in the acquisition of truth" (*Power/Knowledge*, 131). See also Jacques Rancière's concept of "artistic regimes," which he describes as "a specific type of connection between ways of producing works of art or developing practices, forms of visibility that disclose them, and ways of conceptualizing the former and the latter" (*The Politics of Aesthetics*, 20).

11. Theodor Adorno, *In Search of Wagner*, 85.

12. Slavoj Žižek, *The Sublime Object of Ideology*.

13. One finds in Xi's use of *gushi* a fascinating mixture of these levels of meaning, and all the while the term is charged with the discursive power unique to the Chinese communist legacy. That is, with its oral, grassroots implication and popular (even populist) appeal, storytelling has always functioned as a powerful vehicle of mass communication: it aims at casting the past in a new light, as well as presenting a future beyond the conventional imagination. In Apter and Saich's classic *Revolutionary Discourse in Mao's Republic*, the authors even propose that storytelling was the force that generated the solidarity among party members and the people during and after the Yan'an era.

14. Liang Qichao 梁啟超, "Lun xiaoshuo yu qunzhi zhiguanxi" 論小說與群治之關係 (On the relationship between fiction and ruling the people), 2:758.

15. For a detailed discussion of the traditional Chinese understanding of literature as a process of manifestation with regard to the movements of the world, distinct from the Western conceptions of mimesis and representation, see Stephen Owen, *Readings in Chinese Literary Thought*, 20–21. Also see Kirk Denton, *Modern Chinese Literary Thought*, 9.

16. Many things forced Liang to abandon the writing of the novel, including his changing political agenda. See Xia Xiaohong 夏曉虹, *Jueshi yu chuanshi: Liang Qichao de wenxue daolu* 覺世與傳世: 梁啓超的文學道路 (From enlightenment to canonization: the literary road of Liang Qichao), 68–69.

17. For more interpretations of the Chinese Dream, see "Transcript: Xi Jinping's Speech at the Unveiling of the New Chinese Leadership," November 15, 2012, https://www.scmp.com/news/18th-party-congress/article/1083153/transcript-xi-jinpings-speech-unveiling-new-chinese. See also "The Chinese Dream Infuses Socialism with Chinese Characteristics with New Energy," May 6, 2013, https://chinacopyrightandmedia.wordpress.com/2013/05/06/the-chinese-dream-infuses-socialism-with-chinese-characteristics-with-new-energy.

18. David Der-wei Wang, *Fin-de-siècle Splendor*, 301–9.

19. Lu Xun, "Zixu" 自序 (Preface to *Nahan* 吶喊 [A Call to Arms]), 1:417. I am using the translation in Lu Hsun, "Preface to *Call to Arms*," 3.

20. David Der-wei Wang, *The Monster That Is History*, 16–18.

21. Leo Ou-fan Lee, *Voices from the Iron House*, 18.

22. Shen Congwen, "Sange nanzi he yige nüren" 三個男子和一個女人 (Three men and one woman), 8:34.

23. Ibid., 8:34–35.

24. See David Der-wei Wang, *The Lyrical in Epic Time*, 25.

25. *Arabian Nights*, 1:1.

26. Apter and Saich, *Revolutionary Discourse in Mao's Republic*, 75.

27. Ibid.

28. Ibid. Also see Gao Hua 高華 *Hongtaiyang shizenyang shengqide* 紅太陽是怎樣升起的:延安整風運動的來龍去脈 (How did the red sun rise?).

29. Apter and Saich, *Revolutionary Discourse in Mao's Republic*, 34.

30. Ibid.

31. Max Weber, *The Sociology of Religion*, 270. Weber is credited with popularizing the term in a lecture given in 1918 and in *The Sociology of Religion* in 1920. See Eu Jin Chua, "Disenchantment," *Encyclopaedia Britannica*, accessed April 19, 2020, https://www.britannica.com/topic/disenchantment-sociology.

32. Max Weber, *The Protestant Ethic and The Spirit of Capitalism*. For a detailed discussion, see, for example, Malcolm H. Mackinnon, "Max Weber's Disenchantment Lineages of Kant and Channing."

33. Here I am referring to the "real" in Žižek's definition (*The Sublime Object of Ideology*, 47–48.

34. Rey Chow, *Primitive Passions*, 22–23.

35. According to Peter Brooks, the moral occult refers to "the domain of operative spiritual values which is both indicated within and masked by the surface of reality" (*The Melodramatic Imagination*, 5).

36. Walter Benjamin, *Illuminations*, 108–109.

37. John W. Treat, "Arendt in Asia."

38. Seyla Benhabib, "Hannah Arendt and the Redemptive Power of Narrative," 113.

39. For a recent study of Arendt and storytelling, see, for example, Michael Jackson, *The Politics of Storytelling*. Also see Paul Ricoeur, "Action, Story and History."

40. Quoted in Treat, "Arendt in Asia," 425.

41. Hannah Arendt, "Understanding and Politics," 321.

42. Fina Birulés, "Contingency, History and Narration in Hannah Arendt," 123.

43. Mikhail Bakhtin, *Rabelais and His World*.

44. The concept of fabulation first appears in Gilles Deleuze, *Cinema 2*, 145. It was translated as "story-telling" and linked to the "powers of the false." But as Roland

Bogue notes, the concept has related antecedents in Deleuze's discussion of the Nietzschean artist as cultural physician. See Ronald Bogue, "Fabulation," *The Deleuze Dictionary*, accessed March 15, 2020, http://deleuze.enacademic.com/61/fabulation.

45. Ronald Bogue, *Deleuzian Fabulation and the Scars of History*, 46.

46. Gilles Deleuze, *Essays Critical and Clinical*, 26. Also see Gilles Deleuze and Félix Guattari, *What Is Philosophy?*

47. For a historical overview, see Lu Xun, *A Brief History of Chinese Fiction*. Also see Patrick Hanan, "The Development of Fiction and Drama"; Paul S. Ropp, "The Distinctive Art of Chinese Fiction."

48. *Sanyan* refers to three storytelling collection compiled by the late Ming literatus Feng Menglong 馮夢龍 (1574–1646): *Yushi mingyan* 喻世明言 (Illustrious tales to instruct the world, 1620), *Jingshi tongyan* 警世通言 (Comprehensive tales to admonish the world, 1624), and *Xingshi hengyan* 醒世恒言 (Lasting tales to awaken the world, 1627). *Erpai* refers two storytelling collections compiled by the late Ming literatus Ling Mengchu 凌蒙初 (1580–1644) *Chuke paian jingqi* 初刻拍案驚奇; *Erke paian jingqi* 二刻拍案驚奇 (Striking the table in amazement at the wonders; first and second editions, 1628, 1632).

49. The four works are *Sanguo yanyi* 三國演義 (Romance of the three kingdoms), *Xiyouji* 西遊記 (Journey to the West), *Shuihuzhuan* 水滸傳 (Water margin), and *Hongloumeng* 紅樓夢 (Dream of the red chamber).

50. The original is: "史統散而小說興。始乎周季, 盛於唐, 而浸淫於宋。韓非、列禦寇諸人, 小說之祖也。《吳越春秋》等書, 雖出炎漢, 然秦火之後, 著述猶希。迨開元以降, 而文人之筆橫矣。若通俗演義, 不知何昉? . . . 按南宋供奉局, 有說話人, 如今說書之流, 其文必通俗, 其作者莫可考。大抵唐人選言, 入於文心; 宋人通俗, 諧於里耳。天下之文心少而里耳多, 則小說之資於選言者少, 而資於通俗者多。試今說話人當場描寫, 可喜可愕, 可悲可涕, 可歌可舞; 再欲捉刀, 再欲下拜, 再欲決脰, 再欲捐金; 怯者勇, 淫者貞, 薄者敦, 頑鈍者汗下。雖小誦《孝經》、《論語》, 其感人未必如是之捷且深也。" Feng Menglong, *Stories Old and New*, 5–6.

51. Giorgio Agamben, "What Is Contemporary?," 40.

52. C. T. Hsia, "Obsession with China."

53. C. T. Hsia's *A History of Modern Chinese Fiction* remains the most influential book about modern Chinese literary history in the English-speaking world. Although it has been criticized, particularly among leftist circles, for endorsing Cold War ideology, Western liberal humanism, and New Criticism, one cannot overlook its polemical power.

54. Inspired by Deleuzian discourse, I describe immanence as a self-generative agency inherent in any existing entity, as opposed to transcendence that projects the a priori emanation of power from the metaphysical realm.

55. See also the discussion of Lu Xun's concept of darkness in terms of Agamben's concept of the beam of darkness in chapter 5.

56. Václav Havel, "Stories and Totalitarianism," *Index on Censorship*, March 1988, https://journals.sagepub.com/doi/pdf/10.1080/03064228808534381.

Chapter 2

1. C. T. Hsia, "Obsession with China," 536–37.

2. According to Shao Yanjun of Peking University, a leading scholar of Chinese internet literature, as of 2018, there were 400,000,000 subscribers to internet literature and 680,000 contract writers (writers who write under a long- or short-term contract with an internet publishing conglomerate), of whom 320,000 wrote full time. See Shao Yanjun 邵燕君, "Wangluo wenxue shifou keyi tanlun jingdian?" 網絡文學是否可以談論經典? (Can one talk about canonical works of internet literature?).

3. Gilles Deleuze and Félix Guattari, *Anti-Oedipus*.

4. See Clifford Geertz, *Local Knowledge*, particularly the discussion of the interplay between law and fact in the making of local knowledge (ibid., 173); Pierre Bourdieu, "The Force of Law," 838, quoted in Kieran Dolin, *Fiction and the Law*, 11.

5. See Hugh T. Scogin Jr., "Civil 'Law' in Traditional China"; Geertz, *Local Knowledge*, 167–234. In her study of the relationship between literature, law, and philosophy in eighteenth- and nineteenth-century American literature, Wai Chee Dimock describes four forms that constitute the "program of justice": corrective, distributive, compensatory, and revolutionary (*Residues of Justice*, introduction). Dimock's argument is based on rethinking justice as an ontological given and justice as a historical praxis subject to the debate of "commensurability" (ibid.).

6. I am referring in particular to Nancy Armstrong and Leonard Tennenhouse, introduction.

7. Giorgio Agamben, *State of Exception*. See also Walter Benjamin, "Critique of Violence"; Luis Guzmán, "Benjamin's Divine Violence."

8. I am referring to Christopher Prendergast, *The Order of Mimesis*.

9. Yan Fu 嚴復 and Xia Zengyou 夏曾佑, "Benguan fuyin shuobu yuanqi" 本館附印說部緣起 (An announcement of publishing fiction in our press).

10. See David Der-wei Wang, *Fin-de-siècle Splendor*, 36–42.

11. Liang Qichao 梁啟超, "Lun xiaoshuo yu qunzhi zhiguanxi" 論小說與群治之關係 (On the relationship between fiction and ruling the people), 2:758.

12. See, for example, C. T. Hsia, "Yan Fu and Liang Ch'i-ch'ao as Advocates of New Fiction."

13. Liang Qichao 梁啟超, "Yiyin zhengzhi xiaoshuo xu" 譯印政治小說序 (Preface to our series of political novels in translation), 153.

14. Yan and Xia, "Benguan fuyin shuobu yuanqi," 1.

15. Liang Qichao 梁啟超, "Lun xiaoshuo yu qunzhi zhi guanqi," quoted in C. T. Hsia, "Yan Fu and Liang Ch'i-ch'ao as Advocates of New Fiction," 237–238.

16. Jacques Derrida, "Plato's Pharmacy."

17. Juiwo 覺我 (pseudonym of Xu Nianci 徐念慈), "Yu zhi xiaoshuo guan" 余之小說觀 (My view of fiction), in Chen Pingyuan and Xia Xiaohong, 314.

18. Quoted in C. T. Hsia, "Yan Fu and Liang Ch'i-ch'ao as Advocates of New Fiction," 257.

19. See ibid.

20. Lu Xun, "The Diary of a Madman," 18.

21. Marston Anderson, *The Limits of Realism*, 1–26. See also the discussion of Mao Dun in David Der-wei Wang, *Fictional Realism in 20th-Century China*, 67–101.

22. For a classic study of the Yan'an talks and the literary and political practice they inspired, see, for example, Merle Goldman, *Literary Dissent in Communist China*, 1–50.

23. See David Der-wei Wang, *The Monster That Is History*, 161–69.

24. Ibid., 162.

25. For a survey of the modern dimensions of the ideological novel, see Susan Rubin Suleiman, *Authoritarian Fictions*, 1–23 (especially 22–23).

26. This scene appears only in the 2003 edition of *Long Live Youth*, which partly restored Wang Meng's 1956 manuscript. In all the earlier versions of this novel, this scene of over six pages is deleted. See Wang Meng, *Qingchun wansui*, 315–20. Also see Mingwei Song, "The Taming of the Youth."

27. See, for example, Xiaobin Yang, *The Chinese Postmodern*; Xudong Zhang, *Chinese Modernism in the Era of Reform*; Jin Wang, *High Culture Fever*.

28. For a definition of "Maoist discourse" (Mao wenti), see Li Tuo 李陀, "Xuebeng hechu" 雪崩何處 (Where is the avalanche?).

29. David Der-wei Wang, afterword, 244–45.

30. Sigmund Freud, "The Uncanny," 241.

31. For more on Jaroslav Průšek's discussion of the lyrical and the epic modes of modern Chinese literature, see Leo Ou-fan Lee, *The Lyrical and the Epic*. See also David Der-wei Wang, *The Lyrical in Epic Time*, 28–38.

32. Nat Brandt, *Massacre in Shansi*, (Syracuse: Syracuse University Press, 1999), xii. For general background information, see Henrietta Harrison, *The Missionary's Curse and Other Tales from a Chinese Catholic Village*.

33. Li Rui (李銳), *Zhang Mading de Dibatian* 張馬丁的第八天 (The eighth day of Zhang Mading), 213.

34. Ma Ka-fai 馬家輝, *Longtou fengwei* 龍頭鳳尾 (Dragon head, phoenix tale), 172.

35. Eileen Chang 張愛玲, *Qingcheng zhilian* 傾城之戀 (Love in a fallen city), 233.

36. In a broader theoretical context, I am thinking of Agamben's argument in *State of Exception*.

37. Giorgio Agamben, *Homo Sacer*.

38. Michel Foucault, *Power/Knowledge*, 31.

39. See David Der-wei Wang, *The Monster That Is History*, 233-35.

40. For more information about Fang Fang's *Soft Burial*, see, for instance, see Luou Siling 羅四翎 "Zaozuopai weigong, zuojia Fang Fang tan Ruanmai de ruanmai" 遭左派圍攻, 作家方方談《軟埋》的《軟埋》的軟埋" (Attacked by the leftists, writer Fang Fang on the soft burial of her novel *Soft Burial*), *New York Times*, Chinese edition, accessed April 21, 2020, https://cn.nytimes.com/china/20170627/cc27fang-fang/.

41. Yan Geling, *Lufan Yanshi*; Gao Xingjian, *Yigeren de shengjing*.

42. Haiyan Lee, *The Stranger and the Chinese Moral Imagination*, 207–8.

43. Michael Dutton, "Mango Mao," 169. See also Haiyan Lee, *The Stranger and the Chinese Moral Imagination*, 208.

44. Dutton, "Mango Mao," 169.

45. For an overarching description of concentration camp literature, see, for example, Yenna Wu and Philip Williams, *The Great Wall of Confinement*.

46. Hannah Arendt, "Understanding and Politics," 321.

47. Gang Gary Xu, "My Writing, Your Pain, and Her Trauma." For a different argument, see Carlos Rojas, "Without [Femin]ism," 169.

48. Gao Xingjian, "The Case for Literature," accessed March 15, 2020, https://www.nobelprize.org/prizes/literature/2000/gao/25532-gao-xingjian-nobel-lecture-2000-2/.

49. Ibid.

50. Ibid.

51. Paul Ricoeur, *The Symbolism of Evil*. See also Richard Kearney, "On the Hermeneutics of Evil." For a discussion of Ricoeur and suspicion as a condition of possibility, see Alison Scott-Baumann, *Ricoeur and the Hermeneutics of Suspicion*, 73.

52. Gao, "The Case for Literature."

53. Rojas, "Without [Femin]ism," 188. In Rojas's words, "this technique is mirrored, at a more formal level, through the novel's use of shifting personal pronouns to designate different facets of the narrator's persona, as well as the varying degrees of alienation from the perspectives they each represent" (ibid., 189).

54. Gao Xingjian, *One Man's Bible*, 426.

55. Gao 高行健, "Ziyou yu wenxue" 自由與文學 (Freedom and literature) 53. See also Liu Zaifu 劉再復, "Gao Xingjian de ziyou yuanli" 高行健的自由原理 (The principle of Gao Xingjian's freedom), accessed April 21, 2020, http://gb.oversea.cnki.net/KCMS/detail/detail.aspx?filename=HWWX201203009&dbcode=CJFD&dbname=CJFD2012.

56. I am borrowing Leo Strauss's concept in *Persecution and the Art of Writing*.

57. Gao, "The Case for Literature."

58. Wu Ming-yi, *Fuyanren*.

59. See David Der-wei Wang, *Fin-de-siècle Splendor*, 252–312.

60. Mingwei Song, "Chinese Science Fiction Presents the Posthuman Future." I thank Mingwei Song for numerous consultations on Han Song, Liu Cixin, and science fiction in general.

61. Quoted in Lee Yu-lin, “Fabulating a Possible Island: The Symbiosis between Ecology and Indigeneity in Wu Ming-yi’s *The Man with the Compound Eyes*,” unpublished paper.

62. Ibid.

63. Wu Ming-yi, *The Man with the Compound Eyes*, 276. The original is: “他的眼睛跟我們的眼睛不太一樣, 有點不太像是一顆眼睛, 而是由無數的眼睛組合起來的複眼, 像是雲、山、河流、雲雀和山羌的眼睛, 組合而成的眼睛。我定神一看, 每一顆眼睛裏彷彿都各有一個風景, 而那些風景, 組合成我從未見過的一幅更巨大的風景。”

64. Wu Ming-yi, *Fuguang* 浮光 (Floating lights), 151.

65. Ibid., 146.

66. Gilles Deleuze and Fèlix Guattari, *A Thousand Plateaus*, 237.

67. *Santi* (“three body”) refers to a theoretical problem that mathematicians have been trying to solve for the past two centuries. Basic information on the problem in relation to Liu’s novels can be found in Song Mingwei 宋明煒, *Kehuan xiaoshuo xinlangchao* 科幻小說新浪潮 (New wave science fiction in China), 140-91. Also see Mingwei Song, “Chinese Science Fiction Presents the Posthuman Future.”

68. Jia Liyuan 賈立元, *Zhujiu women de weilai* 築就我們的未來 (Achieving our future), 30–46.

69. Liu Cixin, *The Dark Forest*, 484.

70. Nick Richardson, “Even What Doesn’t Happen Is Epic,” *London Book Reviews* 40, no. 3 (February 8, 2018), https://www.lrb.co.uk/v40/n03/nick-richardson/even-what-doesnt-happen-is-epic.

71. The “community of a shared future of mankind” is a concept presented in 2012 by Hu Jintao (then general secretary of the Chinese Communist Party) and advocated by Xi Jinping (the current general secretary). Xi first proposed the concept in an international arena at the Moscow State Institute of International Relations in March 2013, and he mentioned it again in a speech to the World Economic Forum at Davos in January 2017. For more information, see Zhao Qing and Lin Hao, “Commentary: Building a Community with Shared Future for Mankind Key to Maintaining Peace, Prosperity in Asia-Pacific,” June 12, 2019, http://www.xinhuanet.com/english/2019-06/02/c_138111345.htm.

Chapter 3

1. Swedish Academy, “The Nobel Prize in Literature 2012: Mo Yan,” October 11, 2012, https://www.nobelprize.org/prizes/literature/2012/press-release/.

2. Mo Yan, *Life and Death Are Wearing Me Out*, 266.

3. According to the interpretation of Master Shenyan 聖嚴法師, “Too much desire brings pain. Death and rebirth are wearisome ordeals, originating from our thoughts of greed and lust. By lessening desires, we can realize absolute truth and enjoy peace,

freedom, and health in body and mind" (多欲為苦。生死疲勞。從貪欲起。少欲無為。心自在) (*Badareren juejing* 八大人覺經 [Eighth great awakening sutra)], 19).

4. Christopher Prendergast, *The Order of Mimesis*.

5. Michel Foucault, *Le corps utopique suivi de les hétérotopies*, 10. I am using the translation in Xu Shuang, "Traveling through Time and Searching for Utopia," 147.

6. Foucault, *Le corps utopique suivi de les hétérotopies*, 10. The translation is from Xu Shuang, "Traveling through Time and Searching for Utopia," 147.

7. Foucault, *Le corps utopique suivi de les hétérotopies*, 17. The translation is from Xu Shuang, "Traveling through Time and Searching for Utopia," 148.

8. For the fantastic tradition in ancient Chinese literature and its variations, see Yang Yi 楊義, *Zhongguo gudian xiaoshuo shilun* 中國古典小說史論 (History of classical Chinese fiction), chapters 4 and 8; Li Jianguo 李建國, *Tangqian zhiguai xiaoshuo jishi* 唐前志怪小說集釋 (Annotated collection of pre-Tang *zhiguai* fiction). Also see Karl Kao, *Classical Tales of the Supernatural and the Fantastic*, introduction; Kenneth DeWoskin, "The Six Dynasties *Chih-kuai* and the Birth of Fiction."

9. See Yang Yi, *Zhongguo gudian xiaoshuo shilun*, chapters 4, 8, 12, and 20. Also see Chen Pingyuan 陳平原, "Zhongguo xiaoshuo shilun" 中國小說史論 (A history of Chinese fiction), 1495–1506 and 1533–41; Cheng Yizhong 程毅中, *Shenguai qingxia de yishu shijie* 神怪情俠的藝術世界 (The world of the supernatural, the romantic, and the chivalric).

10. Lu Xun, *Zhongguo xiaoshuo shilui* 中國小說史略 (A brief history of Chinese fiction), 230.

11. Ibid. Maruo Tuneki 丸尾常喜 has pointed out Lu Xun's comments on *Hedian* 何典 (What sort of book is this?), a major late Qing novel on the ghostly themes (*Ren yu gui de jiuge* 人與鬼的糾葛 [The entanglements between ghosts and humanity], 162).

12. To be sure, nineteenth-century European realist fiction contains numerous elements of the supernatural, in forms ranging from tales within tales to dream sequences and narrated hallucinations. Verisimilitude was considered to include realistic portrayals of primitive people, women, children, madness, dreams, daydreams, hallucinations, science fiction, and ideology—the spectral according to a positivist standard. A superb example can be found the arch-realist Gustave Flaubert's *The Temptation of St. Anthony*, in which the Christian myth of saintly self-torture is imagined by a deluded disciple of historicism.

13. Zhou Zuoren also said that he did not believe in the immortality of soul ("Gui xianhua" 鬼閒話 [On gossiping about the ghosts], 21).

14. Quoted in Maruo, *Ren yu gui de jiuge*, 215–16. See also Qian Liqun 錢理群, *Zhou Zuoren lun* 周作人論 (A study of Zhou Zuoren), chapter 9.

15. Quoted in T. A. Hsia, *The Gate of Darkness*, 159.

16. See Huang Jinlin 黃金麟, *Lishi, shenti, guojia* 歷史, 身體, 國家 (History, body, nation), chapter 2.

17. See Ban Wang, *The Sublime Figure of History*, chapters 2 and 6.

18. Chiang Kai-shek 蔣介石, "Xin shenghuo yundong gangling" 新生活運動綱領 (Guidelines of the New Life Movement), 30.

19. Ibid., 33–34.

20. See T. A. Hsia, *The Gate of Darkness*, 148; Leo Oufan Lee, *Voices from the Iron House*, chapters 3–4; Wang Xiaoming 王曉明, *Wufa zhimian de rensheng* 無法直面的人生 (A life that cannot be faced up to); Wang Hui 汪暉, "Sihuo chongwen" 死活重溫 (A rekindled dead fire).

21. Quoted in T. A. Hsia, *The Gate of Darkness*, 148. Lu Xun expressed the same feeling in a September 24, 1924, letter to his friend Li Bingzhong: "I have always felt that my soul is filled with something poisonous and ghostly (*guiqi* 鬼氣). I hate it, and want to get rid of it, but I cannot" (*Lu Xun shuxin ji [shang]*, 魯迅書信集上 (Lu Xun's correspondence [part 1], 61).

22. In the wake of T. A. Hsia's study, the Japanese scholar MaruoTuneki has even devoted a book-length study to Lu Xun's obsession with ghosts in his works (*Ren yu gui de jiuge*).

23. Lu Xun, *Yecao* 野草 (Wild grass).

24. The quote is from a statement made by He Jingzhi 賀敬之, one of the coauthors of the Yan'an version of *Baimao nü*. See Meng Yue 孟悦, "*Baimao nü* yanbian de qishi" 白毛女演變的啓示 (The transformations of *The White-Haired Girl* and its significance).

25. Quoted in Dai Jinhua 戴錦華, *Yanban xi de fengfeng yuyu* 樣板戲的風風雨雨 (The stormy history of the model drama) (Beijing: Zhishi chubanshe, 1995), 7–8.

26. Ban Wang, *The Sublime Figure of History*, 1.

27. See David Der-wei Wang, "Nüzuojia de xiandai guihua" 女作家的現代鬼話 (Modernist ghost talk by Chinese women writers).

28. David Der-wei Wang, *The Monster That Is History*, 262–91.

29. The original is: "鬼之為言歸矣" ("Shixun," 3:61).

30. References to the relations between "ghost" and "that which returns" can be found in *Zuozhuan* 左傳 ("If ghosts have an abode to return to, they will not cause terror") and *Liji* 禮記 ("All creatures are destined to die; they return to the earth after death, and that is what 'ghost' means"). See *Zuozhuan* 左傳, "Zhaogong qinian" 昭公七年 (Taipei: Guangwen shuju, 1963), 1291; *Liji* 禮記, "Jiyi" 祭義 (Taieii: Xuesheng shuju, 1981), 757.

31. Sigmund Freud, "The Uncanny." For a discussion of the "uncanny" from a modern spatial point of view, see Anthony Vidler, *The Architectural Uncanny*. Han Shaogong's story adds a twist: a home by the Chinese communist definition is no longer a nuclear, private space as understood in modern Western terms but is instead a space dedicated to collective fulfillment. The strange village that the protagonist returns to is therefore a "home" now twice removed from the nostalgia for prerevolutionary society.

32. Margaret Cohen, *Profane Illumination*, 2 and 12.

33. See Jonathan Crary, *Techniques of the Observer*, 132–34. Also see Terry Castle, "Phantasmagoria."

34. Walter Benjamin, *Charles Baudelaire*, 67–101. Also see Christina Britzolakis, "Phantasmagoria."

35. Theodor Adorno, *In Search of Wagner*, 85. I am using the translation in Andreas Huyssen, *After the Great Divide*, 40.

36. Adorno, *In Search of Wagner*, 85. I am using the translation in Andreas Huyssen, *After the Great Divide*, 41. The original quote is "Its [the phantasmagoria's] perfection is at the same time the perfection of the illusion that the work of art is reality *sui generis* that constitutes itself in the realm of the absolute without having to renounce its claim to image the world." Echoing Anthony Giddens, Harry Harootunian uses the term "phantasmagoric" to describe the "experience of everydayness" in Japan as "the locale—place was penetrated and shaped by practices and knowledges distant and distinct from those received from an immediate history and culture" (*History's Disquiet*, 63. See also Anthony Giddens, *The Consequences of Modernity*, 18–19.

37. Jacques Derrida, *Specters of Marx*, 4.

38. See Peggy Kamuf, "Violence, Identity, Self-Determination and the Question of Justice"; Nigel Mapp, "Specter and Impurity." For more criticism on Derrida's book, see Michael Sprinker, *Ghostly Demarcations*.

39. Quoted in Viren Murthy, *The Political Philosophy of Zhang Taiyan*, 235.

40. Wang Hui 汪暉, *Fankang juewang* 反抗絕望 (Resisting despair), 451–452, quoted in ibid.

41. Wang Hui, "Intuition, Repetition, and Revolution," 702–4.

42. Shi Shuqing 石舒清, *Qingshuili de daozi* 清水里的刀子 (Knife in the Clear Water), 17.

43. Tsering Norbu 次仁羅布, "Fangshengyang" 放生羊 (Sheep of life release).

44. I am grateful for Jannis Chen's discussion of this subject.

45. Gilles Deleuze and Félix Guattari, *A Thousand Plateaus*, 237–38. However, the authors also write, "Cannot any animal be treated in all three ways?" (ibid., 239). Thus, these three kinds of animals are modes of relating to animals, not inherent characteristics of the animals themselves.

46. For a succinct summary of becoming animal, see Gerald L. Bruns, "Becoming-Animal."

47. Deleuze and Guattari, *A Thousand Plateaus*, 243. See also Brent Adkins, *Deleuze and Guattari's* A Thousand Plateaus, 142–44.

48. Wolfgang M. Zucker, "The Demonic," 35.

49. Tsering, "Fangshengyang," 215.

50. Emmanuel Levinas, *Totality and Infinity*, 50–51.

51. Ibid., 201.

52. Syaman, *Tiankong de yanjing.*

53. Hsin-ya Huang, "Re-Visioning Pacific Seascapes," 189.

54. Zhuangzi 莊子, "Qiushui" 秋水 (Autumn water), 6:20. The original is: "子非魚，安知魚之樂"

55. It is significant to note that in the language of Austronesia, where the Tau live, the words for "placenta" and "womb" are also the words for "land" and "sea," respectively. For an argument that Syaman represents the interface between land and sea and conflates the indigenous body with the sea or an island body, see Hsin-ya Huang, "What Does the 'World Atlas' Mean? A Chain of Islands in Oceania. . . . Modern China in Island Perspective," 849. As Huang declares in Tau, "Nu yabu o pongso yam, ala abu ku u (if it were not for the island or ocean, I would not exist)" (ibid.).

56. See Hsin-ya Huang, "Towards Trans-Pacific Ecopoetics," 118 and 135–36. For a general discussion of Taiwanese indigenous narratives, see Kuei-fen Chiu, "The Production of Indigeneity."

57. Donna Haraway, "Anthropocene, Capitalocene, Plantationocene, Chthulucene: Making Kin."

58. As compounds of percepts and affects, blocs of sensations are described as thrusts that act and affect cross sensorial and cognitive territories. See Deleuze and Guattari, *A Thousand Plateaus*, 166.

59. Max Weber, *The Protestant Ethic and The Spirit of Capitalism*. For a detailed discussion, see, for example, Malcolm H. Mackinnon, "Max Weber's Disenchantment Lineages of Kant and Channing."

60. Of course, this is Carl Schmitt's famous theory, expounded in *Political Theology*. I thank Tu Hang for calling my attention to the socialist and postsocialist Sinicization of Schmitt's discourse.

61. Rey Chow, *Visuality, Sexuality, Ethnography, and Contemporary Chinese Cinema*, 26.

62. Walter Benjamin, *The Arcades Project*, 463.

63. Ng Kim-chew 黃錦樹, "Yuhai" 魚骸 (Fish relics). The story won first prize in a fiction contest sponsored by the newspaper *Zhongguo shibao* 中國時報 (China times) in 1996.

64. Ng, "Yuhai," 34–35.

65. See David Der-wei Wang, *The Monster That Is History*, 266.

66. See Chong Fa-hsin and Kyle Shernuk, "An Underground Chinese Malaysian War Novel Is Published."

67. Ng, *Nanyang Renmin Gongheguo Beiwanglu.*

68. For an extensive discussion of imaginary nostalgia, see David Der-wei Wang, *Fictional Realism in 20th-Century China*, 248–89.

69. Ng Kim-chew 黃錦樹 "Qi de gushi" 棄的故事 (Abject stories." Also see David Der-wei Wang, "Wo huali de yinwei yu beishang."

70. Ng Kim-chew, "Qi degushi."

71. See David Der-wei Wang, "Qiannian huaxu zhimeng" 千年華胥之夢 (A thousand-year-old dream of the splendid kingdom of Huaxu).

72. See ibid.

73. Ackbar Abbas, *Hong Kong: Culture and the Politics of Disappearance.*

74. Ibid., 25.

75. Dung Kai-cheung 董啓章, "Wei weilai erzuo dekaoguxue" 為未來而作的考古學 (An archaeology for the," 7. The original is: "董啓章「夢華」二字, 應是世界上所有曾經光輝一時的城市的終極歸結。夢之必破, 華之必衰，似是千古不變的定律。可是, 當時間在寫作中成為永恆的運動, 過去與未來即成就於當下。夢未必虛, 華未必墮, 一切經驗, 一切存在, 一經集之、錄之、誌之, 就可以脫離單一的時空, 成為無限衍生和延伸的世界。"

76. Dung Kai-chung 董啓章, *Dituji* 地圖集 (Atlas), 97. The original is: "虛構 (fiction) 是維多利亞城, 乃至所有城市的本質; 而城市的地圖, 亦必是一部自我擴充、修改、掩飾、推翻的小說。"

77. Wang Dewei, "Shanghen jijing, baoli qiguan" 傷痕即景, 暴力奇觀 (A tableau vivant of scar, a spectacle of violence).

78. Xiaobin Yang, "The Postmodern/Post-Mao-Deng History and Rhetoric in Chinese Avant-garde Fiction," 90.

79. Xiaobin Yang, *The Chinese Postmodern*, 205.

Chapter 4

1. The original is: "黑夜给了我黑色的眼睛 / 我却用它尋找光明" (Gu Cheng, *Selected Poems*, 1).

2. Lowell Dittmer, "Political Culture and Political Symbolism."

3. Wang Meng王蒙, *Ye de yan* 夜的眼 (Eyes of night) 1. The original is: "在夜裡, 眼睛本來是看不清的, 但夜讓人看到了許多白天看不清的東西, 也不禁讓人想起了顧城的那首詩, '黑夜給了我黑色的眼睛, 我卻用它來尋找光明', 有些事情在黑暗深處比在光明處看的更加深切, 更加真實。"

4. Shi Tiesheng 史鐵生, *Mingruo qinxian* 命若琴絃 (Life like a fiddle string), 264. The original is: "目的雖是虛設的, 可非得有不行, 不然琴弦怎麼拉緊，拉不緊就彈不響。"

5. Yan Lianke, *The Day the Sun Died.*

6. Walter Benjamin, "Surrealism," 2:209.

7. Margaret Cohen, *Profane Illumination.*

8. *Faluo* 法螺 refers to a large sea snail (*Charonia tritonis*), the shell of which was used as a musical instrument in Buddhist rituals or like a bugle in military activities. Xu Nianci—an editor, essayist, translator, and fiction writer—was among the most active of the literati in promoting the concepts of progress and science. "A New Account of Mr. Windbag" was modeled on the Japanese short story "Faluo xiansheng

tan" (An account of Mr. Windbag), by Iwaya Sazanami (1870–1933), which was translated into Chinese by Bao Tianxiao 包天笑 (1876–1973). Iwaya Sazanami, the pen name of Iwaya Sueo, was known primarily as a writer of children's stories and plays. The Japanese story was itself an adaptation of the popular fictional adventures of the German Baron Münchhausen (1720–97).

9. Xu Nianci 徐念慈 *Xinfaluo xiansheng tan* 新法螺先生譚 (A new account of Mr. Windbag), 1905), 3.

10. Ibid., 6.

11. Benjamin Schwartz, *In Search of Wealth and Power*, 237–47.

12. Hu Shi 胡適, "Yinian" 一念 (A flash of thought), 27:83. The original is:

我笑你繞太陽的地球，一日夜只打得一個迴旋;
我笑你繞地球的月亮，總不會永遠團圓;
我笑你千千萬萬大大小小的星球, 總跳不出自己的軌道線;
我笑你一秒鐘行五十萬裡的無線電, 總比不上我區區的心頭一念!

13. Quoted in Liu Zaifu 劉再復, *Fangzhu zhushen* 放逐諸神 (Exiling the gods), 144.

14. Guo Moruo 郭沫若, "Tiangou" 天狗, 22. The original is:

我是一條天狗呀!
我把月來吞了,
我把日來吞了,
我把一切的星球來吞了,
我把全宇宙來吞了。
我便是我了! 我是月的光,
我是日的光,
我是一切星球的光,
我是 X 光線的光,
我是全宇宙的 Energy 的總量!

15. See David Der-wei Wang, *Fictional Realism in 20th-Century China*, 60.

16. Mao Tse-tung 毛澤東, "Shijianlun" 實踐論 (On practice), 1:295.

17. Mao Zedong 毛澤東, "Liangge zhongguo1zhimingyun" 兩個中國之命運 (Two fates of China), accessed April 23, 2020, https://www.marxists.org/chinese/maozedong/marxist.org-chinese-mao-19450423.htm. The original is: "我們應當用全力去爭取光明的前途和光明的命運, 反對另外一種黑暗的前途和黑暗的命運。"

18. Mao Zedong 毛澤東 "Shijie shi shuyu nimende" 世界是屬於你們的 (The world belongs to you), accessed May 2, 2020, http://www.people.com.cn/GB/shizheng/252/7955/7958/20020422/714354.html. Mao's remarks were delivered to a group of students on November 17, 1957, when Mao was visiting Moscow.

19. Ban Wang, *The Sublime Figure of History*.

20. Lu Xun 魯迅, "Suixiang lu 41" 隨想錄 41 (Random thoughts 41), 1:341.

21. Lu Xun 魯迅, "Women xianzai zenyang zuofuqin" 我們現在怎樣做父親 (What is required of us as fathers today, 1919), 1:145. In the essay, Lu Xun describes an

episode of a premodern saga *Sui Tang yanyi* 隋唐演義 (The chronicle of the Sui and Tang), in which a heroic bandit supported the lowering gate of a hellish trap at the risk of his own life to let others escape safely.

22. T. A. Hsia, *The Gate of Darkness*, 160.

23. See Leo Lee, *Voices from the Iron House*, chapters 3–4; Wang Xiaoming 王曉明, *Wufa zhimian de rensheng* 無法直面的人生 (A life that cannot be faced up to); Wang Hui 汪暉, "Sihuo chongwen" 死火重溫 (A rekindled dead fire).

24. T. A. Hsia, *The Gate of Darkness*, 162.

25. Eileen Chang, "My Writing," 438.

26. Eileen Chang, *Jinsuoji* 金鎖記 (The story of a golden cangue, 1943), 54. The original is: "一級一級, 走進沒有光的所在。"

27. Chang Hao 張灝, *Youan yishi yuminzhu chuantong* 幽暗意識與民主傳統 (Dark consciousness and the democratic tradition), 21–27 and 69–73.

28. Chang Hao, "Chaoyue yishi yu youhuan yishi" 儒家內聖外王思想之再認與反省 (Transcendental consciousness and dark consciousness), 37.

29. Ibid.

30. Chang Hao, "Youan yishi yuminzhu chuantong," 2–14.

31. Chang Hao, "Chaoyue yishi yu youhuan yishi," 42–43.

32. Ibid., 48. The original is: "誰也不能否認: 政治權威主義，烏托邦心態和政教合一的觀念曾經是近代政治文化的一些主導傾向。同時, 誰也不能否認這些傾向多少以中國傳統遺留下來的聖王觀念為其淵源。"

33. Lee Ming-hui 李明輝, *Rujia shiye xia de zhengzhi sixiang* 儒家視野下的政治思想 (Political Thought in Confucian perspective), 38–43 and 51–53; Hu Ping 胡平 "Rujia renxinglun yu minzhu xianzheng" 儒家人性論與民主憲政 (Confucian humanism and democratic constitution). Also see David Elstein, *Democracy and Contemporary Chinese Philosophy*, 102–4.

34. See, for instance, Chen Zhiqiang 陳志強, *Wanming Wangxue yuanelun* 晚明王學原惡論 (The theory of evil in late Ming Wang Yangming school of thought).

35. For a succinct discussion of the dialectic of virtue and vice, see Wang Fansen 王汎森, "Mingmo Qingchu de renpu yu xingguohui" 明末清初的人譜與省過會 (The Society of Moral Edification in the late Ming and early Qing).

36. For a succinct discussion of the ambivalent distinction between *ren* (benevolence) and *bao* (violence) in late Ming society, see Zhao Yuan's 趙園, *Ming Qing zhiji shidafu zhi yanjiu* 明清之際士大夫之研究 (A study of the intelligentsia of the late Ming and early Qing), 3–22.

37. Quoted in Wang Fansen, "Mingmo Qingchu de renpu yu xingguohui," 682. Also see Chang Hao, *Youan yishi yuminzhu chuantong*, 21–27 and 69–73.

38. Wang Yangming 王陽明, *Wang Yangming quanji* 王陽明全集下 (Complete works of Wang Yangming), 111. The original is: "雖昏黑夜裏, 亦隱隱見得黑白。" See also Bao Yongling 鮑永玲 *Zhongzi yu lingguang* 種子與靈光 (Seed and light), 217.

39. Zhuangzi, *The Complete Works of Zhuangzi*, 78. The original is: "至道之精, 窈窈冥冥; 至道之極, 昏昏默默" ("Zhangzi waipian zaiyou" 莊子外篇在宥 [Zhuangzi, outer chapters], 4:2).

40. Laozi 老子 *Daodejing* 道德經 (The classic of the way), chap. 28, accessed May 2, 2020, http://www.quanxue.cn/ct_daojia/laoziindex.html. See also Bao, *Zhongzi yu lingguang*, chapter 2.

41. Quoted in Lin Ma, "Deciphering Heidegger's Connection with the *Daodejing*," 155.

42. Hölderlin wrote in "Remembrance" (*Selected Poems of Friedrich Hölderlin*, 195):

"But it passes,
Full of dark light,
To me the fragrant cup."

43. Martin Heidegger, "Principles of Thinking," 53.

44. Quoted in Otto Pöggeler, "West-East Dialogue," 64.

45. See Emmanuel Levinas's argument that the narrative is a process of opening to the other—that which is yet to be uttered—vis-à-vis that which is already being said (*Otherwise than Being*, 5–9).

46. C. T. Hsia, "Obsession with China."

47. Giorgio Agamben, "What Is Contemporary?," 44.

48. Ibid., 45.

49. Ibid., 44.

50. Ibid., 46.

51. For a fuller description of the dark matter of the unconscious, see Daniel L. Everett, *Dark Matter of the Mind*, especially the introduction.

52. See P. James E. Peebles, "Dark Matter," *Proceedings of National Academy of Sciences of the United States of America* 112, no. 40 (October 6, 2015), https://doi.org/10.1073/pnas.1308786111.

53. Liu Cixin, *The Three-Body Problem*, 27.

54. Paola Iovene, *Tale of Future Past*, 3–4.

55. Lu Xun 魯迅, "Yesong" 夜頌, 5:203.

56. Ibid.

57. Ibid. Xu Guangping is cited in the footnote to the essay.

58. Ibid.

59. Yan Lianke, *The Day the Sun Died*, 38.

60. Yan first used the term "mythic realism" in *Wodexianshi, wodezhuyi* 我的現實，我的主義 (My reality, my ism).

61. Ibid., 16.

62. Carlos Rojas's translation of a speech that was not published in its entirely.

63. Sophie Beach, "Yan Lianke: Finding Light in China's Darkness," *China Digital*

Times, October 22, 2014, https://chinadigitaltimes.net/2014/10/yan-lianke-finding-light-chinas-darkness/

64. Carlos Rojas's translation.

65. Lu Hsun, "Preface to *Call to Arms*, 3.

66. Lu Xun 魯迅, "Tingshuomeng" 聽說夢 (On dream interpretation), 4:481. The original is: "做夢, 是自由的, 說夢, 就不自由。做夢, 是做真夢的, 說夢, 就難免說謊。"

67. Carlos Rojas's translation.

68. Ibid.

69. Ibid.

70. Jacques Derrida, *Memoirs of the Blind*, 51.

71. Ibid. For a succinct discussion of Derrida's ruin of vision, see Cary Wolfe, *What Is Posthumanism?*, 132–34.

72. Chi Zijian 遲子建 "Shiieshang suoyou de yewan" 世界上所有的夜晚 (All nights in the world), 1.

73. Achille Mbembe, "Necropolitics."

74. Walter Benjamin, *Illuminations*, 109.

75. Hannah Arendt, "Understanding and Politics," 321.

76. Chi, "Shiieshang suoyou de yewan," 38.

77. Chi Zijian 遲子建, "Wodui heian derouqing" 我對黑暗的柔情 (My tender feeling toward darkness), 139. The original is: "如今能看到真正的黑暗的地方, 又有幾處呢? 黑暗在這個不眠的世界上, 被人為的光明撕裂得丟了魂魄 . . . 上帝給了我們黑暗, 不就是送給了我們夢想的溫床嗎?"

78. Lo Yi-chin 駱以軍, *Kuang Chaoren* 匡超人, 133–34. The original is: "前陣子睪丸下方破了個大洞, 自己去葯局買雙氧水消毒, 那洞像鵝嘴瘡愈破愈大, 還發出臭味, 但好像不是花柳病, 而是一種頑強黴菌感染; 同時還發現自己血壓高到一百九, 暈眩無力。"

79. Ibid., 564. The original is: "破雞雞超人是個什麼概念呢? 你想像著, 他是受傷的, 有個破洞在那超人裝最突兀的胯下部位, 那成爲一個最脆弱的窟窿, 傷害體驗的通道入口, 一個痛楚的執念。"

80. Ibid. The original is: "或許猥褻一點的傢伙會這樣羞辱我, '你就是在一個男人的屌上, 又長出了一副女人的屄。'"

81. The term "black hole" was coined in 1967 by the American astronomer John Wheeler. A black hole "can be formed by the death of a massive star. When such a star has exhausted the internal thermonuclear fuels in its core at the end of its life, the core becomes unstable and gravitationally collapses inward upon itself, and the star's outer layers are blown away" ("Black Hole," *Encyclopaedia Britannica*, January 22, 2020, https://www.britannica.com/science/black-hole). After decades when black holes were known only as theoretical objects, the first black hole ever discovered was spotted in 1971. For more information on the black hole, see, for instance, Nola

Taylor Redd, "What Are Black Holes?," Space.com, July 11, 2019, https://www.space.com/15421-black-holes-facts-formation-discovery-sdcmp.html.

82. Lo, *Kuang Chaoren*, 135.

83. Ibid., 426. The original is: "身體軸心空了一個很深的洞的殘障感, 和手部或腳部截肢的不完整感、幻肢感，身體重心偏移的感受不同; 也和古代閹人整個男性荷爾蒙分泌中心被切除的尖銳陰鬱不同 . . . 。那個雞雞上的洞，很像一個活物, 每天都往你不知道那是什麼境地的, 反物質或黯黑宇宙, 那另一個次元, 靈活蹦跳的再長大, 深入。"

84. Shang Wei, *Rulin waishi and Cultural Transformation in Late Imperial China*, 133–45.

85. Lo, *Kuang Chaoren*, 216. The original is: "幾百年前幻燈片裏的搖晃人影印象。"

86. Ibid., 89.

87. Ibid., 63–64.

88. Ibid., 64.

89. Ibid., 353.

90. Ibid., 411. The original is "但那個洞太大了。或者是, 這一個「洞之洞」, 反物質的概念, 在那破裂感, 撕碎感, 死滅, 痛苦的黑暗空無中, 再造一個「第二次的破洞」。"

91. Ibid., 399. The original is: "你不知道這繼續變化的哪一個界面, 是翻出了邊界之外? 也許在第六十九變到第七十變之間? 諸神用手捂住了臉, 悲傷的喊: 「不要啊!」「再翻出去就什麼都不是啦。」但我們其實已在一種臉孔像脫水機的旋轉, 全身骨架四分五裂的暴風, 變成那個反物質、反空間、在概念上全倒過來的維度."

Chapter 5

1. "Strange things" (guaixianzhuang 怪現狀) refers to the title of the late Qing exposé *Ershinian muduzhi guaixianzhuang* 二十年目睹之怪現狀 (Strange things witnessed in the past twenty years), by Wu Jianren 吳趼人 (1866–1910). The novel presents numerous episodes of social absurdities in a pseudo-encyclopedic manner and has been hailed as the most scathing exposure of Chinese reality at the beginning of the twentieth century. "Strange things" has since been used as a phrase to describe Chinese reality at its most grotesque and uncanny.

2. For a fuller discussion of the enormous amount of internet fiction, see Zhan Yubing 戰玉冰, "Wanglu xiaoshuo de shujufa yu lexinglun" 網絡小說的數據法與類型論 (The data method and typology of internet fiction studies).

3. Giorgio Agamben, "What Is Contemporary?", 45.

4. Tao Youzeng 陶佑曾, "Lun xiaoshuo zhi shili jiqi yingxiang" 論小說之勢力及其影響 (On the power of fiction and its impact), originally published in Youxi shijie 遊戲世界 (Playful world) in 1907. The original is: "有一大怪物焉: 不脛而走, 不翼而飛, 不叩而鳴; 刺人腦球, 驚人眼簾, 暢人意界, 增人智力; 忽而莊, 忽而諧, 忽而歌, 忽而哭, 忽而激, 忽而勸, 忽而諷, 忽而嘲; 鬱鬱蔥蔥, 兀兀硞硞, 熱度驟躋極點, 電光萬丈, 魔力千鈞, 有無壟不可思議之大勢力, 于文學界放一異彩, 標一特色, 此何物歟? 則小說是。"

See also Ah Ying 阿英, *Wanqing xiaoshuo congchao* 晚清小說叢鈔 (Compendium of late Qing fiction), 39.

5. Liang Qichao 梁啟超, "Lun xiaoshuo yu qunzhi zhiguanxi" 論小說與群治之關係 (On the relationship between fiction and ruling the people), 2:758.

6. Deleuze and Guattari, *A Thousand Plateaus*, 166.

7. *Shenyi jing* 神異經 (The classic of the divine and the strange), 38:226. The original is: "如虎而犬, 毛長二尺, 人面虎足, 豬口牙, 尾長一丈八尺, 攪亂荒中, 名檮杌。"

8. Tu Cheng-sheng 杜正勝, "Gudai wuguai zhi yanjiu" 古代物怪研究 (A study of ancient monsters).

9. Sima Qian 司馬遷, *Shiji huizhu kaozheng* 史記會注考證 (The record of the grand historian with annotations), 1:3.

10. Zhang Jun 張軍, *Chuguo shenhua yuanxing yanjiu* 楚國神話原型研究 (A study of the mythological archetypes of the Chu), 71. The original is: "檮杌之獸, 能逆知未來。故人有掩捕, 輒逃匿。史以示往來, 故名檮杌。"

11. Mencius 孟子, *Mencius*, "Lilouxia" 孟子·離婁下 (Chapter Lilou 2), 192. I am using the translation in Mencius, *Mencius*, 131. The original is: "晉之乘, 楚之檮杌, 魯之春秋, 一也。"

12. Kong Yingda 孔穎達, *Chunqiu zuozhuan zhengyi xu* 春秋左傳正義序 (Preface to the annotated Chronicle of the Chunqui era by Zuo Qiming), vol. 1, accessed May 2, 2020, http://guji.artx.cn/article/16621.html. The original is: "檮杌者, 嚚凶之類, 興於記惡之戒, 因以爲名。"

13. See David Wang, *The Monster That Is History*, 183–223.

14. Jiang Gui 姜貴, "Zixu" 自序 (Preface), 1. The original is: "紀惡以為戒也。"

15. Chen Sihe 陳思和, "Shilun Yan Lianke de Jianyingrushuo zhongde emoxing yinsu" 試論閻連科的堅硬如水中的惡魔性因素 "On the demonic elements in Yan Lianke's *As Hard as Water*," 33. See also Wolfgang M. Zucker, "The Demonic."

16. See Heraclitus's discussion of daimōn, quoted in Zucker, "The Demonic," 37.

17. Ibid., 35.

18. Ibid., 38.

19. Ibid., 37.

20. Deleuze and Guattari, *A Thousand Plateaus*, 240.

21. Ibid., 243. See also Brent Adkins, *Deleuze and Guattari's* A Thousand Plateaus, 142–44.

22. Gilles Deleuze, *Francis Bacon*, 19, quoted in Gerald L. Bruns, "Becoming-Animal," 711.

23. N. Katherine Hayles, *How We Became Posthuman*.

24. Jacques Derrida, *Without Alibi*, 72 and 210.

25. Ibid., 72. In this analysis, I benefited from Cary Wolfe's *What Is Posthumanism?*, 8–11.

26. Derrida, *Without Alibi*, 72.

27. Ibid., 72–73.

28. Lu Xun 魯迅, "Yuejie lüxing bianyan" 月界旅行辨言 (Introduction to a trip to the moon), 10:163.

29. Lu Xun 魯迅, "Zaoren shu" 造人術 (The art of creating humanity). See also Jia Liyuan 賈立元 "Renxing zhinengji" 人形智能機 (Humanized artificial intelligence).

30. The Japanese text was a loose and truncated rendering of the original, covering only approximately the first seventh of Strong's work and taking considerable liberties with that portion of the text.

31. Lu Xun, "Zaoren shu," 13:93.

32. Quoted in Jia Liyuan, "Renxing zhinengji," 5.

33. Carlos Rojas, introduction.

34. Lu Xun 魯迅, "Wenhua pianzhi lun" 文化偏至論 (On cultural aberrations), 1:51.

35. Lu Xun 魯迅, "Po esheng lun" 破惡聲論 (Toward a refutation of malevolent voices), 8:32.

36. Ibid. I am using the translation in Lu Xun, "Toward a Refutation of Malevolent Voices," 8:30. The original is: "神話之作, 本於古民, 目睹天物之奇瓢, 則逞神思而施以人化。" "僞士當去, 迷信可存。"

37. Lu Xun 魯迅, "Ah Chang yu Shanhaijing" 阿長與山海經 (Ah Chang and the classic of mountains and seas), 2:255.

38. Lu Xun 魯迅 *Zhongguo xiaoshuo shilue* 中國小説史略 (A short history of Chinese fiction), 13.

39. T. A. Hsia, "*The Gate of Darkness*, 162.

40. I am referring to Rob Nixon's *Slow Violence and the Environmentalism of the Poor*. For an interpretation of slow violence, see Nixon's introduction.

41. James Joyce, *Ulysses*, chapter 2.

42. Giorgio Agamben, *Homo Sacer*.

43. Belinda Kong *Tiananmen Fictions outside the Square*, chapter 4. See also, for example, Jess Row, "Circling the Square," *New York Times*, July 13, 2008, https://www.nytimes.com/2008/07/13/books/review/Row-t.html.

44. Ma Jian, *Beijing Coma*, 538.

45. Ibid., 546.

46. Ibid., 555.

47. Guo Pu's 郭璞 annotation to the *Classic of Mountains and Seas*, in *Lidai shanhaijing wenxian jicheng* 歷代山海經文獻集成 (Compendium of materials on the classic of mountains and seas over the past centuries), edited by Wen Qingge 文清閣 (Xi'an: Xi'an ditu chubanshe, 2006), 1:166. The original is: "聚肉形如牛肝, 有兩目; 食之無盡, 尋復更生如故。"

48. Han Song, *Wangling* 亡靈, (Dead souls), 268. The original is: "醫生開出藥方,

發放藥品, 培育病人, 造出下一個宇宙。船就在這些無窮無盡的世界中航行。沒有邊際得汪洋大海喲 ... 永生的醫院呀, 不是天堂, 亦非地獄。孤獨, 徹底的孤獨 ... 但船長相信, 彼岸也許下一刻就會冒泡般的冒出來, 啊, 從那盛滿消毒液的滔滔洪水中咕嘟一聲兀然浮現。"

49. Zhang Fan 張凡 "Yiyao pengke: Han Song Chuangzaole shijie kehuan de xinleixing (Medi-punk: Han Song has created a new model of world science fiction) 醫藥朋克: 韓松創造了世界科幻的新類型, *Gushi zhongguo* 故事中國 (Story China), February 18, 2019, http://www.storychina.cn/frmOnlineStory_Detail.aspx?ID=2950.

50. This refers to the collection of short stories by Han Song, *Kande kongju* 看的恐懼 (The fear of seeing).

51. The campaign was first launched after Mao's Yan'an talks in 1942 and has been repeated many times, as late as 2019. See "Punish before and after, Cure and Save People," accessed April 28, 2020, http://www.people.com.cn/GB/shizheng/252/5303/5304/20010605/481867.html.

52. Han, *Qum*, 140. The original is: "醫生哪怕解剖一千具屍體, 也無法了解生命的全部 ... 所幸還有文學 ... 原來一切不過是文學本質上不是科學, 而是文學。"

53. Ibid., 141. The original is: "講好醫院的故事才最重要。"

54. Lu Xun, "Zixu" 自序 (Preface to *Nahan* 吶喊 [A Call to Arms]), 1:417. I am using the translation in Lu Hsun, "Preface to *Call to Arms*," 3.

Bibliography

Non-Chinese Items

Abbas, Ackbar. *Hong Kong: Culture and the Politics of Disappearance*. Minneapolis: University of Minnesota Press, 1997.

Adkins, Brent. *Deleuze and Guattari's* A Thousand Plateaus: *A Critical Introduction and Guide*. Edinburgh: Edinburgh University Press, 2015.

Adorno, Theodor. *In Search of Wagner*. Translated by Rodney Livingstone. London: NLB, 1981.

Agamben, Giorgio. *Homo Sacer: Sovereign Power and Bare Life*. Translated by Daniel Heller-Roazen. Stanford, CA: Stanford University Press, 1998.

———. *State of Exception*. Translated by Kevin Attell. Chicago: University of Chicago Press, 2005.

———. "What Is Contemporary?" In Giorgio Agamben, *What Is an Apparatus? and Other Essays*, translated by David Kishik and Stefan Pedatella, 39–54. Stanford, CA: Stanford University Press 2009.

Anderson, Marston. *The Limits of Realism: Chinese Fiction in the Revolutionary Period*. Berkeley: University of California Press, 1990.

Apter, David E., and Tony Saich. *Revolutionary Discourse in Mao's Republic*. Cambridge, MA: Harvard University Press, 1994.

Arabian Nights: Tales of 1001 Nights. Translated by Malcolm C. Lyons and Ursula Lyons. Vol. 1. London: Penguin Books, 2008.

Arendt, Hannah. "Understanding and Politics." In Hannah Arendt, *Essays in Understanding, 1930–1954: Formation, Exile, and Totalitarianism*. New York: Schocken, 2005.

Armstrong, Nancy, and Leonard Tennenhouse. Introduction to *The Violence of Representation: Literature and the History of Violence*, edited by Nancy Armstrong and Leonard Tennenhouse, 1–26. New York: Routledge, 1989.

Bakhtin, Mikhail. "Discourse in the Novel." In Mikhail Bakhtin, *The Dialogic Imagination: Four Essays*, edited by Michael Holquist, 259–422. Austin: University of Texas Press, 1981.

———. *Rabelais and His World*. Translated by Helene Iswolsky. Bloomington: Indiana University Press, 2009.

Benhabib, Seyla. "Hannah Arendt and the Redemptive Power of Narrative." In *Hannah Arendt: Critical Essays*, edited by Lewis P. Hinchman and Sandra K. Hinchman. Albany: State University of New York Press, 1994.

Benjamin, Walter. *The Arcades Project*. Translated by Howard Eiland and Kevin McLaughlin, Cambridge, MA: Belknap Press of Harvard University Press, 1999.

———. *Charles Baudelaire: A Lyric Poet in the Era of High Capitalism*. Translated by Harry Zohn. London: Verso, 1983.

———. "Critique of Violence." In Walter Benjamin, *Selected Writings*, edited by Marcus Bullock and Michael Jennings, 1:236–52. Cambridge, MA: Belknap Press of Harvard University Press, 1996.

———. *Illuminations*. Translated by Harry Zohn. Edited and with an introduction by Hannah Arendt. New York: Harcourt Brace Jovanovich & World, 1968.

———. "Surrealism: The Last Snapshot of the European Intelligentsia." In Walter Benjamin, *Selected Writings*, edited by Howard Eiland and Michael W. Jennings, vol. 2. Cambridge, MA: Harvard University Press, 1996.

Birulés, Fina. "Contingency, History and Narration in Hannah Arendt." In *Ágnes Heller and Hannah Arendt: A Dialogue*, edited by Ángel Prior and Ángel Rivero, 117–25. Newcastle upon Tyne, UK: Cambridge Scholars Publishing, 2018.

Bogue, Ronald. *Deleuzian Fabulation and the Scars of History*. Edinburgh: Edinburgh University Press, 2010.

Bourdieu, Pierre. "The Force of Law: Toward a Sociology of the Juridical Field." *Hastings Law Journal* 38, no. 5 (1987): 814–38.

Brandt, Nat. *Massacre in Shansi*. Syracuse, NY: Syracuse University Press, 1999.

Britzolakis, Christina. "Phantasmagoria: Walter Benjamin and the Poetics of Urban Modernism." In *Ghosts: Deconstruction, Psychoanalysis, History*, edited by Peter Buse and Andrew Stott, 72–91. London: St. Martin's Press, 1999.

Brooks, Peter. *The Melodramatic Imagination: Balzac, Henry James, Melodrama, and the Mode of Excess*. New Haven, CT: Yale University Press, 1976.

Bruns, Gerald L. "Becoming-Animal (Some Simple Ways)." *New Literary History* 38, no 4 (2007): 703–20.

Castle, Terry. "Phantasmagoria: Spectral Technology and the Metamorphosis of Modern Reverie." *Critical Inquiry* 15, no. 1 (1988): 26–61.

Chang, Eileen. "My Writing." Translated by Wendy Larson. In *Modern Chinese Literary Thought: Writings on Literature, 1893–1945*, edited by Kirk Denton, 436–42. Stanford, CA: Stanford University Press, 1997.

Chiu, Kuei-fen. "The Production of Indigeneity: Contemporary Indigenous Literature in Taiwan and Trans-Cultural Inheritance." China Quarterly 200 (December 2009): 1071–87.

Chong Fa-hsin and Kyle Shernuk. "An Underground Chinese Malaysian War Novel Is Published: Revolution, Body and the Chinese Malaysian Leftist Narrative." In *A New Literary History of Modern China*, edited by David Der-wei Wang, 635–40. Cambridge, MA: Belknap Press of Harvard University Press, 2017.

Chow, Rey. *Primitive Passions: Visuality, Sexuality, Ethnography, and Contemporary Chinese Cinema*. New York: Columbia University Press, 1995.

Cohen, Margaret. *Profane Illumination: Walter Benjamin and the Paris of Surrealist Revolution*. Berkeley: University of California Press, 1993.

Crary, Jonathan. *Techniques of the Observer: On Vision and Modernity in the Nineteenth Century*. Cambridge, MA: MIT Press, 1992.

Deleuze, Gilles. *Cinema 2: The Time-Image*. Translated by Hugh Tomlinson and Robert Galeta. Minneapolis: University of Minnesota Press, 1989.

———. *Essays Critical and Clinical*. Translated by Daniel W. Smith and Michael A. Greco. Minneapolis: University of Minnesota Press, 1997.

———. *Francis Bacon: The Logic of Sensation*. Translated by Daniel W. Smith. Minneapolis: University of Minnesota Press, 2003.

Deleuze, Gilles, and Félix Guattari. *Anti-Oedipus: Capitalism and Schizophrenia*. Translated by Robert Hurley, Minneapolis: University of Minnesota Press, 1983.

———. *A Thousand Plateaus: Capitalism and Schizophrenia*. Translated by Brian Massumi. Minneapolis: University of Minnesota Press, 1987.

———. *What Is Philosophy?* Translated by Hugh Tomlinson and Graham Burchell. New York: Columbia University Press, 1994.

Denton, Kirk. *Modern Chinese Literary Thought: Writings on Literature, 1893–1945*. Stanford, CA: Stanford University Press, 1996.

Derrida, Jacques. *Memoirs of the Blind: The Self-Portrait and Other Ruins*. Translated by Pascale-Anne Brault and Michael Naas. Chicago: University of Chicago Press, 1993.

———. “Plato’s Pharmacy.” In Jacques Derrida, *Dissemination*, translated by Barbara Johnson, 63–171. Chicago: University of Chicago Press, 1981.

———. *Specters of Marx: The State of the Debt, the Work of Mourning, and the New International*. Translated by Peggy Kamuf. London: Routledge, 1994.

———. *Without Alibi*. Translated and edited by Peggy Kamuf. Stanford, CA: Stanford University Press, 2002.

DeWoskin, Kenneth. “The Six Dynasties *Chih-kuai* and the Birth of Fiction.” In *Chinese Narrative*, edited by Andrew Plaks, 21–52. Princeton, NJ: Princeton University Press, 1977.

Dimock, Wai Chee. *Residues of Justice: Literature, Law, Philosophy*. Berkeley: University of California Press, 1997.

Dittmer, Lowell. “Political Culture and Political Symbolism: Toward a Theoretical Synthesis” *World Politics* 29, no. 4 (1977): 552–83.

Dolin, Kieran. *Fiction and the Law: Legal Discourse in Victorian and Modernist Literature*. New York: Cambridge University Press, 1999.

Dutton, Michael. “Mango Mao: Infections of the Sacred.” *Public Culture* 16, no. 2 (2004): 161–88.

Elstein, David. *Democracy and Contemporary Chinese Philosophy*. New York: Routledge, 2015.

Everett, Daniel L. *Dark Matter of the Mind: The Culturally Articulated Unconscious*. Chicago: University Press of Chicago, 2016.

Feng Menglong. *Stories Old and New*. Translated by Shuhui Yang and Yunqin Yang. Seattle: University of Washington Press, 2000.

Freud, Sigmund. "The 'Uncanny.'" In Sigmund Freud, *The Standard Edition of the Complete Psychological Works of Sigmund Freud*, translated and edited by James Strachey with Anna Freud, 17:219–52. London: Hogarth Press, 1976.

Foucault, Michel. *Discipline and Punish: The Birth of the Prison*. Translated by Alan Sheridan. New York: Vintage, 1995.

———. *Le corps utopique suivi de les hétérotopies*. Paris: Nouvelles Editions Lignes, 2009.

Gao Xingjian. *One Man's Bible*. Translated by Mabel Lee. New York: Harper Collins, 2002.

Geertz, Clifford. *Local Knowledge: Further Essays in Interpretive Anthropology*. New York: Basic Books, 1983.

Giddens, Anthony. *The Consequences of Modernity*. Stanford, CA: Stanford University Press, 1990.

Goldman, Merle. *Literary Dissent in Communist China*. Cambridge, MA: Harvard University Press, 1967.

Gu Cheng. *Selected Poems*. Edited by Sean Golden and Chu Chi-yu. Hong Kong: Renditions, 1987.

Guzmán, Luis. "Benjamin's Divine Violence: Unjustifiable Justice." *New Centennial Review* 14, no. 2 (2014): 49–63.

Hanan, Patrick. "The Development of Fiction and Drama." In *The Legacy of China*, edited by Raymond Dawson, 115–43. Oxford: Oxford University Press, 1964.

Haraway, Donna. "Anthropocene, Capitalocene, Plantationocene, Chthulucene: Making Kin." *Environmental Humanities* 6, no. 1 (2015): 159–65.

Harootunian, Harry. *History's Disquiet: Modernity, Cultural Practice, and the Questions of Everyday Life*. New York: Columbia University Press, 2000.

Harrison, Henrietta. *The Missionary's Curse and Other Tales from a Chinese Catholic Village*. Berkeley: University of California Press, 2013.

Hayles, N. Katherine. *How We Became Posthuman: Virtual Bodies in Cybernetics, Literature, and Informatics*. Chicago: University of Chicago Press, 1999.

Heidegger, Martin. "Principles of Thinking." Translated by Andrew J. Mitchell. In *The Piety of Thinking*, edited by James G. Hart and John C. Maraldo. Bloomington: Indiana University Press, 1976.

Hölderlin, Friedrich. *Selected Poems of Friedrich Hölderlin*. Translated by Maxine Chernoff and Paul Hoover. Richmond, CA: Omnidawn, 2008.

Hsia, C. T. "Obsession with China: The Moral Burden of Modern Chinese Literature."

In C. T. Hsia, *A History of Modern Chinese Fiction*, 533–54. New Haven, CT: Yale University, 1971.

———. "Yan Fu and Liang Ch'i-ch'ao as Advocates of New Fiction." In *Chinese Approaches to Literature from Confucius to Liang Ch'i-ch'ao*, edited by W. Allyn Rickett, 221–57. Princeton, NJ: Princeton University Press, 1978.

Hsia, T. A. *The Gate of Darkness*. Seattle: University of Washington Press, 1968.

Huang, Hsin-ya. "Re-Visioning Pacific Seascapes." In *Landscape, Seascape, and the Eco-Spatial Imagination*, edited by Simon Estok, Jonathan White, and I-Chun Wang, 179–96. New York: Routledge, 2016.

———. "Towards Trans-Pacific Ecopoetics: Three Indigenous Texts." In Hsin-ya Huang and Clara Shu-Chun Chang, *Aspects of Transnational and Indigenous Cultures*, 118–36. New Castle upon Tyne, UK: Cambridge Publishing, 2014.

———. "What Does the 'World Atlas' Mean? A Chain of Islands in Oceania. . . . Modern China in Island Perspective." In *A New Literary History of Modern China*, edited by David Der-wei Wang, 846–50. Cambridge, MA: Belknap Press of Harvard University Press, 2017.

Huyssen, Andreas. *After the Great Divide: Modernism, Mass Culture, Postmodernism*. Bloomington: Indiana University Press, 1986.

Iovene, Paola. *Tale of Future Past: Anticipation and the End of Literature in Contemporary China*. Stanford, CA: Stanford University Press, 2014.

Jackson, Michael. *The Politics of Storytelling: Variations on a Theme by Hannah Arendt*. Chicago: University of Chicago Press, 2013.

Kamuf, Peggy. "Violence, Identity, Self-Determination and the Question of Justice: On *Specters of Marx*," In *Violence, Identity, and Self-Determination*, edited by Hent deVries and Samuel Weber, 271–83. Stanford, CA: Stanford University Press, 1997.

Kao, Karl. *Classical Tales of the Supernatural and the Fantastic*. Bloomington: Indiana University Press, 1987.

Kearney, Richard. "On the Hermeneutics of Evil." *Revue de Métaphysique et de Morale* 2 (2006): 197–215.

Kong, Belinda. *Tiananmen Fictions outside the Square: The Chinese Literary Diaspora and the Politics of Global Culture*. Philadelphia: Temple University Press, 2012.

Lawrance, Alan. *China since 1919, Revolution and Reform: A Sourcebook*. New York: Psychology Press, 2004.

Lee, Haiyan. *The Stranger and the Chinese Moral Imagination*. Stanford, CA: Stanford University Press, 2014.

Lee, Leo Ou-fan, ed. *The Lyrical and the Epic: Studies of Modern Chinese Literature*. Bloomington: Indiana University Press, 1980.

———. *Voices from the Iron House: A Study of Lu Xun*. Bloomington: Indiana University Press, 1987.

Levinas, Emmanuel. *Otherwise than Being: Or beyond Essence*. Translated by Alphonso Lingis. Pittsburgh, PA: Duquesne University Press, 1981.

———. *Totality and Infinity: An Essay on Exteriority*. Translated by Alphonso Lingis. Pittsburgh, PA: Duquesne University Press, 1969.

Lin Ma. "Deciphering Heidegger's Connection with the *Daodejing*." *Asian Philosophy* 16, no. 3 (2006): 149–71.

Liu Cixin, *The Dark Forest*. Translated by Joel Martinson. New York: Tor Books, 2015.

———. *The Three-Body Problem*. Translated by Ken Liu. New York: Tor Books, 2014.

Lu Hsun. "A Madman's Diary." In Lu Hsun, *Selected Stories of Lu Hsun*, translated by Hsien-yi Yang and Gladys Yang. Beijing: Foreign Languages Press, 1960.

———. "Preface to Call to Arms." In Lu Hsun, *Selected Stories of Lu Hsun*, translated by Hsien-yi Yang and Gladys Yang, 2–5. Beijing: Foreign Languages Press, 1960.

———. "Toward a Refutation of Malevolent Voices." Translated and annotated by Jon Eugene von Kowallis. *boundary 2* 38, no. 2 (2011): 39–62.

———. *See also* Lu Xun.

Lu Xun. *A Brief History of Chinese Fiction*. Translated by Gladys Yang and Yang Hsien-yi. Beijing: Foreign Languages Press, 1959.

Ma Jian. *Beijing Coma*. Translated by Flora Drew. New York: Picador, 2009.

Mackinnon, Malcolm H. "Max Weber's Disenchantment Lineages of Kant and Channing." *Journal of Classical Sociology* 1, no. 3 (2001): 329–35.

Mao Tse-tung 毛澤東. "Shijianlun" 實踐論 (On practice). In Mao Tse-tung, *Selected Works of Mao Tse-tung*, 1:295–309. Beijing: Foreign Languages Press, 1967.

Mapp, Nigel. "Specter and Impurity: History and the Transcendental in Derrida and Adorno." In *Ghosts: Deconstruction, Psychoanalysis, History*, edited by Peter Buse and Andrew Stott, 92–124. London: St. Martin's Press, 1999.

Mbembe, Achille. "Necropolitics." *Public Culture* 15, no. 1 (2003): 11–40.

Mencius. *Mencius*. Translated by D. C. Lau. London: Penguin, 1970.

Mo Yan. *Life and Death Are Wearing Me Out*. Translated by Howard Goldblatt. New York: Arcade, 2018.

Murthy, Viren. *The Political Philosophy of Zhang Taiyan: The Resistance of Consciousness*. Leiden, the Netherlands: Brill, 2011.

Nixon, Rob. *Slow Violence and the Environmentalism of the Poor*. Cambridge, MA: Harvard University Press, 2011.

Owen, Stephen. *Readings in Chinese Literary Thought*. Cambridge, MA: Harvard Council on East Asian Studies, 1992.

Pöggeler, Otto. "West-East Dialogue: Heidegger and Lao-Tzu." In Gram Parkes, ed., *Heidegger and Asian Thought*, 47–78. Honolulu: University of Hawaii Press, 1987.

Prendergast, Christopher. *The Order of Mimesis: Balzac, Stendhal, Nerval, Flaubert*. Cambridge: Cambridge University Press, 1986.

Rancière, Jacques. *The Politics of Aesthetics: The Distribution of the Sensible*. Translated by Gabriel Rockhill. New York: Continuum, 2004.

Ricoeur, Paul. "Action, Story and History: On Re-Reading *The Human Condition*." *Salmagundi* 60 (Spring–Summer 1983): 60–72.

———. *The Symbolism of Evil*. Translated by Emerson Buchanan. New York: Beacon, 2016.

Rojas, Carlos. Introduction to "The Germ of Life." Special issue, Modern Chinese Literature and Culture 23, no. 1 (2011): 1–16.

———. "Without [Femin]ism: Femininity as Axis of Alterity and Desire in Gao Xingjian's 'One Man's Bible.'" *Modern Chinese Literature and Culture* 14, no 2 (2002): 163–206.

Ropp, Paul S. "The Distinctive Art of Chinese Fiction." In *The Heritage of China: Contemporary Perspectives*, edited by Paul S. Ropp, 308–34. Berkeley: University of California Press, 1990.

Schmitt, Carl. *Political Theology: Four Chapters on the Concept of Sovereignty*. Translated with an introduction by George Schwab, with a foreword by Tracy Strong. Chicago: University of Chicago Press, 2005.

Schwartz, Benjamin. *In Search of Wealth and Power: Yen Fu and the West*. Cambridge, MA: Belknap Press of Harvard University Press, 1964.

Scogin, Hugh T., Jr. "Civil 'Law' in Traditional China: History and Theory." In *Civil Law in Qing and Republican China*, edited by Kathryn Bernhardt and Philip C. C. Huang, 13–41. Stanford, CA: Stanford University Press, 1994.

Scott-Baumann, Alison. *Ricoeur and the Hermeneutics of Suspicion*. London: Bloomsbury, 2011.

Shang Wei. *Rulin waishi and Cultural Transformation in Late Imperial China*. Cambridge, MA: Harvard Center for Asian Studies, 2003.

Song, Mingwei. "Chinese Science Fiction Presents the Posthuman Future." In *A New Literary History of Modern China*, edited by David Der-wei Wang, 951–58. Cambridge, MA: Belknap Press of Harvard University Press, 2017.

———. "The Taming of the Youth: Discourse, Politics, and Fictional Representation in the Early PRC." *Journal of Modern Literature in Chinese* 9, no. 2 (2009): 108–38.

Sprinker, Michael, ed. *Ghostly Demarcations: A Symposium on Jacques Derrida's* Specters of Marx. London: Verso, 1999.

Strauss, Leo. *Persecution and the Art of Writing*. New York: Free Press, 1952.

Suleiman, Susan Robin. *Authoritarian Fictions: The Ideological Novel as a Literary Genre*. Princeton, NJ: Princeton University Press, 1993.

Treat, John W. "Arendt in Asia: Responsibility and Judgment in Nanjing and Hiroshima." *Harvard Journal of Asiatic Studies* 77, no. 2 (2017): 407–35.

Vidler, Anthony. *The Architectural Uncanny*. Cambridge, MA: MIT Press, 1992.

Wang, Ban. *The Sublime Figure of History: Aesthetics and Politics in Twentieth-Century China*. Stanford, CA: Stanford University Press, 1997.

Wang, David Der-wei. Afterword to *Running Wild: New Chinese Writers*, edited by David Der-wei Wang, 238–58. New York: Columbia University Press, 1994.

———. *Fictional Realism in 20th-Century China: Mao Dun, Lao She, Shen Congwen*. New York: Columbia University Press 1992.

———. *Fin-de-Siècle Splendor: Repressed Modernities of Late Qing Fiction, 1849–1911*. Stanford, CA: Stanford University Press, 1997.

———. *The Lyrical in Epic Time: Modern Chinese Intellectuals and Artists through the 1949 Crisis*. New York: Columbia University Press, 2015.

———. *The Monster That Is History: History, Violence, and Fictional Writing in 20th-Century China*. Berkeley: University of California Press, 2004.

Wang Hui. "Intuition, Repetition, and Revolution: Six Moments in the Life of Ah Q." Translated by Natasha Gentz and Carlos Rojas. In *The Oxford Handbook of Modern Chinese Literatures*, edited by Carlos Rojas and Andrea Bachner, 702–21. Oxford: Oxford University Press, 2016.

Wang, Jin. *High Culture Fever: Politics, Aesthetics, and Ideology in Deng's China*. Berkeley: University of California Press, 1996.

Weber, Max. *The Protestant Ethic and The Spirit of Capitalism*. Translated by Peter Baehr and Gordon C. Wells. New York: Penguin Books, 2002.

———. *The Sociology of Religion*. Translated by Ephraim Fischoff. New York: Beacon, 1971.

Wolfe, Cary. *What Is Posthumanism?* Minneapolis: University of Minnesota Press, 2010.

Wu Ming-yi, *The Man with the Compound Eyes*. Translated by Darryl Sterk. New York: Pantheon, 2014.

Wu, Yenna, and Philip Williams, eds. *The Great Wall of Confinement: The Chinese Prison Camp through Contemporary Fiction and Reportage*. Berkeley: University of California Press, 2004.

Xu, Gang Gary. "My Writing, Your Pain, and Her Trauma: Pronouns and 'Gendered' Subjectivity in Gao Xingjian's *Soul Mountain* and *One Man's Bible*." *Modern Chinese Literature and Culture* 14, no. 2 (2002): 99–129.

Xu Shuang. "Traveling through Time and Searching for Utopia: Utopian Imaginaries in Internet Time-Travel Fiction." In *Utopia and Utopianism in the Contemporary Chinese Context*, edited by David Wang, Angela Leung, and Yingde Zhang, 146–58. Hong Kong: University of Hong Kong Press, 2020.

Yan Lianke. *The Day the Sun Died*. Translated by Carlos Rojas. New York: Grove, 2018.

Yang, Xiaobin. *The Chinese Postmodern: Trauma and Irony in Chinese Avant-Garde Fiction*. Ann Arbor: University of Michigan Press, 2002.

———. "The Postmodern/Post-Mao-Deng History and Rhetoric in Chinese Avant-Garde Fiction." PhD diss., Yale University, 1996.

Zhang, Xudong. *Chinese Modernism in the Era of Reforms: Cultural Fever, Avant-Garde Fiction, and the New Chinese Cinema*. Durham, NC: Duke University Press, 1997.

Zhuangzi. *The Complete Works of Zhuangzi*. Translated by Burton Watson. New York: Columbia University Press, 2013.

Žižek, Slavoj. *The Sublime Object of Ideology*. London: Verso, 1989.

Zucker, Wolfgang M. "The Demonic: From Aeschylus To Tillich." *Theology Today* 26, no. 1 (1969): 34–50.

Chinese Items

Ah Ying 阿英. *Wanqing xiaoshuo congchao: Xiaoshuo xiqu yanjiujuan* 晚清小説叢鈔: 小説戲曲研究卷 (Compendium of late Qing fiction: Research materials on fiction and drama). Beijing: Zhonghua shuju,1960.

Bao Yongling 鮑永玲. *Zhongzi yu lingguang: Wang Yangming xinxue yuxiangtixi tonglun* 種子與靈光: 王陽明心學喻象體系通論 (Seed and light: A study of the metaphorical system of Wang Yangming's thought of heart or mind). Shanghai: Shanghai shudian chubanshe, 2012.

Chan Koon-chung 陳冠中. *Jianfeng Reign: Xinzhongguo wuyoushi* 建豐二年: 新中國烏有史 (The second year of the Jianfeng reign: A uchronia of new China). Taipei: Ryefield, 2015.

Chang, Eileen張愛玲. *Jinsuoji* 金鎖記 (The story of a golden cangue). In Eileen Chang, *Chuanqi* 傳奇 (Romance). Taipei: Huangguan chubanshe, 1973.

———. *Qingcheng zhilian* 傾城之戀 (Love in a fallen city). In Eileen Chang, *Chuanqi* 傳奇 (Romance), 198–245. Taipei: Huangguan chubanshe, 1973.

Chang Hao 張灝. "Chaoyue yishi yu youhuan yishi: rujia neisheng waiwang sixiang zhizairen yu fanxing" 儒家內聖外王思想之再認與反省 (Transcendental consciousness and dark consciousness: The rethinking of and reflection on the Confucian concept of "inside the saint" and "outside the king"). In Chang Hao, *Zhanghao zixuanji* 張灝自選集 (Selected works by Chang Hao). Shanghai: Shanghai jiaoyu chubanshe, 2002.

———. *Youan yishi yuminzhu chuantong* 幽暗意識與民主傳統 (Dark consciousness and the democratic tradition). Taipei: Lianjing chuban gongsi, 1989.

Chen Pingyuan 陳平原. "Zhongguo xiaoshuo shilun" 中國小說史論 (A history of Chinese fiction). In Chen Pingyuan, *Chen Pingyuan xiaoshuoshi lunji* 陳平原小說史論集 (Collection of works on Chinese fictional history by Chen Pingyuan). Shijiazhuang: Hebei renmin chubanshe, 1996.

Chen Sihe 陳思和. "Shilun Yan Lianke de Jianyingrushuo zhongde emoxing yinsu" 試論閻連科的堅硬如水中的惡魔性因素 "On the demonic elements in Yan Lianke's *As Hard as Water*." *Xiandai zuojia pinglun* 現代作家評論 (Contemporary writers review) 4 (2002): 31–44.

Chen Zhiqiang 陳志強. *Wanming Wangxue yuanelun* 晚明王學原惡論 (The theory of evil in the late Ming Wang Yangming school of thought). Taipei: National Taiwan University Press, 2018.

Cheng Yizhong 程毅中, ed. *Shenguai qingxia de yishu shijie* 神怪情俠的藝術世界 (The world of the supernatural, the romantic, and the chivalric). Beijing: Zhongyang dangxiao chubanshe, 1994.

Chi Zijian 遲子建. "Shiieshang suoyou de yewan" 世界上所有的夜晚 (All nights in the world). In Chi Zijian, *Shiieshang suoyou deyewan* 世界上所有的夜晚 (All nights in the world). Taipei: Fulin wenhua, 2008.

———. *Shijieshang suoyou deyewan* 世界上所有的夜晚 (All nights in the world). Taipei: Fulin wenhua, 2008.

———. "Wodui heian derouqing" 我對黑暗的柔情 (My tender feeling toward darkness). In Chi Zijian, *Chi Zijian sanwen* 遲子建散文 (Essays of Chi Zijian), 135–39. Hangzhou: Zhejiang wenyi chubanshe, 2014.

Chiang Kai-shek 蔣介石. "Xin shenghuo yundong gangling" 新生活運動綱領 (Guidelines of the New Life Movement). In Chiang Kai-shek, *Xin shenghuo yundong shiliao* 新生活運動史料, 30–34. Taipei: Zhongyang wenwu gongyingshe, 1963.

Dai Jinhua 戴錦華. *Yanban xi de fengfeng yuyu* 樣板戲的風風雨雨 (The stormy history of the model drama). Beijing: Zhishi chubanshe, 1995.

Dung Kai-cheung 董啓章. *Dituji: Yige xiangxiang de chengshi de kaoguxue* 地圖集: 一個想像的城市的考古學 (Atlas: An archaeology of an imaginary city). Taipei: Unitas, 1997.

———. "Wei weilai erzuo dekaoguxue" 為未來而作的考古學 (An archaeology for the future). In Dung Kai-chung, *Menghualu* 夢華錄 (Dream of splendor), 7–10. Taipei: Lianjing, 2011.

Gao Hua 高華. *Hongtaiyang shizenyang shengqide* 紅太陽是怎樣升起的?延安整風運動的來龍去脈 (How did the red sun rise? The rectification movement of Yan'an). Hong Kong: Chinese University Press, 2000.

Gao Xingjian 高行健. *Yigeren de shengjing* 一個人的聖經 (One man's bible). Taipei: Lingking Publications, 1999.

———. *Ziyou yu wenxue* 自由與文學 (Freedom and literature). Taipei: Lingking Publications, 2014.

Guo Moruo 郭沫若. "Tiangou" 天狗. In Guo Moruo, *Guo Moruo ji* 郭沫若集 (Works of Guo Moruo), 22. Guangzhou: Huacheng chubanshe, 2006).

Han Song 韓松. *2066: Huoxing zhaoyao meiguo* 2066: 火星照耀美國 (2066: Mars over America). Shanghai: Shanghai renmin chubanshe, 2012.

———. *Kande kongju* 看的恐懼 (The fear of seeing). Beijing: Renmin youdian chubanshe, 2012.

———. *Qumo* 驅魔 (Exorcism). Shanghai: Shanghai wenyi chubanshe, 2017.

———. *Wangling* 亡靈 (Dead souls). Shanghai: Shanghai wenyi chubanshe, 2018.

Hu Ping 胡平. "Rujia renxinglun yu minzhu xianzheng: Yu Zhang Hao jiaoshou shangque" 儒家人性論與民主憲政：與張灝教授商榷 (Confucian humanism and democratic constitution: A dialogue with Professor Zhang Hao). *Zhongguo luntan* 中國論壇 (Chinese tribune) 347 (1991): 111–17.

Hu Shi 胡適. "Yinian" 一念 (A flash of thought). In Hu Shi, *Hushi zuopinji* 胡適作品集 (Works of Hu Shi), 27:83. Taipei: Yuanliu, 1990.

Huang Jinlin 黃金麟. *Lishi, shenti, guojia: Jindai zhongguo shenti de xingcheng, 1895–1937* 歷史, 身體, 國家: 近代中國身體的形成 (History, body, nation: The formation of the modern Chinese body, 1895–1937). Taipei: Lianjing chuban gongsi, 2001.

Jia Liyuan 賈立元. "Renxing zhinengji: Wanqing kehuan xiaoshuo zhongde shenxin gaizao xushi" 人形智能機: 晚清科幻小說中的身心改造敍事 (Humanized artificial intelligence: Mental and bodily transformation in late Qing science fiction). *Zhongguo xindai wenxue* 中國現代文學 (Modern Chinese literature) 35 (2019): 3–28.

———. *Zhujiu women de weilai: Jiushi niandai zhijin Zhongguo kehuan xiaoshuo zhongde zhongguo xiangxiang yanjiu* 築就我們的未來: 九十年代至今中國科幻小說中的中國形象研究 (Achieving our future: A study of China's image in Chinese science fiction since the 1990s). Master's thesis. Beijing Normal University, 2010.

Jiang Gui 姜貴, "Zixu" 自序 (Preface). In Jiang Gui, *Jin taowu zhuan* 今檮杌傳 (A history of *taowu* of modern times; also titled Xuanfeng 旋風 [Whirlwind]). Tainan: Chunyulou, 1957.

Lee Ming-hui 李明輝. *Rujia shiye xia de zhengzhi sixiang* 儒家視野下的政治思想 (Political thought in Confucian perspective). Taipei: Guoli Taiwan daxue chuban zhongxin, 2005.

Li Jianguo 李建國, ed. *Tangqian zhiguai xiaoshuo jishi* 唐前志怪小說集釋 (Annotated collection of pre-Tang *zhiguai* fiction). Taipei: Wenshizh chubanshe, 1987.

Li Rui 李銳. *Zhang Mading de Dibatian* 張馬丁的第八天 (The eighth day of Zhang Mading). Taipei: Ryefield, 2012.

Li Tuo 李陀. "Xuebeng hechu" 雪崩何處 (Where is the avalanche?). Preface to Yu Hua, *Shibasui chumn yuanxing* 十八歲出門遠行 (Going out for a trip at the age of eighteen), 3–7. Taipei: Yuanliu chuban gonsi, 1991.

Liang Qichao 梁啟超. "Lun xiaoshuo yu qunzhi zhiguanxi" 論小說與群治之關係 (On the relationship between fiction and ruling the people). In Liang Qichao, *Yingbingshi wenji dianjiao wenji* 飲冰室文集點校 (Ice drinker studio collection of writings, annotated edition), 2:758–60. Kunming: Yunan jiaoyu chubanshe, 2001.

———. "Yiyin zhengzhi xiaoshuo xu" 譯印政治小說序 (Preface to our series of political novels in translation). In Liang Qichao, *Yinbingshi wenji dianjiao* 飲冰室文集點校 (Ice drinker studio collection of writings, annotated edition), 1:153. Kunming: Yunan jiaoyu chubanshe, 2001.

Liu Cixin 劉慈欣. *Santi* 三體 (The three-body problem: a trilogy comprising *Santi* 三體 [The three-body problem]; *Heian senlin* 黑暗森林 [Dark forest]; and *Sishen yongsheng* 死神永生 [Death's end]). Chongqing: Chongqing chuban jituan, 2014.

Liu Zaifu 劉再復, *Fangzhu zhushen* 放逐諸神 (Exiling the gods). Hong Kong: Tiandi chuban, 1994.

Lo Yi-chin 駱以軍. *Kuang Chaoren* 匡超人. Taipei: Ryefield, 2018.

Lu Xun 魯迅. "Ah Chang yu Shanhaijing" 阿長與山海經 (Ah Chang and the classic of mountains and seas). In Lu Xun, *Lu Xun Quanji* 魯迅全集 (Complete works of Lu Xun), 2:250–257. Beijing: Renmin wenxue chubanshe, 2005.

———. *Lu Xun shuxin ji (shang)* 魯迅書信集上 (Lu Xun's correspondence [part 1]). Beijing: Renmin wenxue chubanshe, 1976).

———. "Moluo shili shuo" 摩羅詩力說 (A treatise on the Mara Poet). In Lu Xun, *Lu Xun Quanji* 魯迅全集 (Complete works of Lu Xun), 1:65–120. Beijing: Renmin wenxue chubanshe, 2005.

———. "Po esheng lun" 破惡聲論 (Toward a refutation of malevolent voices). In Lu Xun, *Lu Xun Quanji* 魯迅全集 (Complete works of Lu Xun), 8:25–40. Beijing: Renmin wenxue chubanshe, 2005.

———. "Suixiang lu 41" 隨想錄 41 (Random thoughts 41). In Lu Xun, *Lu Xun Lu Xun Quanji* 魯迅全集 (Complete works of Lu Xun), 1:325. Beijing: Renmin wenxue chubanshe, 2005.

———. "Tingshuomeng" 聽說夢 (On dream interpretation). In Lu Xun, *Lu Xun Quanji*, 4:481–485. Beijing: Renmin wenxue chubanshe, 2005.

———. "Women xianzai zenyang zuofuqin" 我們現在怎樣做父親 (What is required of us as fathers today). In Lu Xun, *Lu Xun Quanji* 魯迅全集 (Complete works of Lu Xun), 1:134–149. Beijing: Renmin wenxue chubanshe, 2005.

———. *Yecao* 野草 (Wild grass). In Lu Xun, *Lu Xun Quanji* 魯迅全集 (Complete works of Lu Xun), vol. 2. Beijing: Renmin wenxue chubanshe, 2005.

———. "Yesong" 夜頌 (Ode to night). In Lu Xun, *Lu Xun Quanji* 魯迅全集 (Complete works of Lu Xun), 5:203–220. Beijing: Renmin wenxue chubanshe, 2005.

———. "Yuejie lüxing bianyan" 月界旅行辨言 (Introduction to a trip to the moon). In Lu Xun, *Lu Xun lunchuangzuo* 魯迅論創作 (Lu Xun on creative writing), 339. Shanghai: Shanghai wenyi chubanshe, 1983.

———. "Zaoren shu" 造人術 (The art of creating humanity). In Lu Xun, *Luxun Quanji* 魯迅全集 (Complete works of Lu Xun), 13:93–95. Beijing: Renmin wenxue chubanshe, 2005.

———. *Zhaohua xishi* 朝花夕拾 (Morning flowers plucked at sunset). In Lu Xun, *Luxun Quanji* 魯迅全集 (Complete works of Lu Xun), vol. 2. Beijing: Renmin wenxue chubanshe, 2005.

———. *Zhongguo xiaoshuo shilue* 中國小說史略 (A brief history of Chinese fiction). Reprint. Hong Kong: Qingwen shuwu, 1972.

———. "Zixu" 自序 (Preface to *Nahan* 吶喊 [A call to arms]). In Lu Xun, *Lu Xun Quanji* 魯迅全集 (Complete works of Lu Xun), 1:437–443. Beijing: Renmin wenxue chubanshe, 2005.

Ma Jian 馬建. *Rouzhitu* 肉之土 (Fleshy earth). Taipei: Yunchen chubanshe, 2008.

Ma Ka-fai 馬家輝. *Longtoufengwei* 龍頭鳳尾 (Dragon head, phoenix tale). Taipei: Xinjingdian Press, 2016.

Maruo Tuneki 丸尾常喜. *Ren yu gui de jiuge: Lu Xun xiaoshuo lunxi* 人與鬼的糾葛: 魯迅小説論集 (The entanglements between ghosts and humanity: An analysis of Lu Xun's fiction). Translated by Qin Gong. Beijing: Renmin wenxue chubanshe, 1995.

Master Shenyan 聖嚴法師. *Badareren juejing* 八大人覺經 (Eighth great awakening sutra). Taipei, Fagu wenhua, 2005.

Mencius 孟子. *Mencius*, "Lilouxia" 孟子·離婁下 (Chapter Lilou 2). In Mencius, *Mengzi yizu* 孟子譯注 (Annotated Mencius), annotated by Yang Bojun. Taipei: Hanjing wenhua, 1987.

Meng Yue 孟悅. "*Baimao nü* yanbian de qishi: Lun Yan'an wenyi de lishi duozhi xing" 白毛女演變的啓示: 論延安文藝的歷史多質性 (The transformations of *The White-Haired-Girl* and its significance: On the polyphony of history in Yan'an literature). In *Zai jiedu: Dazhong wenyi yu yishi xingtai* 再解讀: 大衆文藝與意識形態 (Reinterpretation: Popular literature and ideology), edited by Tang Xiaobing 唐小兵, 68–89. Hong Kong: Oxford University Press, 1993.

Mo Yan 莫言. *Shensi pilao* 生死疲勞. (Life and death are wearing me out). Taipei: Ryefield, 2007.

Ng Kim-chew 黄錦樹. *Nanyang Renmin Gongheguo* 南洋人民共和國備忘錄 (Memorandum of the People's Republic of South Seas). Taipei: Lingking Publications, 2013.

———. "Qi de gushi: Gebifangjian de liefeng: Lun Lou Yi-chin" 棄的故事: 隔壁房間的裂縫——論駱以軍 (Abject stories: cracks in the room next door—on Lou Yi-chin." In Lou Yi-chin 駱以軍, *Qian beihuai* 遣悲懷 (Banished sorrow), 339–57. Taipei: Maitian chuban, 2001.

———. "Youjian fuyu" 猶見扶餘 (As if seeing Fuyu). In Ng Kim-chew, *Youjian fuyu* 猶見扶餘 (As if seeing Fuyu). Taipei: Ryefield, 2014.

———. "Yuhai" 魚骸 (Fish relics). In *Yuhai*, edited by Yang Ze 楊澤, 29–45. Taipei: China Times, 1997.

Qian Liqun 錢理群. *Zhou Zuoren lun* 周作人論 (A study of Zhou Zuoren). Shanghai: Shanghai renmin chubanshe, 1991.

Shao Yanjun 邵燕君. "Wangluo wenxue shifou keyi tanlun jingdian?" 網絡文學是否可以談論經典? (Can one talk about canonical works of internet literature?). In *Zhongguo wangluo wenxue ershinian: dianwenji* 中國網絡文學二十年: 典文集 (Chinese internet literature of the past twenty years, a volume of canonical works), edited by Shao Yanjun 邵燕君 and Xue Jing 薛靜, 1–23. Guilin: Lijiang chubanshe, 2019.

Shen Congwen. "Sange nanzi he yige nüren" 三個男子和一個女人 (Three men and one woman). In Shen Congwen, *Shen Congwen quanji* 沈從文全集 (Complete works of Shen Congwen), 8:18–36. Taiyuan: Beyue wenyi chubanshe, 2009.

Shenyi jing 神異經 (The classic of the divine and the strange). Annotated by Zhang Hua 張華注. In *Biji xiaoshuo daguan* 筆記小說大觀 (A compendium of fictional sketches), 38: 226. Taipei: Xinxiang shuj, 1985.

Shi Shuqing 石舒清. *Qingshuili de daozi* 清水里的刀子 (Knife in the clear water). Yinchuan: Ningxia chubanshe, 2008.

Shi Tiesheng 史鐵生. *Mingruo qinxian* 命若琴絃 (Life like a banjo string). Nanjing: Fenghuang wenyi chubanshe, 2011.

"Shixun" 釋訓 (Interpretation and glossing). In *Erya* 爾雅 ([Elegant and proper diction), vol. 3. Shanghai: Shanghai guji chubanshe, 1977.

Sima Qian 司馬遷. *Shiji huizhu kaozheng* 史記會注考證 (The record of the grand historian with annotations). Annotated by Kametarō Takigawa 瀧川龜太郎. Taipei: Hongye shuju, 1980.

Song Mingwei 宋明煒. *Kehuan xiaoshuo xinlangchao* 科幻小說新浪潮 (New wave science fiction in China). Shanghai: Shanghai wenyichubanshe, 2020.

Syaman Rapongan 夏曼藍波安. *Tiankong de yanjing* 天空的眼睛 (Eyes in the sky. Taipei: Lingking Publications, 2012.

Tsering Norbu 次仁羅布. "Fangshengyang" 放生羊 (Sheep of life release). In Tsering Norbu, *Fangshengyang*. Tianjin: Baihua wenyi, 2015.

Tu Cheng-sheng 杜正勝. "Gudai wuguai zhi yanjiu: Yi zhong xintaishi he wenhuashi de tansuo (weiwan chugao)" 古代物怪研究: 一種心態史和文化史的探索 (A study of ancient monsters: A survey of a zeitgeist and cultural history, unfinished manuscript). *Dalu zazhi* 大陸雜誌 (Dalu magazine), 104, no. 1 (2002):1–14.

Wang, David Der-wei 王德威. "Nüzuojia de xiandai guihua" 女作家的現代鬼話 (Modernist ghost talk by Chinese women writers). In David Der-wei Wang, *Zhongsheng xuanhua: Sanling yu baling niandai de zhongguo xiaoshuo* 眾聲喧嘩: 三十年代與八十年代的中文小說 (Heteroglossia: Chinese fiction of the 1930s and 1980), 227–38. Taipei: Yuanliu chuban gongsi, 1988.

———. "Qiannian huaxu zhimeng: Dung Kai-chueng, Meng Yuanlao, Menghuati xushi" 千年華胥之夢: 董啓章, 孟元老, 華胥體敘事 (A thousand-year-old dream of the splendid kingdom of Huaxu: Dung Kai-chung, Meng Yuanlao and the Huaxu narrative style). In *Kaifeng: Dushi jiyi yu wenhua xiangxiang* 開封: 都市記憶與文化想像 (Kaifeng: Urban memory and cultural imaginary), edited by Chen Pingyuan 陳平原, David Wang 王德威, and Guan Aihe 關愛和. Beijing: Peking University Press, 2013.

———. "Wo huali de yinwei yu beishang: Lo Yi-chin de siwang xushi" 我華麗的淫猥與悲傷: 駱以軍的死亡敍事 (My magnificent sadness and perversity). In Lou Yi-chin 駱以軍, *Qian beihuai* 遣悲懷 (Banished sorrow), 7–30. Taipei: Maitian chuban, 2001.

———. *See also* Wang Dewei.

Wang Dewei. "Shanghen jijing, baoli qiguan" 傷痕即景, 暴力奇觀 (A tableau vivant of scar, a spectacle of violence). Introduction to Yu Hua, *Xu Sanguan maixie ji* 許三觀賣血記 (Xu Sanguan the blood donor), 1–23. Taipei: Maitian chuban gonsi, 1997.

Wang Fansen 王汎森. "Mingmo Qingchu de renpu yu xingguohui" 明末清初的人譜與省過會 (The Society of Moral Edification in the late Ming and early Qing), *Zhongyang yanjiuyuan lishi yuyan yanjiusuo jikan* 歷史語言研究所集刊 (*Journal of the Institute of History and Philology*) 63, no. 3 (1993): 679–712.

Wang Hui 汪暉. *Fankang juewang* 反抗絕望 (Resisting despair). Beijing: Sanlian, 2008.

———. "Sihuo chongwen" 死火重溫 (A rekindled dead fire), in Wang Hui, *Sihuo chongwen* 死火重溫 (A rekindled dead fire) 413–34. Beijing: Renmin wenxue chubanshe, 2000.

Wang Meng 王蒙. *Qingchun wansui* 青春萬歲 (Long live youth). Beijing: Renmin wenxue chubanshe, 2003.

———. *Ye de yan* 夜的眼 (Eyes of night). Changchun: Shidai wenyi chunbanshe, 2001.

Wang Xiaoming 王曉明. *Wufa zhimian de rensheng* 無法直面的人生 (A life that cannot be faced up to). Taipei: Yeqiang chubanshe, 1996.

Wang Yangming 王陽明. *Wang Yangming quanji: Chuanxilu xia* 王陽明全集: 傳習錄下 (Complete works of Wang Yangming: Instructions for practical learning, part 2). Shanghai: Shanghai guji chubanshe, 1992.

Wu Ming-yi 吳明益. *Fuguang* 浮光 (Floating lights). Taipei: Xinjingdian, 2014.

———. *Fuyanren* 複眼人 (The man with the compound eyes). Taipei: Xinjingdian chubanshe, 2016.

Xu Nianci 徐念慈. *Xinfaluo xiansheng tan* 新法螺先生譚 (A new account of Mr. Windbag). Shanghai: Xiaoshuolin, 1905.

Yan Fu 嚴復 and Xia Zengyou 夏曾佑, "Benguan fuyin shuobu yuanqi" 本舘附印說部緣起 (An announcement of publishing fiction in our press). In Chen Pingyuan 陳平原 and Xia Xiaohong 夏曉虹, eds., *Ershi shiji zhongguo xiaoshuo lilun ziliao* 二十世紀中國小說理論資料 (Critical materials on fiction theory in twentieth-century China), 1:1–12. Beijing: Beijing daxue chubanshe, 1989.

Yan Geling 嚴歌苓. *Lufan Yanshi* 陸犯焉識 (Convict Lu Yanshi). Beijing: Zuojiachubanshe1, 2011.

Yan Lianke 閻連科. Rixi 日熄 (The day the sun died). Taipei: Ryefield, 2015.

———. *Wodexianshi, wodezhuyi* 我的現實, 我的主義 (My reality, my ism). Beijing: Zhongguo renmin daxue chubanshe, 2011.

Yang Yi 楊義. *Zhongguo gudian xiaoshuo shilun* 中國古典小說史論 (History of classical Chinese fiction). Beijing: Zhongguo shehui kexue chubanshe, 1995.

Yu Hua 余華. *Diqitian* 第七天 (The seventh day). Beijing: Xinxing chubanshe, 2013.

Zhan Yubing 戰玉冰. "Wanglu xiaoshuo de shujufa yu lexinglun: yi 2018nian de 749 bu zhongguo wanglu xiaoshuo weikaochaduixian" 網絡小說的數據法與類型論: 以2018 年的749 部中國網絡小說為考察對象 (The data method and typology of internet fiction studies: based on a survey of 749 internet novels in 2018). *Zhongguo xiandai wenxue* 中國現代文學 (Modern Chinese literature) 35 (2019): 65–88.

Zhang Jun 張軍. *Chuguo shenhua yuanxing yanjiu* 楚國神話原型研究 (A study of the mythological archetypes of the Chu). Taipei: Wenjin chubanshe, 1994.

Zhao Yuan 趙園. *Ming Qing zhiji shidafu zhi yanjiu* 明清之際士大夫之研究 (A study of the intelligentsia of the late Ming and early Qing). Beijing: Beijing daxue chubanshe, 1999.

Zhou Zuoren 周作人. "Gui xianhua" 鬼閒話 (On gossiping about the ghosts). In Zhou Zuoren, *Guadouji* 瓜豆集 (Melons and beans). Shanghai, 1937.

Zhuangzi 莊子. "Qiushui" 秋水 (Autumn water). In Zhuangzi, *Zhuangzi jishi* 莊子集釋 (Annotations of Zhuangzi), edited by Guo Qingfan 郭慶藩, 6:20. Beijing: Zhongguo shudian, 1988.

———. "Zhangzi waipian zaiyou" 莊子外篇在宥 (Zhuangzi, outer chapters). In Zhuangzi, *Zhuangzi jishi* 莊子集釋 (Annotations of Zhuangzi), edited by Guo Qingfan 郭慶藩, 4:2. Beijing: Zhongguo shudian, 1988.

Index

The Author

DAVID DER-WEI WANG is the Edward C. Henderson Professor of Chinese Literature and Comparative Literature at Harvard University. His publications include *The Lyrical in Epic Time: Modern Chinese Intellectuals and Artists through the 1949 Crisis*; *The Monster That Is History: History, Violence, and Fictional Writing in 20th-Century China*; and *Fin-de-Siècle Splendor: Repressed Modernities of Late Qing Fiction, 1849–1911*. He is also editor of the Harvard/Belknap edition of *A New Literary History of Modern China*.

Library of Congress Cataloging-in-Publication Data

NAMES: Wang, Der-wei, author.

TITLE: Why fiction matters in contemporary China / David Der-wei Wang.

DESCRIPTION: Waltham: Brandeis University Press, 2020. | Series: The Mandel Lectures in the Humanities at Brandeis University | Includes bibliographical references and index. | Summary: "Contemporary discussions of China tend to focus on politics and economics, giving Chinese culture little if any attention. Why Fiction Matters in Contemporary China offers a corrective, revealing the crucial role that fiction plays in helping contemporary Chinese citizens understand themselves and their nation. Where history fails to address the consequences of man-made and natural atrocities, David Der-wei Wang argues, fiction arises to bear witness to the immemorial and unforeseeable. Beginning by examining President Xi Jinping's call in 2013 to "tell the good China story," Wang illuminates how contemporary Chinese cultural politics have taken a "fictional turn," which can trace its genealogy to early modern times. He does so by addressing a series of discourses by critics within China, including Liang Qichao, Lu Xun, and Shen Congwen, as well as critics from the West such as Arendt, Benjamin, and Deleuze. Wang highlights the variety and vitality of fictional works from China as well as the larger Sinophone world, ranging from science fiction to political allegory, erotic escapade to utopia and dystopia. The result is an insightful account of contemporary China, one that affords countless new insights and avenues for understanding" —Provided by publisher.

IDENTIFIERS: LCCN 2020028867 (print) | LCCN 2020028868 (ebook) | ISBN 9781684580262 (cloth) | ISBN 9781684580279 (paperback) | ISBN 9781684580286 (ebook)

SUBJECTS: LCSH: Chinese fiction—20th century—History and criticism. | Chinese fiction—21st century—History and criticism. | Literature and Society—China—History—20th century.

CLASSIFICATION: LCC PL2443 .W2443 2020 (print) | LCC PL2443 (ebook) | DDC 895.13/609—dc23

LC record available at https://lccn.loc.gov/2020028867

LC ebook record available at https://lccn.loc.gov/2020028868